Frederic Huntington

**Christ in the Christian year and in the life of man**

Sermons for laymen's reading

Frederic Huntington

**Christ in the Christian year and in the life of man**
*Sermons for laymen's reading*

ISBN/EAN: 9783337104887

Printed in Europe, USA, Canada, Australia, Japan

Cover: Foto ©Lupo / pixelio.de

More available books at **www.hansebooks.com**

# CHRIST IN THE CHRISTIAN YEAR

AND IN

# THE LIFE OF MAN

SERMONS FOR LAYMEN'S READING

(ADVENT TO TRINITY)

BY THE
RT. REV. F. D. HUNTINGTON, D.D.
BISHOP OF CENTRAL NEW YORK

NEW YORK
E. P. DUTTON AND COMPANY
713 BROADWAY
1878

This volume owes its existence to a letter received by the author, some months ago, from a presbyter in one of our western dioceses highly esteemed in the Church at large and of wide experience in its service. He believes that there is still need of printed sermons to be read in churches, and gives some reasons why the present publication should be made. Although it would not have been undertaken but for his advice and request, he is in no manner responsible for what the book contains.

This suggestion having been adopted, it became necessary to accept whatever limitations it imposed both as to matter and method. Preferences which otherwise might be reasonably indulged, as respects topics and their treatment, lines of abstract thought and completeness of discussion, must to some extent be sacrificed. The frequent appearance of italics, a blemish on the pages to the eye of taste, is to be accounted for in the same way. It was also thought that to most readers certain obvious aspects and explanations of the principal Church-seasons might be supposed to be already sufficiently familiar.

Let it be stated as according to the author's general conception of preaching that the aim in each individual discourse should be rather to give a sense of reality, in the particular truth there presented, than to exhaust subjects; to create in the hearers as vivid and abiding an impression as may be of some distinct department of Christian doctrine or duty, comprehending only such relations of idea and fact as seem most suitable to that end. Several important topics, pertaining to the domain of Church-instruction, are reserved for another volume.

The author ought frankly to add that in allowing these sermons, many of which were written for a parochial ministry, to go to press, he could not bring himself to consider merely their use in lay reading. He would modestly hope that some of them, while help ing a soul here and there to live heartily for God, may also at least indicate a belief that the men of this country and this time, especially if somewhat thoughtful and right-hearted, are to find a solution of many theological and speculative difficulties by subordinating everything else in Christian teaching to the fact of the Incarnation of our Lord, Son of God and Son of Man, and to the power of His person as the Giver of life, the only true and eternal life, through the divine channels of His grace, to mankind. The best promises of the thinking and working world appear to encourage this anticipation. May it not be expected that, as this profound and inspiring verity takes its due place, many doubts arising in the spheres of physical science and metaphysical philosophy will disappear, not by a process of dialectics or controversy but by a fair construction of that Word which is "the Word of life" just because it has for its substance Him who is the living and everlasting "Word made flesh" and "dwelling among us"?

It would seem to follow naturally in the line of this view that the higher rather than the lower range of motives is to be addressed by the pulpit, in appeals for faith and obedience, for manliness and godliness. Had there been in the homiletics and general religious literature of the last two hundred years a more distinct and rugged realism, a more visible relation between the supernatural elements of revelation and the production of character in Christian people, and had piety been represented rather as spiritual health in the entire man than as a special and somewhat exceptional not to say abnormal sentiment, the scepticism of the "common-sense" school in England with the humanitarian and literary rationalism of Germany, France, and the United States would have had less plausibility and been less destructive.

F. D. H.

# CONTENTS.

|  | PAGE |
|---|---|
| ADVENT SUNDAY, | 1 |
|     Christ's First Coming. | |
| SECOND SUNDAY IN ADVENT, | 11 |
|     Christ's Second Coming. | |
| THIRD SUNDAY IN ADVENT, | 29 |
|     Christ in Judgment. | |
| FOURTH SUNDAY AFTER ADVENT, | 41 |
|     The Righteousness of God, and Uprightness in Man. | |
| CHRISTMAS-DAY, | 55 |
|     The Man Christ Jesus. | |
| SUNDAY AFTER CHRISTMAS, | 66 |
|     Faith Outliving its Special Occasions. | |
| SECOND SUNDAY AFTER CHRISTMAS, | 73 |
|     New and Old.—Beginning of the Year. | |
| FIRST SUNDAY AFTER EPIPHANY, | 83 |
|     The Epiphany Goodness. | |
| SECOND SUNDAY AFTER EPIPHANY, | 94 |
|     The Soul Sought by Christ and Seeking Him. | |
| THIRD SUNDAY AFTER EPIPHANY, | 105 |
|     The Law of Christian Enlargement. | |
| FOURTH SUNDAY AFTER EPIPHANY, | 117 |
|     The Saviour in the Ship. | |

|  | PAGE |
|---|---|
| FIFTH SUNDAY AFTER EPIPHANY, | 128 |
| Two and Two before His Face. | |
| SIXTH SUNDAY AFTER EPIPHANY, | 141 |
| Instant Obedience. | |
| SEPTUAGESIMA SUNDAY, | 152 |
| The Foremost Desire. | |
| SEXAGESIMA SUNDAY, | 164 |
| Sons and Daughters in the Family of Christ. | |
| QUINQUAGESIMA SUNDAY, | 175 |
| One Weak Spot. | |
| ASH-WEDNESDAY, | 186 |
| The Yoke and Burden already Easy and Light. | |
| FIRST SUNDAY IN LENT, | 196 |
| The Throng and the Touch. | |
| SECOND SUNDAY IN LENT, | 207 |
| Supplication the Church's Power. | |
| THIRD SUNDAY IN LENT, | 219 |
| Purity and its Safeguards. | |
| FOURTH SUNDAY IN LENT, | 232 |
| Strength out of Weakness. | |
| FIFTH SUNDAY IN LENT, | 243 |
| A Heavenly Mind Here. | |
| PALM SUNDAY, OR SUNDAY BEFORE EASTER, | 255 |
| Spiritual Waste and Wealth. | |
| GOOD FRIDAY, | 265 |
| The Water and the Blood. | |
| EASTER-DAY, | 280 |
| The Power of the Resurrection. | |

|  | PAGE |
|---|---|
| FIRST SUNDAY AFTER EASTER, . . . . | 293 |
| How the Risen Christ is Seen. | |
| SECOND SUNDAY AFTER EASTER, . . . . | 307 |
| What is Heaven? | |
| THIRD SUNDAY AFTER EASTER, . . . . | 320 |
| Why there will be no more Sea. | |
| FOURTH SUNDAY AFTER EASTER, . . . . | 335 |
| Alone at Athens. | |
| FIFTH SUNDAY AFTER EASTER, . . . . | 350 |
| The Human Society in the City of God. | |
| ASCENSION-DAY, . . . . . . . | 362 |
| The Heavens Opened. | |
| SUNDAY AFTER ASCENSION, . . . . . | 372 |
| Unprofitable Gazing. | |
| WHITSUN-DAY, . . . . . . . | 384 |
| Leadings of the Holy Spirit. | |

# CHRIST'S FIRST COMING.

### *Advent Sunday.*

"THE Word was made flesh, and dwelt among us, and we beheld His glory."—*St. John* i. 14.

BY a People numbering nearly four millions of souls there is a celebration to-day of the coming into this world of the greatest and best of all the Sons of men. What is wonderful, if we judge in the way the world has been apt to judge of men these thousands of years, is that He is the greatest *because* He is the best. Under that order of ideas which ruled till He came, still holding its own in vast dull communities where He is unknown or unwelcomed, and each trying to maintain itself within the bounds of His nominal empire, the greatest men have been soldiers who conquered and killed their kind; princes of fortune who bought, hired, and bribed men; or, in social states a little higher, students and thinkers who led and entertained them by knowledge or speech. That is, power and command and hence commemoration belonged to certain men by virtue of what they *had*, not by what they *were*. Now came a new order, bringing new estimates of human welfare, new aims for human life, new foundations for strong states and grand institutions, a new law and impulse for civilization; in a word, a new standard by which to measure and test what is really noblest and most glorious for man—man the individual, man in the family, man in the nation; yes, for humanity itself. Thenceforth the greatness of any man was to be reckoned not by what he has, but by what he is. Character was to be king.

No revolution could be so radical, so wide, so prolific of real results as this. It goes to the roots of life, and sooner or later everything on earth must be touched by it. Why? Because the life of man and the life of God were to be brought together, and made one. Hitherto, even by the nation that knew most of Him, God was thought of, worshipped, obeyed, as living apart from the world; over it, to be sure, exalted above it, but separate from it. Looking through the Old Testament we do not often find God spoken of as entering into the heart of His child, dwelling in man's soul, or as making even the holiest of His saints or the purest of His prophets a "partaker of the divine nature." Yet it must be just that, and only that, which could create in a man the highest conceivable or possible goodness; because God is the Good One, and His life the only perfect life. If humanity could only receive that divine life into it, be quickened, enlarged, transfigured by it, share its eternal vigor and beauty, that would be indeed its "new creation." How could this be? It would be, if a man, still remaining man, a child "born of a woman," should be also, by some life-giving mystery not unlike that of the first creation, a partaker of the life of God,—be divine, one with the Father. Through Him the vital heavenly goodness enters into mankind. Through His heart, as its channel, its organ, its "living way," God's life pours itself into all the sons of men that will receive it by this Son of Man. We shall have only to be united with Christ, the human

Brother, spiritually, inwardly, to be united also at once with God; for God is in Him; and we are joined to the whole Christ. That is possible for all men that live.

And now this coming in flesh is what has taken place. It is the Advent-fact. Is it strange that four hundred millions of people remember it to-day, and rejoice in it, with chants and hymns, with Eucharist and spiritual communion? It is the regeneration of our race. There is a new creation. There is a second Adam. "The first man Adam," says St. Paul, "was made a living soul"; but the soul was a natural soul, and the life was nature's life, limited, with seeds of imperfection and death in it. The Greeks called it *psyche*, and St. Paul uses their word. "The last Adam was made a quickening spirit." By Him life, life imperishable, everlasting, is given to those who want to live, and do not want to die. "As in Adam all die," or live a dying life, "so in Christ shall all be made alive," or live directly, spiritually, from God. This is the Incarnation. Read the first chapter of St. John. We get only a partial notion of the coming of Christ when we think of Him as coming, as other historical persons have come, from without, or even from above, in the ordinary sense of "above." He "comes forth" from God, and God comes forth in Him, to receive willing, believing, obedient men into Himself. We ourselves are new-born in Him, and live forever,— live a divine life, sons and daughters of the Lord Almighty. "Whosoever will," may.

No matter what the enterprise, skill, wit, energy, combinations, or bravery of men may do, there is nothing to be done, or remembered, like this. All other comings and goings in history must turn around this, make room for this, look up to this. The kingship of character is enthroned. A Christian immortality is constituted.

We are enabled to live the highest life. Heaven begins on earth. The Word is made flesh and dwells among us. God and man are at one.

The face of society was changed because its heart was changed. Instead of wearing any longer a look of hate and greed and cruelty, there came flashing and glowing into its expression the look of love, purity, mercy. This was the Advent-light. The world silently began to be another world. And the Power set working to bring this change about made it unlike all other revolutions. It wrought without violence, noise, ambition, or parade, "not with observation." It went on not by destruction, but construction; not tearing down, but building up. When the sword was drawn it was because human hands were used, and the obstinacy of the old system would let a path be made for the new in no other way. Generally it moved in among the kingdoms of this world according to the great anthem that announced it when it was born, peacefully seeking glory for God by good-will to men,— spreading as morning is spread upon the mountains, as a harmony spreads through the spaces and arches of a sanctuary. Hence, inasmuch as it must take an organic form, after its Living Head, and be a kingdom, it was called a Kingdom of Life. Life was a great word with it. Its founder was the life-giver. "I am come," He said, "that they might have life, and might have it more abundantly." The change was first in the seats of life, within, — coming gradually out into doings or fruit, as the way of life is,— from a hidden seed to root, germ, blade, and ear; into common labor, elevating it; into homes, purifying them by honoring woman and consecrating childhood; into commerce, hallowing it by the spirit of integrity; into education, making the training of conscience and faith, our loftiest capacities, the crown of all other culture; into worship, directing it to the One God, worshipped in spirit and in truth.

We know precisely when this new Age, regenerating humanity, came visibly in. The Divine Power did not come as an idea, or a book, or a system, or a code of laws, or a bundle of maxims. Great and good things have come in all these shapes. But the Life of life came in a man, born as a child, growing as a youth, living as other men live. It was not, then, Christianity that renewed the race, it was Christ; not abstract Truth, but a Personal Force, "made flesh." Nor did He come to disappear, but to remain. We Christians are not a backward-looking people. His Church holds Him fast, clinging to Him by her faith, and keeping His presence fresh by commemorative ordinances, and by Christ-like work. Is it not clear what our Advent-observance ought to be?

True enough, too true, the new Life was not kept pure. What river of Truth running through the world ever was? The Giver or His Apostles never promised such a miracle. The old selfish kingdom crept back and crowded into the Church. The promise was that the Life, however perverted, should never be lost. It never was. Again and again, when most in peril, it has reasserted its original healing power. It is slow work, but it goes on. So every year, besides the millions who praise the Lord that has come, millions more who do not acknowledge Him are glad to live in the Christendom He has created. There is a believing modern science, and a believing modern literature. What is to be said of a science and a literature which undertake to discredit the Author of the age which makes their existence possible?

But this is not all. Men have another kind of want. Without the Life of God in them they become conscious of their poverty and peril. Bad men know that they are bad. A sense of guilt wakes up and torments them. At least it haunts their dreams. The kingdom of Christ's righteousness stands before them, witnessing against them. The Life of God in the Son of Man judges them. They feel it around them, though not within them. They know what its holy fruits are, and that they ought to be bringing them forth, and are not. Through frivolous employments and dissipated nights the irreligious youth, the flighty, prayerless woman, carry with them a feeling, partly smothered, partly drugged, but never dead,—a feeling that springs up again, comes back, wakes in the night, seizes them when they are alone, making them confess secretly that they are not right, not safe, not friends with God; and yet God is Almighty. What will the end be? They are afraid to look at themselves honestly. Perhaps they despise themselves and the hollow life they are living. They wish they were out of it. The sense of sin that pours its confession in the fifty-first Psalm, and cries out in the publican's prayer, is stirred in them. Had Christ not come, that saving discontent might have slumbered still. In heathendom they might have been content. Jesus said, "If I had not done among them the works which none other man did, they had not had sin." The unjust, unclean rich man looks round him on his broad estate, and it does not satisfy. It shrinks, as he looks at some poor brave neighbor filled with the life of Christ. A shadow falls across all the comfort and splendor. It falls from a dark spot within him. His experiment at living without God is failing, and he is aware of it. What is it all for? It occurs to him that the coffin will be as indispensable an article in the furniture of his house as any. What then? Will that be really the end? Christ's coming sunders the world of men into two sorts, right and left. So, by thousands, men are revealed to themselves as sinful,—if left to themselves lost. How shall they find peace, how be forgiven, how know that they have God reconciled for their Friend? That question, too, Christ comes to answer. No other ever did,—no naturalist, no moralist, no positive philosopher. Then it appears that Christ came not only to live, and to give life by living, but to die, and give life to men dead in sin, by dying. He suffers. He bears the cross. Mysteriously but with a certainty that grasps and holds the conviction of the believers of every age and land, that suffering and that cross disclose the worth of a soul's life so redeemed. The Divine Life is Love, a Love that is willing to give a mortal life for undeserving, disobedient brother-men. Law is not loosened; it stands. The eternal contradiction between right and wrong is not confused. But in faith the penitent feels the love, and lives. This is atonement. Christ comes to put away sins by the sacrifice of Himself.

We have infirmities which are not sins. In ways partly known and partly unknown they may be fruits of disobedience; but they are not distributed among persons in proportion to their deserving. Still, they are a part of moral discipline. At its very best, this life is "compassed" with them. To the last the little ship sails heavily freighted with sorrows. Of how many kinds these sorrows are! And then death separates us. The good die young. The saints cease from their beneficent service. The prophets do not live forever. Can we bear it? In imagination—thank God not otherwise—we can put ourselves out into that bleak desert, a Christless world. We ask there, and then ask here, will these graves ever open? Shall I see the face of my mother, my child, my friend, whose spirit was rich in the gifts and graces of God? See it in an eternity of blessed, unbroken, undivided life? I know that I shall. Jesus Christ has come, has died, has risen from the dead. Because He lives, His follower, one with Him, shall live also. The resurrection is not only His. It is the resurrection of every believer on earth. The life-power is common to both. It is within the Christian heart. When the undying Christ liveth in us, we can never die. Be His, and you are already immortal, mortality being swallowed up of life. The glorious expectation enlarges itself. In the day of His appearing you shall appear, and with Him. "We know not what we shall be, but we know that we shall be like Him." We know that none of us need die eternally. Countless households in every Christian country, knowing what it is to mourn for the dead, awake this morning to worship a risen Redeemer, and to realize the strength of the beatitude, "Blessed are they that mourn, for they shall be comforted." Let it come close to your bereavement. "Thy brother shall rise again." You say, "Obscurity overhangs the future state." Obscurity perhaps, but not uncertainty. It is of the first Coming that we are the children now, not of the second. Eye hath not seen the place, the mode, the scenery, the employments. All in due time; all in order. "We shall see as we are seen; know as we are known." Jesus Christ has come for this,—a Helper of infirmities, holding us in the hand of His most sure promise, till the day break and the shadows flee away. We have seen the three-fold character and power of Advent. It brings the life of God into humanity; forgiveness of sin and peace to every faithful heart; boundless and endless comfort to sorrow, even though it be the sorrow of death.

The drawback with all stated and repeated observances is that we keep them outwardly, not inwardly. We say over the religious words; we go through the decent forms; perhaps we think the appropriate religious thoughts. "Advent! Oh, yes; it is good to keep Advent. It is well that Christ came":—and we go away with almost as little love of Him, almost as much of the old selfishness, pride, passion, which He died to deliver us from, as before; almost as much uncharitableness or insincerity dropping from our lips; to renew to-morrow the poor life of getting, hoarding, competing, being amused, eating, drinking, dressing, as if these things were ends,—"without God."

What is it really to *keep* an Advent-season? The religious repetition will not give us the Christ, whether as the Renewer of the world's life, or the Pardoner of sin, or the Conqueror of death. The worth of the observance is only that it helps us to a deeper, inner union with our Lord, and likeness to Him. Words are not saviours. Is this social state we live in such as Christ came to frame? Is its spirit His? Are its fashions moulded by the principles of His righteousness? Your daily business,—is it a Christian service? Your family manners and conversation,—are they such that if Christ were to make His advent there, He would find Himself at home in your house? Your hidden life, that secret world within you which no housemate, neighbor, friend, ever sees, the "inner man,"—is it renewed day by day so as, more and more brightly, to reflect His image?

It is remarkable that, while the Scriptures for Advent-Sunday are greatly concerned with the august events to which they point, we find in them searching directions for our present, every-day conduct; rebukes for common sins; familiar dangers mentioned by name. Examine the "Epistle" especially. What does it signify? This, without a doubt: that our true preparation for our Lord's approach is holy living. Mark the ascending scale. Debts are to be paid. Elementary commandments are to be re-studied down to their roots. The new Christian year is to be the beginning of a new period of spiritual life; the young are to strike into a new line of Christian action; all are to set up higher standards of Christian honor; "the night is far spent"; a "day" of unprecedented splendor, lighting us on to unprecedented labors, is mounting into the sky. And when all duties, with their loftiest motives, are to be comprehended in a single precept, it can be no other than this: "Put ye on the Lord Jesus Christ."

# CHRIST'S SECOND COMING.

*Second Sunday in Advent.*

"WHEREFORE if they shall say unto you, Behold, He is in the desert; go not forth: behold He is in the secret chambers, believe it not. For as the lightning cometh out of the east, and shineth even unto the west; so shall also the coming of the Son of Man be."—*Matt.* xxiv. 26, 27.

I SHALL assume that there is some interest on your part, and at the same time some uncertainty, as to what the Scripture teaching of the future coming of the Son of Man really is. Both have always been found to exist among Christians, though the *interest* of the question has been much livelier and more general at some particular periods of the Church than others, being generally strongest in times of great social disturbance and danger, like the several epochs of persecution under the Roman emperors, the first uprising of modern liberty in conflict with European despotism, the struggles between the people and the crown in England, involving the integrity of the national Church, in the middle and latter part of the seventeenth century, and again in the great social and political agitations of our own day. Such intensely wrought states of the public mind naturally direct the attention forward to the final issue, giving activity and acuteness to the sense of future change, somewhat as the jar of the atmosphere by travel on the highway, or the jostle of machinery, is said to quicken in deaf persons the sense of hearing. But there never was a time when the true followers of Christ were indifferent to His promise of meeting them face to face, and receiving them into a wider fellowship and an everlasting kingdom.

There are some real difficulties, we ought candidly to acknowledge, in discovering how much the inspired writings were intended to reveal. Hence we shall lay it down at the outset, and remember it all along, that there are two provinces to be kept entirely distinct. One is the province of what the Scriptures plainly and undoubtedly declare, as by all Christians to be believed, and as being in some way necessary to a complete life and godliness. The other province includes much matter less essential, matter of inference and construction less vitally related to the edifying of the soul and its salvation, where room is given for a lawful difference of interpretation, and for variety of opinion. Even here we all have the duty of investigation, and the responsibility of it; truth is never a matter of indifference; every topic that the Bible touches deserves a reverent regard. Yet the dividing line is one that ought to be respected, and in relation to few subjects more than this one. Revelation tells us with wonderful clearness what all men ought to believe and ought to do. The disclosure to us of necessary doctrine and duty, if not obvious at first sight in every part, can be understood on a very reasonable amount of pains, even by unlettered and common minds, if the attempt is lighted up by that inward illumination of the Holy Spirit which shines on our darkness in answer to prayer. But round about this region of positive teaching, resting on absolute authority, there lies another region, still scriptural, of intimation and suggestion, of allusion and probability, of things half unveiled, prospects dimly disclosed and intended so to stand till we are lifted into loftier places and broader light, perhaps till we have "open vision for the written word." These shadows and half-lights of Revelation, these things seen as through a glass darkly, have their divine uses and even their peculiar glories in the exercise of our patience, the feeding of simple faith, and the discipline of humility. The mischief is that curiosity and audacity are often tempted to take what belongs to this matter of religious suggestion and throw it over into the province of dogmatic assertion, requiring to be received as religious fact, and perhaps with some defined theory of the fact, what God meant us to behold only with wonder, trust, and hope. The mischief is manifold. It intermixes mortal mistakes with God's unadulterated truth. It colors the uncolored beam of Heaven. It repels candid inquiries by a tone of arbitrary presumption. Worse than all, it draws the soul aside from her direct and practical work, of doing her Lord's will, into a thousand very tempting and seductive, but wholly irrelevant, lines of thought, quite foreign from the building of men up in righteousness, in love, and in holy obedience.

St. Matthew tells us that a short time before the Saviour's suffering and departure from the world, as He went out of the temple at Jerusalem for nearly or quite the last time, His disciples called his attention to the grandeur and durability of the structure. He simply amazed and alarmed them at the moment by informing them that a destruction was awaiting the building so violent and complete that not one stone would be left upon another. The topic was not pursued at the time in so public a place. But a little later in the day, on their evening walk to Bethany, as they sat down privately on the Mount of Olives, and, looking westward, saw those superb towers of marble and gold standing firm against the twilight sky, where the fading sunshine must have appeared to them like a sad symbol of that declining and vanishing national enthusiasm which for centuries had kindled the hearts of their ancestors toward that hallowed spot, they renewed the conversation, begging their Master to tell them when this startling prediction should be accomplished, and what signs they might expect beforehand of the great catastrophe. Nor was this all. Mark what else they included in their inquiry. They said: "What shall be the sign of *Thy coming*, and of *the end of the world?*" which seems to show that they associated together the sacking of the Holy City with the final crash of the whole terrestrial order, either regarding the local ruin as to be simultaneous with the general dissolution, or else as somehow leading on or pointing to it. This opened the whole subject, and Jesus proceeded with that august prediction which the Evangelists have recorded, where every word is weighty with the solemnity of the judgment.

Now, without a minute scrutiny here of each phrase in detail, but embracing in the same view with the entire passage all the other teachings of Christ and His several Apostles on the subject, — which are certainly capable of being reduced into entire harmony with each other, — we may reach, and put down before us, as it appears to me, a few satisfactory statements, or doctrines if you choose, which pretty much exhaust what we have just referred to as the plainly revealed and therefore essential truth in the whole matter. And this we get at, remember, not by an attempt to make out a foregone conclusion, or to square Scripture to any favorite view, but simply by bringing all the pertinent passages together, placing them side by side, observing their several connections, ascertaining the meaning of the original as well as the translated terms, and declaring the result.

1. First, then, both Christ and His Apostles speak repeatedly of a second coming of the Son of Man, in such a sense as forbids us to confound the second with the first. The two are put entirely apart in time, though they are internally and morally connected with each other; the one preparing the way for the other, and each being in fact fragmentary and unintelligible without the other. The one coming, however, as a historical fact, is past,—having given birth to a new age, the Gospel and the Church; the other is yet to be. They are respectively the beginning and the end, in time, of one design, the redemption and training of mankind, from sin to holiness, from an old life, which was death, into a life everlasting, in an immortal society. We are all living, throughout this Christian dispensation, in the intermediate stage of this glorious proceeding. It is a kind of transition-period. As compared with eternity, it is all but a short term,—a narrow strip between two boundless seas. Could we really conceive of eternity, or could we so be lifted up as to look down on the immensity stretching on each side of this whole Christian era, it would no doubt appear like a mere thread across the field of vision. Yet, it is sufficient for the discipline of a living race, including millions of souls. So we stand here, each individual life but a speck on that narrow belt, and here we make our choice. We look behind and before. The Gospel tells us, over and over, in every variation of the plainest language, that Christ has come in our flesh and nature once, and has removed every possible hindrance to our living with Him forever. It tells us just as explicitly that He has gone, like a travelling prince, to receive for Himself a kingdom, and

that He is coming again to reign in that kingdom, with His own people, and that, in connection with that, the whole period of trial, of choice, will end. So the Church has ever believed and taught, and so she prays in her repeated Advent collect. Her Advent season reaffirms and illustrates the truth. From Sunday to Sunday she holds up many Scripture lessons to keep it ever in mind. Her living Head is to come a second time.

2. In the next place, that coming is personal and literal. Look at all the language and all the accompanying descriptions, and you will see that no loose talk of "figures of speech" will explain away this lucid and repeated declaration, or the mysterious fact it announces. Whatever accommodations of the literal language we may find, they must all grow up around this one unmistakable, foretold *fact*, and grow out of it. We may call signal social revolutions, reforms in government, the emancipation of slaves, or great accessions of knowledge or charity, new comings of Christ. The figure is intelligible; but they are not comings of *Him*. They may be comings of the impersonal power and principles of His religion,—partial blessings reminding us of the one great blessing that includes them all; but *He* is to come. "Ye shall *see* the Son of Man (not His ideas but Him) coming in power and great glory." Either by the gathering of His people, or by His own celestial movement, "Every eye shall *see* (not His works but) Him." Besides, certain particular miraculous events and tokens are mentioned as attending His appearing.

Nor, again, will it do to tamper with Holy Scripture by such a theory of interpretation as that *His coming* means *our going*. The death or departure of the individual is one thing; the Bible often mentions that, meaning just what it says. The Lord's coming is another; it will be but once again for all men; there will be a time for it; it will be sudden and bright, like the light that shineth from east to west. We have no data, no experience, no critical apparatus, to measure such a fact by. That is not our business. We are learners to be taught.

> "Thou hast spoken, I believe,
> Though the oracle be sealed."

3. Thirdly, this great coming is to be connected with a separation of the good from the bad, the believers from the deniers, the spiritually alive from the spiritually dead. Hence it is always spoken of as a Judgment; because each one then goes to his own place, and finds his portion where he has chosen it. That begins to be the case, inwardly, with every man, now. But it becomes the outward, literal, terrible fact, not till then. It is not declared that the whole process of final adjudication to heaven or hell is finished then; it is rather made to appear that after another long period some mysterious ordeal will try the faithful once more; but the external judgment begins: and hence how well it is for us to entreat, as we do, that by His first coming the hearts of the disobedient may be so turned, and the works of darkness be so cast off, that at His second coming in majesty to judge the world, we may be found an acceptable people, and rise to the life immortal!

4. The chapter of St. Matthew, however, in the common-sense interpretation of it, obviously has *some* reference to a kind of coming of Christ which was to take place in the lifetime of the generation that was on the stage while the Saviour was speaking. It was to be

in some way connected with the invasion of the Roman armies and the downfall of the capital and temple of the Jews, in that century. This is the first of two main difficulties. Men have said, If the Messiah meant to predict a great coming in His kingdom at the end of the Christian age, why did He employ terms that distinctly point to what was to take place so soon, and at Jerusalem, and call that His coming? To answer that, consider that the disciples were questioning Him on that very point, the overthrow of the Temple. The reply to them must be a part of His discourse.

But consider, further, that it is one of what we may call the laws or canons of prophetic writing, that the language employed may have reference to two different persons or times,— the one, and the less important, too near to the speaker; the other and the greater fulfilment being found in some remoter and grander personage or event to come. Thus, for instance, if you examine those Psalms of David which contain prophecies of the Messiah, you see that they are so composed as to be in part and at first applicable to David himself, and his own personal fortunes; but you look again, and see that there is prophetic language there which will not suit any other personage than the Son of God; and in fact Christ and the Evangelists expressly declare that it was written of Him. The human subject is made a groundwork and a type, to exhibit the Divine King that was to be. So of some of the predictions of Isaiah. The same principle must be heeded in interpreting these predictions of our Lord. You find a part of the phraseology referring explicity to Palestinian history, and of that part He says, "This generation shall not pass away till all these things are fulfilled." It is said that "this generation" may refer to the national life of the Jews. It is *possible*.

Others have said those words mean the whole Christian Dispensation, which appears to us to be forced and improbable. Yet at the same time you find, in the same discourse, expressions that show the speaker to have been looking forward down the track of ages, to a much wider and mightier consummation. For He goes on to say that *all nations* shall be alarmed and aroused at this final appearing; that it shall be preceded by unprecedented disorders and antagonisms; that the Gospel must first be preached to all nations; that signs shall appear before it such as the world has not yet witnessed. Moreover, studying the passage more carefully, you will notice that the change of reference is gradual; and that, while Christ begins with dwelling almost entirely on incidents of the fall of the City and Temple, He rises, as He proceeds, till in the latter part the words befit His world-wide manifestation, and that alone.* Admit the rule of a double application, one immediate and the other remote, which for some cause or other is evidently according to the supernatural genius and usage of the prophetic spirit, and difficulties disappear. Each portion of God's Word becomes consistent with itself, with other portions, with the character of the author, and with what was known of human history outside of it.

5. We come now to what, with many minds, has been a greater difficulty, viz., that inspired writers, Apostles, signify their expectation that Christ's second advent would take place during their own natural life. Were they mistaken, and mistaken teachers of others? A vast amount of ingenious effort has been made to break the force of this objection without sacrificing

---

* The order of sentences seems not intended by the Evanglists to be exact. See St. Luke.

the infallibility of the record. For the most part it has failed by taking the purely external or philological method, and without sounding spiritually the depths of the Evangelic purpose. I need not even specify the various hypotheses. Let us honestly take the language of honest men in its ordinary acceptation. What, then, shall we say? To me all difficulties are cleared by the following proposition, which I think commends itself as reasonable, reverential, and in harmony not only with the drift of the doctrine we have presented, but with the doctrine of inspiration which the faith of the Church Catholic has held from the beginning: *The purpose of Revelation, in this matter, was to create in Christians, not a belief that Christ would come at any particular hour in history, but a belief that He is always at hand, and that all Christians should at all times and in all places be ready, as men that stand with their lamps trimmed and burning, to meet Him personally.* The date of the event was no part of the Divine communication. On that point the writers were left to their human faculties, and if they misapprehended, it was only the plainer evidence that they were but men. In other words, it was of importance that the mind of the Church should be always regarding the Lord and Head as nigh, but not to have the chronology settled. The Bible makes its usual preference of moral and religious impression above accuracy in the letter. There was, in fact, no practical error. For the writers were as careful to caution the Church against impatience and over-confidence as against the opposite. That generation passed; and no future one could be misguided by their expressions. In regarding it as their solemn duty to be ever waiting, and watching, and hasting unto the coming of the day, as one of them ardently expresses it, even though they were individually to die in martyrdom, or in their beds, they were unquestionably and blessedly right.

In proportion as we rise, in thought, toward the immensity of the life of God, and have "the mind of the Spirit," the whole period of history shrinks, great distances dwindle, epochs are pressed together, and "a thousand years are as one day."

Besides, the highest authority in modern physical science, in astronomy, and geology, and chemistry, harmonizes singularly enough as to the issue with the Apostolic language. It concludes that the machinery of the material universe is wasting, its movements are slackening, its balance is slowly loosening, and that a general catastrophe is inevitable. The sneer of the scientific sceptic of the last century is silenced by the science of to-day.

We may say that, in the Bible predictions generally, borrowing a phrase from the fine arts, what we may call *historical perspective* is lost sight of. We are not told at what intervals from each other, or always in just what order, these majestic events, by which eternity seems to open down into time, shall follow on. Chronology is not the object. The *facts* are what we are to know, and receive, and feed upon in our hearts by faith. The moment we begin to try our petty arithmetic on them we miss the mark, and lose our way. We all know that, even with ourselves, the moments of tremendous peril, when awful events are casting their colossal shadows about us, are just the time when the ordinary measure of succession drops out of sight. We look across the great tract and see other great conjunctions, as if they were nigh at hand. Christ Jesus is not enclosed in time, but time is all in Him. The regular sequence of incidents is broken up; common occurences are dwarfed; and we see nothing else but Him,—His first mediatorial ministry, His present ineffable life, His future glorious appearing and reign;—we see *Him* as an object of supreme affection. So that the intense life of faith, begotten in the first disciples, at the miraculous stirring age of the very presence and sacrifice of the Saviour, would be the very condition of things where everything *between* would be forgotten, and the believer would look on straight to the great consummation and end of all, and would behold it as if that were the one transcendent and even near event,— as, to the traveller straining his eyes to the mountain top before him, the higher the peak the narrower the intervening plain appears. This, therefore, would become the appropriate and forward-looking attitude which the Church and the Christian would always hold,— an attitude of hopeful, ardent, believing expectation,—"looking for and hasting unto the coming or day of the Lord."

The chief elements in the practical, animating power of that expectation are that it assures us of the unity and sure completion of the "redeeming work" for which the Son of God took our nature upon Him; it promises the end of that long conflict of evil with good of which this world has been the defiled and weary theatre,— wet, so many thousand years, with the tears of the wronged and the blood of the just, and resounding with groans of remorse; it preannounces the victory and the eternal peace; it welcomes to the throne the Leader and Shepherd in whose dear cause the good soldier has fought, faithful to his life's end. It anticipates the eternal festival when, not only in the right of possession but in the actual and loyal submission and praise of saints, the earth shall be the Lord's and the fulness thereof.

[Here, if I understand the record, the realm of what is essential to Christian doctrine in the passage ends. There are other points which different schools have insisted on as necessary parts of it, sometimes with unwarranted assurance. As matters of opinion, as constructions of what the Scriptures *imply* rather than reveal, they may be correct, or may not be. They cannot be held or taught as authoritative matter, nor are they included in the Catholic system of truth. Thus, there have been ambitious attempts to fix the year, by computation on many different data or bases, when the present dispensation will be wound up and the Son of Man come to close the probationary age. They have all offended common-sense by the extravagance of their mode of dealing with numbers, and every one of them has broken down by the simple passage of time. The very starting-point of them was a departure from faith to mathematics, — and the mathematics turned out to be about as weak as the faith. The marvel is the greater, because the statement in the Acts is so explicit that the Father hath hid the times and seasons in His own power; while it might have been supposed that the Saviour had given His followers the most impressive and conclusive lesson of reserve and modesty, when He declared it as a part of the condescension of His incarnation and humility, that so long as He was in the flesh the day and hour were hidden even from the Son himself.

[Similar bold ventures have been made toward determining precisely who that "Man of Sin" is, that, before the end comes, is to gather up, as St. Paul says, and embody in himself somewhere all the malign infidelity and blasphemy of modern irreverence and conceit, whether as pope, autocrat, or philosopher, exalting himself above all that is called God, and showing himself that he is God. But these transgressors over the line of written truth have only published their own presumption, and contradicted one another.

[A favorite accessory to the revealed doctrine is that of the regathering of the tribes of Israel in their Judean home, and the restoration of the Holy City. There is certainly a great deal of apparent Scripture encouragement for that bright and tenacious hope of the Hebrew. It seems to me that, on the whole, the preponderance of prophetic testimony favors it. But I cannot be blind to the grave questions which arise, both exegetical and historical, holding many able minds in suspense as to the part the Jew is yet to play, and arraying others on the negative side; and so I cannot help wondering at the unqualified confidence of men in what strikes me as a cheerful probability, of which we must humbly wait the verification, rather than an evangelically affirmed certainty.

[Much the same may be said of those decided opinions we sometimes hear advanced respecting the exact order of events in the final disposition of things in the last days, and the ultimate fate of this planet. Such speculations are utterly worthless. A little more faith, hope, and charity would be better than the best of them. All we know is that such changes in our globe as have been wrought in the past geologic periods, and as reason declares to be probable at any time, only universal, are foretold in the Bible as to happen some time or other,— "the elements shall melt with fervent heat"; that the resources of Omnipotence are infinite; that the universe is vast, beyond the utmost stretch of the amplest imagination; that the souls of the righteous are in the hands of God alone, where no torment shall touch them; and that though this earthly house of our tabernacle were dissolved, we have a building of God, eternal and indestructible, where, though we know not what we shall be, we know that we shall be like Christ, and with Him, seeing Him as He is.

[Biblical criticism is a much profounder thing than many prompt and confident people have suspected, requiring both learning and modesty. If the Bible were a text-book of the observatory or laboratory, or a treatise of natural history, or a simple narrative of facts, it would be comparatively easy to pronounce on all its contents and meanings. But remember, it contains specimens of almost every kind of composition known in literature, written at intervals reaching over nearly two thousand years, abounds in the boldest and most poetic forms of speech, and yet conveys to us the few simple truths relating to our relations and duties to God through Christ, which make up, for every wayfaring man and child, the way of salvation. Oh, the plainness of the way! The longer I live, the more I stand in awe of its simplicity, and give God thanks for it, and the more I disesteem the artificial systems that are built upon it, or used to overlay and crowd it aside. But when we go beyond that open learning of the heart, we must be guarded against shallow interpretations and catch-words. A few Greek and Hebrew clauses are not enough. It needs the largest appreciation, and most comprehensive scope, and ripest maturity, of any study in this world. You may take almost any crude fancy or pet system to the Bible, and find something plausible in those free and affluent pages to support it. And so books that have the look and air of scholarship have often abused and deluded thousands, who thought they were eating the Bread of Life. Where the Word of God is plain we can walk with firm steps. Repentance toward God and faith in the

Lord Jesus Christ are very intelligible words. But when we go over from certainty to conjecture, let it be with slow, careful, and unpretending steps.]

"If they shall say unto you, Behold, He is in the desert; go not forth: behold, He is in the secret chambers; believe it not."

Here are two opposite yet ever-present dangers. One is that of fancying that our Saviour and our salvation are to be found in some extraordinary, out-of-the-way fashion of religious manifestation: "Behold, He is in the desert." Anything looks attractive and promising in religion, to some temperaments, which lies aside from the commonplace path of familiar well-doing. *That* soon tires and grows distasteful. A very prevalent temptation hides under this innocent-looking passion for novelty. We imagine, with the sons of Zebedee, that we should do better in some other and more favorable condition. We fail to see that there is a deep sense in which Christ presents Himself to us now under the forms of common persons and things that we meet in our households and business. If we saw Him, and knew Him, and felt Him there, by faith, all this dull routine would take on a new interest, and rise into new dignity. The old prophets, with their rough exterior, haggard aspect, sharp cry, and fierce eloquence, used to make their appearance by coming out of solitary and desert places. So excitable people, wanting some stimulus to whet their dull desire, looked out into the wilderness. Only blow a trumpet, and point to a new John or Jeremiah, and the Church will seem to be awaking to new life. Christ is coming. But no; Go ye not forth, He solemnly says. He comes to you, in His own time and way. Invite Him where you are. Open to Him your heart, without changing your place. Most of us have to become acquainted with Him, and learn to sit at His feet, where our lot is cast, or we never find Him at all. There is a fringe of desert lying all around us, and there are novelties enough coming out of it, and voices enough to cry, "Lo, there is Christ, in some new ritualism, or new revivalism, or new rationalism." Believe it not. It is a false Christ. The old creeds, the old duties, the old ordinances, the old prayers, and praises, and confessions; the old charities, kindnesses, graces, forbearances, — the sweeter for being old,— keep to these; fill them up with a fervent, thankful, holy heart. And when Christ has any new disclosure or gift to make to you, it shall meet you there, shining through all the sky of your inner life, from east to west, and making for you, in the stronger light of His love, new heavens and a new earth.

The other danger is that we shall fancy that our Saviour and our salvation are to be found in particular states of our own interior feeling: "Behold, He is in the secret chambers." The first was superstition; this is fanaticism. The first fostered a fickle and shallow restlessness; this fosters a self-opinionated, self-confident, and fastidious indolence. The one is the religion of social excitement; the other of a dreamy sentimentality. The one makes an idol of an outward scene or symbol; the other of a complacent sensibility. One is led by the multitude; the other by an idol in the heart. One is an Athenian agitator; the other an Oriental mystic. These sentimentalists are always asking, "How do I feel? Am I happy? Is my frame exalted? Is my inner sense acute and high?" But, ah! mistaken dreamer, Christ is not there. Come out of your secret chambers; you may go there, and shut your door, only to pray and commune with Him, for refreshment, after and before your busy work in the world. Frames of feeling are no tests of your progress. An honest, healthy, robust, out-of-door faith is what you want. Plain duties, homely piety, cheerful submission, regular worship,—Christ is waiting for you in all of these. In the morning, take up the morning's cross. Walk with Christ all day. Working under Him is watching for Him. And then, whether He shall come at the first watch, or in the second, or at noon-day, or at evening, Blessed is the servant whom He shall find so watching!

# CHRIST IN JUDGMENT.

## *Third Sunday in Advent.*

"For we must all appear before the judgment seat of Christ."—
II. *Cor.* v. 10.

In the four weeks of Advent we regard Him who was to come, and who has come, and who is to come again, not only in His other characters, but as our Judge.

There are some parts of the truth that God will have delivered which make the messenger stand in awe of his message. It is so with what is revealed of the retributions of eternity. In whatever degree we realize the words we speak, we shall wish those words to have very little that can be called our own in them. We shall be anxious that they shall only represent, as simply as possible, the announcements that are made on the authority from which there is no appeal.

Indeed, there is so much of this judgment-language in all portions of the Bible that I shall set myself smaller limits yet, and only attempt to open before you what is taught us by it from the lips of the Saviour himself. It is not so much in the hearing of many warnings as it is in the realizing and remembering of a few; it is not so much in having the scenes of final judgment made familiar as it is in making the outlines clear and strong, so that we shall see whatever we do see as definite and undeniable realities,—that we are to expect deep and practical impressions. This is the way of the Scriptures. They do not deal much, like many of their weak interpreters, in elaborate descriptions of that Great Day of Reckoning, or of the sufferings beyond. What they are earnest to have us all know, and feel, and remember, is that there is a Reckoning, and that the Justice and Love of the Son of God and Son of Man will control and guide it. What they would make certain to us is that our everlasting life is in actual peril from our daily temptations; that the Judge is just; and that there can be no change in His judgment. Grounded in these certainties their one entreaty is, "Be ye ready."

You hear it said that the judgment is going on now; that we are judged from hour to hour. That is true, and a truth of very awful and startling import, which ought never to be forgotten. In one sense our own character and conduct judge us. What we really are determines our condition. Every new message from the Spirit of God judges us. We are always taking sides, for God or against Him. In the presence of a pure and noble Person we are always judged,—sent to the right hand or the left. By conscience, by the choice between right and wrong, we are sundered terribly, one from another, at this moment. By His very coming on earth amongst men Christ in that sense judges men. But that is not all. It is not the only judgment. It is not that Judgment to Come, of which our Lord so plainly declares that it *shall be* hereafter.

Men are swayed by their best sympathies. I find, from a generous thinker, an English preacher, who has had great popularity in our day, these sentences: "Christ's preaching differed from that of John the Forerunner, in that it was not a ministry of terror. He seldom appealed to fear. Christ taught that God is love.

He instructed in those parables which required thoughtful attention, and a gently sensitive conscience. He spoke didactic, calm discourses, very engaging, but with little excitement in them,—which assuredly, if any one were to venture so to speak before a modern congregation, would be stigmatized as a moral essay." Fair minds will recognize at once a certain amount of truth in this very one-sided statement. The question is one of fact: Did Christ appeal to the dread of retribution?

There can be no question at all that He, the Son of the God of Love, the highest of all Teachers, places love, as a motive, far above fear; that He will rather have men come to Him as their Friend than as their Judge; that He would have them cling to righteousness for the righteous One's sake, and put faith in God for His goodness, rather than be scourged into the Kingdom by threats of penalty and the terror of torment. Let this be granted, for it is precious and momentous truth. Where it is forgotten, let it be reaffirmed. But having granted it we shall only be in the better position to see how defective and superficial these statements quoted are, taken as a full description of Christ's Gospel. What man might be and ought to be, in his susceptibility to the higher range of impressions is one thing; but what he really is, in his spiritual poverty and dulness, is what Christ mercifully considers.

We are not at liberty to take an ideal Christendom, the conception of which we owe to the loftier elements of our own religion, and attempt to square to that the words of Him who came to stir and move the world that now is by "the powers of the world to come." That is the true love which moves by the *surest* path, not always the shortest or most agreeable, to its end,— the welfare of the beloved.

We should expect, therefore, that this loving Lord and Master, who knows so well what is in man, would present not a part but *all* of the grand motives that constrain men to newness of life, to repentance and faith, to the conquest of self, and the glory of goodness; and therefore that He would sometimes take away the veil from the misery and horror that belong to the second death; that ·He will bid His servants sometimes call men to "flee from the wrath to come," and by "the terrors of the Lord,"—of the Lord—to persuade men; that he would show that God has not forgotten to be just, *because* He has not forgotten to be gracious, but that He governs the world by law,—blessed and righteous law, which is "the mother of our peace and joy," —just as truly now as before the Gospel pity and redemption came.

We turn to the actual instructions of the Saviour to refute the assertion that He spoke only " calm, didactic discourses," addressed to men's hopes and affections, "with little excitement in them." We open, at the beginning, that Sermon on the Mount, which it is pretended is so far from anything that excites the *fear* of punishment or judgment. It has proceeded but a little way when we find the Teacher threatening the people, that unless their righteousness shall exceed the righteousness of the Scribes and Pharisees, they shall "in no case enter into the Kingdom of Heaven." A little further, and we hear Him say, "Whosoever is angry with his brother without a cause, shall be in danger of the judgment; and whosoever shall say, Thou fool, shall be in danger of hell fire." A little further, and he cries, with the repetition of a fearful emphasis, "If thy right eye, or thy right hand, cause thee to sin, pluck it out, or cut it off, and cast it from thee; for it is profitable for thee that one of thy members should perish, and not that thy whole body should be cast into hell." A little further yet, in the same Divine Sermon, He begins to speak very solemnly of "the broad way which leadeth to destruction," and "the narrow way which leadeth unto life," and the "few that find it." Then He passes to *warn* those that come to the gate, crying, "Lord, Lord," without doing His will, that at a certain day He will profess unto them, "I never knew you; depart from me, ye that work iniquity." Then comes the parable,—which is only a picture and prophecy of the last judgment,—of the house on the rock and the house on the sand, with destruction as the penalty of folly. Only one chapter further forward He calls up the vision of many coming from the East and the West, with the unworthy and false children of the Kingdom "cast out into outer darkness; there shall be weeping and gnashing of teeth." We turn a leaf or two, and the same faithful voice, loving as ever, but faithful just because it is loving, is exclaiming, "Fear Him who is able to destroy both soul and body in hell." In the next chapter, He is upbraiding, tenderly, the people before whom His mighty works have been done,—just as they are done before so many of us,—"in vain,"—"because they repented not";—"it shall be more tolerable, in the day of judgment, for Tyre and Sidon, than for you." ("Thou that art exalted to heaven shalt be brought down to hell.") Just after, He rebukes the impious blasphemy against the Holy Ghost, with a threat which almost silences our lips,—"It shall not be forgiven him, neither in this world, neither in the world to come." This He follows with the almost equally appalling declaration,—"Every idle word that men shall speak, they shall give account thereof in the day of judgment." When He has spoken the parable of the tares of the field, He finishes and applies it with the words,—"The tares are the children of the wicked one; the enemy that sowed them is the devil; the harvest is the end of the world, and the reapers are the angels. So shall it be in the end of this world. The Son of Man shall send forth His angels, and they shall gather out of His kingdom all things that offend, and them which do iniquity, and shall cast them into a furnace of fire: there shall be wailing and gnashing of teeth." When He has delivered the parable of the net cast into the sea, he explains, "So shall it be at the end of the world: the angels shall come forth and sever the wicked from among the just, and shall cast them into the furnace of fire." Out of the sorrow and burden of His soul, He cries, weeping," Woe unto the world because of offences! Woe to that man by whom the offence cometh!" He shows the forgiven servant who had no compassion on his fellow servant as "delivered to the tormentors"; and he says, "*So likewise* shall my Heavenly Father do also unto you, if ye from your hearts forgive not every one his brother their trespasses." In a different parable yet, wicked men are miserably destroyed; the kingdom is taken from them; and on whomsoever the stone of retribution falls, "it will grind him to powder." In still another parable, the guest that pushes his way in, without the wedding garment of holiness, prepared for him at the door, is bound hand and foot, and taken away, and cast into utter darkness. Of one class of sinners before His face He asks, as if the burden of an unutterable grief pressed upon him in having exhausted every resource of mercy for them in vain,— "How can ye escape the damnation of hell?" The exhortation to watch and be ready is followed by the example of the drunken and reckless servant whose portion is cut suddenly asunder, leaving him to weep and groan in agony. You know how the parable of the wise and foolish virgins ends,—with the solemn and final shutting of the door; that of the talents, with the stripping and shame of the faithless servant; and, above all, that of the shepherd king, the Son of Man in his glory, dividing and separating the sheep from the goats, on the right hand and the left,—the blessed and the cursed,— *these* going away into everlasting punishment, but the righteous into life eternal!

You will see, dear friends, that there must be some limit set to these proofs and confirmations. I have only collected these from a portion of the first of the four Records of Christ's public ministry. So He preached. So He came testifying of the judgment to come. You hear His words. Mine are nothing. Ponder His. Ask yourselves what they mean. Take them in their natural, obvious, and tremendous import. What shall we say of a writer who, having the New Testament before his eyes, tells us Jesus preached gently always, and did not preach terror? Are these the "didactic, calm discourses, very engaging, but with little excitement in them"? *Is it* so unlike the preaching of the Baptist, crying, "The axe is laid unto the root of the tree: every tree that bringeth not forth good fruit is cut down and cast into the fire"; "Whose fan is in his hand, and He will thoroughly purge His floor, and gather the wheat into His garner; but the chaff He will burn with unquenchable fire"? Are these those placid parables which "required only thoughtful attention, and a gently sensitive conscience," sounding "to a modern congregation like moral essays"?—these with their fire, and sifting, and separating, and shutting doors, and sundering of soul from soul, and opening of the house of torment, and punishment everlasting? Let us at least receive our Master's words as they stand. It will go ill with us if we alter them, if we reject them. Prejudice, the power of a preconceived idea, works strange results of interpretation. We have not to rewrite the Gospel of our Lord. He who knew all our necessities gave it all for our salvation. And since we must all stand before His judgment seat, He has told us beforehand, so that repenting and believing we might stand there with joy,—not with grief,—to pass from it to the right hand, and not the left, of the Son of Man in His glory, our Shepherd, and our King.

The question is not about the imagery, but whether the imagery has a meaning; not whether the terms are partly figurative, but whether the figures have a reality behind them.

It has become a habit to confuse the strong and simple declarations made here with subordinate and irrelevant speculations as to the mode, the time, and the place. The text sweeps these all away, and our poor subterfuges and evasions with them. "For we must all appear before the judgment seat of Christ," not here or there, or at any foretold hour, or in any scenery that is described: only, "we *must* appear."

The infirm and worldly heart, clinging to its wrong indulgencies, half-conscious of its guilt, seizes on a screen from the blaze of the judgment throne. "This notion of judgment is harsh,—Jewish;—Christianity is all tenderness; God is too good to cast even the worst of His rebellious and sinful subjects from Him."

Argument in its place; not here. We are out of that sphere. "We must all appear before the judgment seat of Christ." We *must*. The first fact we are to think of respecting the judgment is the certainty of it. The Scriptures never say, our Lord never says, that it is something which *may* take place, but which some possible contingency in the future course of the world may prevent. Whatever else may fail or prosper,—enterprises, governments, expeditions, colonies, campaigns, intentions, — their failure or their success will not touch the decree that has fixed one day beyond them all,—the judgment. There is scarcely one human interest, institution, undertaking, of which we can predict the course for twenty-four hours; but far above all their chances, independent of them all, subject to no chance, no reconsideration, no postponement, is the judgment. The whole frame-work of order in outward nature may be broken to pieces; the heavens be wrapped together like a scroll, the elements melt with fervent heat, the planet be refashioned, or burnt, or drowned, the stars be loosened from their circles, and clash together, or fly apart,—these revolutions would only make more sure the fulfilment of the whole prophecy, and their inevitable end will be the judgment. So doubtful and ignorant are we about everything in our own personal lives and fortunes, from this hour onward, that we can be said to be perfectly sure of only two events to come: "It is appointed unto men once to die, and after this the judgment." And "now," says the Apostle, "God commandeth all men everywhere to repent; because He hath appointed a day in the which He will judge the world in righteousness." It *must be.*

The second fact is the universality of it. We must *all* appear. *Here* the individual sometimes escapes notice either by retiring from society, or by being lost in its crowd. There the one kind of concealment will be just as hopeless as the other. There will be room enough for all, and yet the personal soul of each, with its individual character, with the sign of Christ its Lord or the sign of His adversary upon it, will stand out as sharply distinguished as if no other soul had ever been related to it, or shared its experience. They will come from lonely deserts and from thickly populated cities, from scattered houses far back in villages, from border-dwellings on the edges of forests, from solitary cells in hills and on plains, from homes that resound now with voices of life, from chambers of dreary sickness where a charitable visitor entered to break the stillness only once in the long week, from the field of war where great armies fought together, and from the same field the night after the battle when the spirit of the dying soldier went up to meet its God alone; but they will all be there; *we* shall all be there; every one. There will be no excuse taken, and there will be no absence to be excused. Merchandise, the farm, marriage, mental promises, getting a livelihood, calls of business, sceptical habits of mind, companies and journeys of pleasure, doubts about being accepted,—these will have no force to keep one bidden guest away, and all are bidden. Every name will be called,—those that have been written in the Book of Life, and the names of those that have heard the Gospel preached Sunday after Sunday, and year after year, and yet would not turn to take the cross and follow Christ. Every member of this present congregation will be there, and that may be the next time we shall *all* be assembled in one another's presence without one left out. Obscurity, insignificance, weakness, youth, poverty, ignorance,—those natural extenuations that we so often plead for not taking up responsibilities here, will not keep any out there; many that were last shall be first, and so, also, many that were first shall be last. Station and dignities and wealth and honors will avail nothing to obtain an exemption or a substitution. The guilty, the careless, the sensualist, the mocker, the trifler, the old man here that is coming to his grave with his heart hard and selfish, the merchant here who imagines he has no time to be a Christian, the scholar that dreams he can make learning and accomplishments pass for repentance toward God and faith in the Lord Jesus Christ, the profane swearer, the scandal-monger and uncharitable tale-bearer, the proud, resentful woman, the wilful boy who is trying to forget his mother's prayers, the vain girl who thinks of every dress for her body but that one which will be put on her for her burial,—*all* of us must appear before the judgment seat of Christ.

The third fact is that we must *appear* there; that is, we must be not only present, but our true characters must be made manifest; what is here kept hidden must come to light. We pray, every Sunday, to Him "to whom all hearts are open, and from whom no secrets are hid." In that day, this Searcher and Reader of our hearts will take us up, and deal with us. Faith will stand out boldly. Purity will shine in garments white as the light. Long-abused innocence will get its due. Misunderstood charity and wrongly suspected integrity will come forth out of their cloud, in triumph and joy. "Holy and humble men of heart" will be seen for what they are.

Deception and concealment will have had their crafty way long enough. Masks will fall off. Disguises will be stripped aside. The cunning sagacity that has covered up the lurking passion, or the cool calculation, will lose its self-possession. Whatever wicked thing we have been at most pains to conceal will be written out as with a pen of fire on our foreheads. There will be only one covering for our shame,—and that the robe of the mercy promised to them who believe. There is a fountain for uncleanness. Purge me in that, and I shall be clean! Wash me in that, and I shall be whiter than snow!

The only thing further that it much concerns us to know of the judgment is that He who then reveals our hearts and fixes our condition, the Judge, is the Son of God and the Son of Man. Repeatedly Christ says that His work, while on earth, in His first coming, is not judgment. Here "I judge no man." Here He ministers life; will we receive it? Here He offers grace; will we accept it? Here He opens the way into His kingdom; will we enter? Here He suffers and dies, the one perfect, sufficient, only sacrifice; can we believe, confess, and live? There, on His throne, all judgment is committed unto Him, " because He is the Son of Man." He knows all man's infirmity, to have compassion; all man's sympathy with evil, to punish. It is not then the time of salvation. The time of salvation is now. Our opportunity is to-day. In *that* day, every work will be brought into judgment, and every secret thing. Every work! Every secret thing!

# THE RIGHTEOUSNESS OF GOD, AND UPRIGHTNESS IN MAN.

*Fourth Sunday after Advent.*

"RIGHTEOUSNESS and judgment are the habitation of His throne."—*Psalm* xcvii. 2.

"PETER answered and said unto her, Tell me whether ye sold the land for so much. And she said, Yea, for so much. Then Peter said unto her, How is it that ye have agreed together to tempt the Spirit of the Lord? Behold, the feet of them that have buried thy husband are at the door, and shall carry thee out."—*Acts* v. 8, 9.

IN the first passage we are shown the principles upon which the universe is carried on through the everlasting ages. They are very simple, though they are very grand. First, there is a living God, living now, not passing away with passing periods, or a mere tradition of the old Bible-days, but alive all days.

Next He has a "Throne"; not only a life, not only a dwelling-place, not only boundless fields to work in, and not only a kind heart, but a throne. The psalm begins, "The Lord reigneth." This world, with everybody in it, is not only under a government, but under a personal Governor. Modern science is right about everything being done by law; only revelation uncovers to science a secret of its own. Behind the law is a Law-giver and a Judge,—a truth of quite as much practical value to us, in the long run, as the other. The history of man on the globe is not a spontaneous generation. The machine of nature is not running itself. The seasons and the harvests, the streams and the stars, house-keeping, schools, trade, politics, are not the human contrivance of "perpetual motion." There may be a good deal of meaning in such popular words as "self-reliance," "independence," "the power of the will," "man the master of circumstances," "dignity of human nature"; but then, after all, there is a Throne, and One sits on it who is not man. We talk of self-reliance, but the reliance at least is upon Him. Of Him, it is finally found out, we are never independent. As to the power of the will, when it has done its best, it brings up against another Will, more powerful than itself, immeasurably more. There turn out to be circumstances of which we are not masters, by any means. The stopping of pulse and breath is one of them. Human nature has, to be sure, a kind of dignity, but there is a greatness infinitely more royal, and a glory more glorious.

Then we know what the Throne is made of, and what He who occupies it keeps there forever with Him. We are not governed by caprice, by impulse, by policy, by passion, by indiscriminate indulgence. There are principles of this rule over us, and their names are given,—"Righteousness and judgment are the habitation of His throne." They are not there now and then; they inhabit or abide there. They inhere in the character of the living King.

Over all this world, then—this is what the first passage says—over you and me, personally—reigns the living, righteous, just Lord.

The second passage discloses a different sight. It takes us to the opposite extremity of the moral kingdom,—from the top to the bottom. "Self-reliance," separating itself from God as far as it can, has made its experiment, worked out its ambitious result of "independence," and here it is. "Tell me whether ye sold the land for so much. She said, Yea, for so much." The doctrine of the dignity of human nature, left to itself, breaking away from the "Throne," has come to this; and it does not appear to good advantage. It appears with a fraud branded on its forehead, a false invoice in its hand, and a lie upon its lips, the criminal victim of a capital execution. "Then fell she down straightway at his feet and yielded up the ghost; and the young men came in and found her dead, and carrying her forth buried her by her husband. And great fear came upon all the Church." No matter whether the miracle happens once or every day. It is simply the type of a law inevitable and universal. Whether the outer stroke should ever be repeated or not, it was only the visible sign of a thing that is always going on while the world stands,—unrighteousness blasted, lying exposed, the cheating man and the cheating woman, in spite of their skill in concealment, sent down at last to misery.

In the two parts of the text, therefore, we have the same foundation-truth of our religion,—*personal integrity the criterion of life or death.* In the first it shines out in the splendor of the great white Throne, with the rainbow bending its glorious beauty around it. In the last it is thundered forth along the low line of an earthly horizon, out of a horror of great darkness, lit up only by the lightning-flash of God's "consuming fire."

Among the characteristics of the times we are living in there is one not much mentioned by the many popular speakers, who seem to think the men they speak to are to be benefited chiefly by being assured how much wiser and better and more "progressive" they are than any of their fathers were, who suppose the age is to be instructed by being flattered, and that the country needs to be glorified rather than to be purified; which was certainly not the way of the old prophets. The characteristic I mean is dishonesty. I am not discrediting any of the actual modern merits,—intelligence, enterprise, invention, philanthropy. Grant all these, in large degree. Nevertheless, they do not bring with them honesty in proportion. Falsehood and fraud flourish along with them, in spite of them, and in some cases by the help of them. From the vulgar sediment of society up to its highest summits there spreads a tremendous force of selfish materialism—call it sharpness or call it crime—by which men reach after and snatch and call their own, for use or for show or for hoarding, what is not theirs. It is stolen property, only stolen ingeniously and indirectly, and in such ways that the old forms of law, which under took to punish outright robbery, fail to overtake them. Not in a few rare spots, but in every spot where two or three hundred people live together, a part of these people consume, or lay up, or waste, what belongs to other people, and what they have managed to get by some species of deception. What natural production of the earth is there, meant for the sustenance or comfort of man, that is not adulterated by some degrading mixture, or shortened in the measure? Do not the devices of Anglo-Saxon traffic repeat, in faithful exactness, the devices of the Jew, denounced by the prophet, making the ephah of the seller small, and the shekel of the buyer large; selling the refuse for wheat, and "falsifying the balance by deceit"? What line of mechanical work is there, where the base material, or the shabby construction, or the overcharge, does not disgrace the handicraft?

What branch of commerce without its delusive labels, its broken promises, its advertising fictions, its postponed payments, its calculated bankruptcies, its hollow contracts? Men who will not suffer their respectability to be challenged, look one another in the face, and with a mutual jugglery of knavish tricks conspire to grow rich by villany. The brilliant audacities of the great commercial centres have their lame and creeping copies, hardly less cruel or calamitous, back in the little rural villages, in sight of grave-yards where sleep the ashes of clean-handed ancestors, living and dying, in their day, in the faith of a God who has righteousness and judgment for the habitation of His Throne. Outside the Church are financial Ahabs and social Jezebels. Inside are Ananias and Sapphira, tacitly agreeing together to lie to the Holy Ghost, pretending to give to God, for missions or Bible societies, a hush-money fragment of what they have seized from their fellow-men. Too often there is no Peter with the courage to search out their sin,—" Tell me whether ye sold the land for so much." The grand difficulty with our popular piety is that it is still trying to find a way, in this nineteenth century of the Gospel, of serving two gods together.

If our national Christianity is to maintain its respect, it will have to deal with these abominations somewhat more directly, more fearlessly, and more personally, than it is doing now. Greatly to their credit, our cotemporary moralists have undertaken to investigate crime, its sources, its statistics, and its correction. But the criminals are of two classes. One class, ill-bred, ill-fed, ill-clad, with little knowledge, bad examples, and strong temptations, take what they have no right to take, and render no equivalent. Another class, better clothed, better educated, with a better chance of living honestly, perhaps holding offices and entertaining flattering assemblies, do precisely the same thing. The first class perform their lawless work in the dark; and so do these. The detected felons sometimes put on masks; and what else but a mask are good manners over an unprincipled heart? The vagrant robbers occasionally come together and lay out their schemes and count their booty. The gentlemanly robbers who haunt the lobbies of Legislatures, the municipal chambers, the bribable courts — tramps of the commercial highways — understand each other with an instinct just as keen, and a cunning just as infamous. Now, if this is all true, and if the habitation of the living God is righteousness and judgment, then what is sure to come by and by, when the King, patient as He is, uncovers that Throne, and the Judge finally brings these souls, one by one, to the reckoning? Are we any safer than Ananias and Sapphira? Is this a safe country? With all its advantages, its celebrations of what it has done, and its loud predictions of what it is going to do, is America resting, secure and approved, this Advent, at the foot of God's righteous judgment seat?

"Tell me whether ye sold the land for so much; and she said, Yea! for so much."

Is there any remedy? The remedy will be found by finding through what popular mistakes the mischief has crept in, and by raising against them the everlasting principles of the Bible-morality, the old-fashioned safeguards of personal uprightness, on the staunch commandments of a God of righteousness.

The unguarded conversation of men is the natural revelation of them; of their moral standards, if they have any, and of their lack of them if they have none. We hear people continually debating whether some line of action will be lucrative, prudent, or agreeable; politic, reputable, or successful; whether it will serve some interest, or baffle some opponent, or advance some party. But how often, in all the thoroughfares of society, do we hear an open question shut and concluded by the short, swift, clear argument of a Christian tongue? "This is right, and because it is right, it must be done, cost what consequences it may; that other thing is wrong, and therefore it cannot be touched, let it promise to pay what it will." In the clamoring of calculation and profit, how often is the simple voice of Duty audible and decisive?

Looking for causes, we find that, among the virtues which the people honor, we have been trying a good deal, of late, to make the softer virtues answer for the sturdier, and philanthropy for all the rest. It happened by a natural reaction. In the feudalism and vassalage of the middle ages, and under the monarchies of the old world, the tendency ran to physical cruelty. Life was cheap. Liberty was crushed. The lower classes were not too good to suffer any sort of deprivation. The slave was at the mercy of the master; and where that is true, mercy always gives place, sooner or later, to wrath. When the free spirit arose, and more equal forms of civil society were planted, the milder compassions and gentler sensibilities of Christian people came uppermost. So far as the moral feelings were aroused at all, the impulse was to make everybody comfortable in condition and happy in mind. But there is something higher than that. Wrongs were righted, not always because they were wrongs, and because rights are sacred, but because suffering is disagreeable. If a malefactor was seized by the arm of justice, and shut up in prison, an indiscriminate sympathy, thinking nothing of the safety of society, went about to stir up public sympathy in his behalf, sent flowers and pictures and carpets to his cell, tried to shorten his term of punishment, and, if possible, to get him out of the hands of the law altogether. Now, it must be a hard heart which does not recognize in these kindly impulses the working of the spirit of Christian charity. Such ameliorations were needed, in a degree, and they came, and blessed were they by whom they came. But, after all, God does not govern mankind by an unqualified pity, but by mercy balanced with justice; by tenderness harmonized with severity,— the severity itself sometimes being merciful. In mortal progress the pendulum swings from one extreme to another. Probably in the old social order there were some upright and downright traits, intermixed with coarser ones, which, as sons of a God of righteousness, we could not afford to let go, and which we shall have to bring back, and plant side by side with our yielding charities and fair humanities, before we shall throw off this disgrace of dishonesty. There must be more respect for reality, and less for show; more willingness to be poor, if God wills it; less anxiety to hang out the signals of success; more simplicity and less extravagance. Nor is there any such thing possible as atoning for a fraudulent getting of money by giving a part of it away. Ananias laid a part of the proceeds of the land at the Apostle's feet for the use of the Church. It is known of one of the foremost of American statesmen that he was in the habit of bestowing munificent alms impulsively on mendicant people about him, and letting his debts go unpaid. What a wretched world this would be if the Almighty turned His ordinances of truth into a confusion of unprincipled indulgences like that! Kindness is always lovely, but kindness will not save us from the consequences, if we do not pay what we owe, or if we take more than our due. An age of mingled philanthropy and dishonesty is not an age of the reign of Christ, whose name is "the Lord our righteousness."

Another mistake pertains to the realm of religion. In almost any of our communities you may set ten persons to inquire into the religious state of their neighbors, and in nine cases of the ten the first question will be about feelings; not, What are your convictions of truth, your principles of conduct, the root and ground of your faith in God, or in the solid and fixed facts of a revealed Gospel and historical kingdom of our Lord? but, What is your feeling? not, What are you standing on? not whether a holy Christ has your loyal and unflinching obedience; not how far you are practically pledged to a righteous Master,—which are certainly the chief matters now, as they were in the days and the preaching of the Apostles,—but rather whether the sensibilities are lively and the devout emotions enthusiastic. Religious feeling is one of the fruits of the Spirit—one of them; it has much to do in kindling and sustaining religious exertion. But feeling is certainly the most irregular element in our composition, and it so far depends on outward conditions that it makes one of the least trustworthy tests of the actual frame of a Christian soul before God. Feeling belongs to the passive part of our nature; principle to the active part. Feeling depends on a sensitive surface; principle on depths of moral purity. We feel spontaneously, and often whether we would or not. There is no principle and no duty without a direct exertion of the will. Feeling may be sudden; duty is deliberate. Feeling may be transient; duty is constant. Feeling changes with temperament, with states of health and nerves, with a thousand fickle external influences.

Principle is independent of all physical or alterable circumstances, moves straight on through all moods and climates, sails by fixed stars, and is the same secure and glorious thing through all the shifting seasons, though the mountains of prosperity were torn up and cast into the sea.

It deserves to be considered, therefore, whether the emotional type of piety is, on the whole, the only or the strongest type, or is calculated to carry a man bravely and uprightly through all the temptations of the market and society, of public and private life. Let us hope that the sturdy common-sense of this people will repudiate any ministration that addresses itself chiefly to a sentimental fancy, whether in the gusty appeals of open-air conventicles, in sensational pulpits, or in the scenery of church chancels. Is it not likely that some part of the loose dealings, and false accounts, and violated covenants, which have frightened the propriety and shocked the better sense of all Christian bodies, are traceable to this idea, that religion is concerned entirely with emotions, and not with character? Ananias and his wife had just come into the church, been baptized, joined the Christian community, and their feelings were so far wrought upon that they wanted to follow where the popular current was then setting, and to throw their private estate into the common treasury, though that was no part of the Christian obligation, as St. Peter taught them. What was their sentimental ardor worth? It did not save them from being both, one after the other, wound up in shrouds and carried out to a dishonored burial. It appears to me that, even within the recollection of living men, the Christian Faith has come to be less and less regarded as a commanding and mighty power from Heaven, a voice of authority, a law of holy life, but more and more as an easy-going guide to future enjoyment, to a universal happiness and an indiscriminate salvation. Who can believe these horrible insults to morality would go on cursing our cities, and corrupting our young men, if the offenders looked up above a hireling police, a venal judiciary, and a cowardly public opinion, and believed those simple words, "Thou, God, seest me, who wilt by no means clear the guilty"? The Gospel is a gift of grace; but if it does not keep the disciple out of the schemes of sharpers and liars, the grace has miscarried. The Gospel is love; but it has a law-element in it, too, which the saintliest Christian never outgrows. The Old Testament goes into the New. The Saviour says explicitly He came not to destroy the law, but to fill it full, and that He is coming again to judge every follower by his deeds. If you cut the New Testament apart from the Old, your one Bible is gone, and rationalism will pick the fragments to pieces at its leisure. We want that elder and eternal Testament which gives us the text—"Righteousness and judgment are the habitation of His throne." See how that word "righteous" studs all the Scripture-pages, and how the glorious reality it represents is the steadfast foundation of the welfare of souls, from the first creation on to the new heavens and the new earth.

We read public reports of ardent religious agitations. Not a syllable shall my lips speak in disparagement of religious revivals. Till there is more thought for things unseen, in these uncounted dwellings around us, which have now no veneration, no Lord's Day, no prayer, no sacrament, no Advent, and no realized God, we can ill afford to despise any honest attempt to waken the dead to life. But we are certainly not wrong if, with God's Bible in our hands, we urge that the religion that is revived shall revive with it honesty, fair dealing, veracity, chastity, plain living and faithful work; shall bring on a new epoch of duty,—courageous, clean-handed, sweet-hearted duty, irreproachable and incorruptible duty—fearing God and keeping His commandments.

How wise it would be, too, if, in the disorganizing social questions and the depressing commercial reverses of the time, we could come to look at these problems more in the daylight of duty, and less under the delusive glamour of speculation! When markets are overloaded and the wheels of industry hang idle; when merchants go to their counting-rooms in the morning, not to see how much money they can make, but how little they can lose; when the charities of the Church are shrivelled, and hope dies out of the hearts of the poor, not for the want of bounty but for the want of work; do not imagine you can go to the bottom of the matter by some disputed theory of currency or political economy. Take God's law with your account-book. Admit, frankly, that enterprise and commerce have been living, these last years, too much on false pretenses. Own that where business professed that it was done on solid capital, it has been done on bubbles of air; that you have walked in vain shadows, and called those shadows property; that you have promoted to places of honor men who have asked to be trusted when there was nothing to trust,—men shocked at no duplicity, sticking at no excess, ashamed of no dishonor! How can any financial philosophy or turn of political parties repair ruins wrought by sins like these?

You return from the out-of-door vexations, for peace, to your home. But remember that even home, where virtue generally makes its last retreat, if without this

Christian principle of right, is no safer than the exchange or the street. Marriage loses its sacredness, and along with its sanctity its joy. Domestic life is tossed into a troubled, angry strife. License and self-will, pagan deities, stalk out of their old Pantheon, and become the household gods of a degenerate and heathenized Christendom. Men look at women through a mist of passion, and women look at men as rival claimants for privilege and power. Who can marvel that the fountains of young life are poisoned, and that the foundations of social honor are loose? The relations of man and woman will not grow healthier—they will be worse disordered—till we hear less about "rights," and more of *what is right*; less of the clashing of their spheres, and more of their mutual obligations. Were every "incompatible" husband and wife to take at once the simple spirit of duty for their reconciliation, resolved to do what is nobly and tenderly right, in the mutual bond that has bound them divinely and indissolubly together, a new age would begin in the soiled history of American families, and cleaner blood would run in the veins of the generations coming. We need apostolic households, no less than an apostolic Church; and it is an Apostle who, when he has said, "Wives obey your husbands," says with equal emphasis, "Husbands, love your wives, and be not bitter against them,"—and what gentleness in his reason!—for "The husband is the head of the wife, as Christ of the Church."

Begin with your children. Speak cheerfully, but reverently and solemnly, to them of the righteousness of God. Tell them He is their Father, and tell them He is their Judge. Show them His face of compassion; show them His Throne of retribution. Teach them that He loves the good; teach them that He hates lying, and lust, and all iniquity, and that, for His goodness's sake, He will sweep those who do not hate them finally into tribulation. Take care, yourselves, to touch not the unclean thing, so that your counsel to your sons and daughters be not a mockery. Shake off the first dishonest penny from your fingers, as the Apostle shook the venomous viper into the fire. Stand in awe of your conscience; stand in awe of the King of kings. Expect and welcome, from the ministry of Christ, searching messages. Pray for prophets who will rebuke you, as their ancient predecessors did Israel, for robbing man by any fraud, for robbing God by keeping back the offerings at His altar which He requires at your hands. Turn to old Isaiah, and listen to the burden of his advent vision:

"Hear, O Heaven, and give ear, O Earth, for the Lord hath spoken. I have nourished and brought up children, and they have rebelled against me. Wash you; make you clean. Cease to do evil; learn to do well. Seek judgment; relieve the oppressed; right the fatherless; plead for the widow. Zion shall be redeemed with judgment, and her converts with righteousness. Say ye to the righteous, It shall be well with them, for they shall eat the fruit of their doings. Woe unto the wicked; it shall be ill with him, for the reward of his hand shall be given him. The mouth of the Lord hath spoken it."

# THE MAN CHRIST JESUS.

### *Christmas Day.*

"AND they shall call His name EMMANUEL, which being interpreted is, GOD WITH US.—*St. Matthew* i. 23.

THE form of the sentence is prophetic. The Evangelist expressly quotes it from the Book of prophecy where it originally stood. Isaiah, sometimes called the evangelist among the prophets, because his mind was so deeply acquainted with the spirit of Christ, wrote it as a promise to his people. Through them it was a promise to the world. Blind and lost humanity had gone wrong, groping and stumbling down the slope of four thousand evil years. Had it been only man that was offended, then some better man, large of brain and large of heart, might have been the mediator. But the Prophet saw deeper than that. With the Psalmist, he knew that the human heart must cry out, "Against Thee, Thee only," O *my God*, "have I sinned." Some mightier Saviour must come. Even the Heaven of heavens is moving itself in mercy. "Ask thee a sign of the Lord thy God; ask it either in the depth or in the height above. The Lord himself shall give you a sign. Behold, a virgin shall conceive, and bear a Son." "In the beginning was the Word, and the Word was with God, and the Word was God. He was in the world,—that world which was made by Him,—and the world knew Him not." "In

Him was life"; original, absolute, eternal, uncreated life. So, virgin-born, God came in great humility as man,—Emmanuel,—and we, with undeserving eyes, beheld His glory, the glory as of one only begotten of the Father, full of grace and truth. How have we beheld Him? Has it been with a joy like John's? Has it been with a faith like Mary's? Have we knelt, bringing our offerings to Him with the sages, or worshipped Him in simplicity of heart, with the shepherds?

Secondly, the Mediator was to come in the purity and the power of a sinless human character. Here, again, notice how simple and natural the prophet's language is. The child to be born "shall know to refuse the evil and choose the good." Heavenly knowledge! "To depart from evil, that is understanding." This Christ to come shall be the perfect Man. In Him all virtues, all graces, shall meet. They shall not only meet but harmonize in Him, blending together into one matchless manhood. It shall not be as in all other men, the grandest specimens of virtue, where some disproportion spoils the symmetry; excess or defect, one-sidedness or limitation, clinging to the highest minds. But everything in Him shall be tempered faultlessly together: energy with patience, dignity with tenderness, forbearance toward the guilty with indignation at wrong, command with obedience, courage with humility, the fortitude of heroes and martyrs with the sensibility of woman, and the ripe experience of saints with the artlessness of a child. It was "that *holy* thing" of which the angel spoke so mysteriously and awfully to Mary, which "should be born of her," as "the Son of God." He would be the man with men. He would be humanity's one consummate immaculate example. He would be the world's one stainless human soul.

This was the second part of the world's one real want: First, Divine redemption for the sins that are past. Secondly, a holy Man. We, my friends, are a part of the human world; and you and I, if we have attained at all to a spiritual life, must join in with the cry of this longing of human hearts for a Christ. Give us, O Giver of all good gifts, one Leader like ourselves; one glorious human Person that we can love immeasurably and forever, and the more we love Him be the more exalted; one King that our loyalty can cling to, without abatement or misgiving, till we die, and then not die eternally. Let Him be one of us, that we may be one in Him. Let Him be no strange, distant demigod, belonging neither to heaven nor earth, too unearthly for our affections, and yet too mortal for our worship. But let Him be born here,—on this familiar, sinful earth, which feels human to our human feet; in some Bethlehem village, where men and women work and weep, and children play in the streets; and if it be in a stable-manger, so much the better for the encouragement of our faith that He really means to minister to us, and to take the form of a servant, and to put pride altogether away;— though He was rich with the wealth of heaven and earth before, to become poor for our sake. Let Him grow up in a carpenter's family, that He may make all our common labor sacred, and have a place in every humble house on the globe. Though He is to be the conqueror of all nations and all ages, let us see Him first as a filial boy at home, subject to the order of the house, obedient to His mother, growing into His lordship over the race through these steps of pious subordination. Above all, let Him, for our poor sinful nature's sake,—let Him be tempted, like as we are, that He may know how to succor and pity and love us who are tempted. Complete, and spotless, and triumphant in His holiness, let us nevertheless find Him facing our adversary,—in actual struggles,—in the wilderness, hungry for earthly bread; on the temple-top, with the pride of personal display before Him; at the mount, beholding the kingdoms of worldly dominion lying helpless within the grasp of His ambition, yet refusing them. Alone, out among the hills, when the world of men has misunderstood, worried, rejected Him, with the night wind on His heated face, let us catch the words of peaceful prayer from His lips. Though He is to overcome death, passing through it, and rising from it, yet, since we all dread it, let us hear Him entreat, under its agony, "If it be possible, let this cup pass from Me." Let us meet Him weeping sometimes at the grave of His friend, and by all this thorough and utter humanity in Him, let Him be to us a brother, while He is a Saviour; Mary's child, while He reigns over the kingdom of David,—the Son of Man, as He is the Son of God,—God himself, in His wondrous way, *with us.* Emmanuel!

When this yearning of mankind was taken up into the guidance and inspiration of God, it became prophecy. The voice became articulate. A "more sure word," as the Apostle says, "holy men of old spoke as they were moved by the Holy Ghost." One of the most expressive titles of our Lord condenses and conveys all this that I have been trying to say. He was the "Desire of all nations," and accordingly the Evangelist, in the passage of the text, while he records the blessed nativity at Bethlehem, adds to the narrative, "Now all this was done, that it might be fulfilled which was spoken of the Lord by the prophet." Some puzzled students, looking not much below the literal sense lying on the surface, have wondered at this language, and disputed about it. "Is it credible," they have asked, "that God in heaven should order such grand transactions as make up the Messiah's ministry, merely for the purpose of fulfilling certain old predictions, written by men ages before?" But there is a profounder view of the unity between prophets and evangelists than this. And where do we find it, but in the very significance and strength of those desires we have just seen in the whole mind and heart of the nations of men, seeing them there just because we feel them first in ourselves;— desires for a Divine propitiation, for a perfect Master, Leader, Lord, to love, and trust, and follow,—to love more than life, to follow through all hurt and peril with joy, to trust for everlasting salvation? In order that these longings of the human heart,—fed on prophecy, divinely instructed, made a preparation for Christ, gathered up and clothed in miraculous authority in great illuminated seers like Isaiah and Zechariah,—might be fulfilled, He was born, and died. Herein was love. Nothing here is beneath the dignity of the covenants and revelations of Heaven. It is the answer of God's eternal purpose to the cry of His penitent family, in the gift of the Emmanuel, our Saviour.

And now these things that I have been saying to you, as our Christmas morning thought, are a declaration,— only not in the usual formulas of theological discussion, —of the one fact which lies central and life-giving, at the heart of all our Christian thoughts and hopes. The name that the creeds and standards of the Church have always given it is the Incarnation,—or the doctrine of God in Christ, made flesh, and dwelling with us. Ready as Christians have been, however, to give that blessed truth this place in words, there is too much reason to fear it does not possess the soul of Christendom as the joyful conviction it ought to be, lightening all our darkness, scattering all our fear, sanctifying all our life. We cover it up with strange and gloomy draperies of unreal phraseology, technical traditions, or sectarian disputes. It is not blessed truth at all then, but is robbed of its blessedness. Let it stand out in its own simple, fresh, and glorious splendor, and what loveliness of moral beauty, what majesty of disinterested sacrifice, what gladness of relief and consolation, what beam of hope is there, that does not meet and mingle in its mercy? In the whole world of realities there is nothing so real, or so comforting to us, as this. *Emmanuel!*

Further, we come short of the full grandeur of the Gospel when we take the clause, "God with us," as signifying only *one among us*,—a Deity moving among individuals, outside of them all, and, however friendly and gracious, still an external Person, saving them only by a work wrought all above them. Christ's atonement is *no* mechanical device in the Divine counsels, brought in at an unexpected emergency in the world's fortunes, paying the price of men's sins in a mercantile equivalent adjusted by contract, after which the Redeemer retires to contemplate His ransomed beneficiaries from afar off. Oh, friends in Christ, friends *in* Christ, we have a dearer, warmer, holier faith. When it is said that, in Emmanuel, God is *with us*, it is meant that His very nature is wrought into our nature, if in faith and baptism we *receive Him*, and ours into His. In the true Incarnation all humanity is, in a certain sense, taken up into the embrace of God. Henceforth all the world is saved, and no soul born of woman,—no man, no child, —needs to be an alien or outcast from the Father's House. It only needs that the energetic command be heeded,— "Repent and be baptized; come in faith; accept your heritage; be born of water and of the Spirit; awake to the spiritual privileges and holy living of the family order and affection around you." Then new beauty will robe the earth; new joy will encompass it like an atmosphere! Now we have a meaning for the angels' song,—" Glad tidings of great joy to all people"; "Glory to God in the highest; on earth peace; good-will to men." Old things *are* passed away; behold all things are become new.

It is a remark of the historian Guizot, and it doubtless contains a sound philosophy, for all history confirms it, that "there never can be a great moral revolution without its being concentrated in some great personage." Doubtless, loyalty, everywhere, must have a leader. But the practical assurance which this Feast of the Nativity repeats to us reaches far beyond that, and comes home to the heart's experience of those that are themselves sore let and hindered in running the race that is set before them. Christ not merely takes His place in history; but all history takes place in Him. He is large enough, comprehensive enough, compassionate enough, to take in all the experience, the souls, the lives, the burdens, the sorrows, of all nations and all ages. See at once what a higher and holier character this truth puts on the much-abused dogma of the dignity of human nature. Human nature without the incarnation is the least dignified of all things: it is weak, inconstant, vulgar, guilty, lost. As for anything it is in itself, only conceit and vanity could call it noble, and hence it is that the doctrine of the dignity of human nature, held without the Church-truth of Christ's divinity and incarnation, has proved but a thin and feeble force to convert mankind, to raise society, or to send out missions to the heathen. Its fatal infirmity, in the lack of this fundamental and vitalizing fact of the Gospels, has emptied even its honest and eloquent advocates of spiritual power. But let it be seen that human nature is uplifted and ennobled in the Divine humanity of Christ, Son of Man and Son of God, and forthwith it wears a grandeur as if the majestic bearing and outlines of the Divine Man were visibly reflected upon it. Education is a new thing now: it is a sacred training in a sacred school. Social reform is a new thing: for it is no visionary scheme of an indefinite "progress," all whose forces are secular, and whose civilization is unconsecrated, never on its knees, and never at sacraments; but it is a restoration of this divine image in man. Philanthropy is a new thing: no longer bitter, headstrong, factious; but reverential, genial, generous, and orderly. Christ's human nature is the nature of all classes and conditions of men,—the slave's nature, the poor man's nature, the pagan's nature; and when He died, with the crucifixion and anguish of that nature, on the cross, it was that all these might be lifted to the glory of spiritual liberty and light, and their sins be blotted out. Here centre and here rest all solid hopes of a bright and happy future for mankind; not in economic schemes, or bills of rights, or civil constitutions, or policies of a godless self-elevation and self-reliance. They rest in the reverent spirit of the Church of God, with her hopeful and all-animating certainty of an incarnate Lord, a God with us, who is the Son of Man: *Emmanuel.*

Then, too, it will begin to appear what Christ's own people may be, acknowledging their membership, confirmed and alive in His body. Take the Holy Scriptures and see how often Christ is there spoken of as an indwelling Christ, present now, formed within, living in the believer and the believer in Him, the very Life of life.

Take our service of the Holy Communion of His body and blood; study its sublime scriptural language; and you find how intimate and inward is this membership of the disciple and communicant with his Lord by faith. Light even breaks in on that almost inexplicable and incredible saying of St. Peter, that by the "exceeding great and precious promises" of the Word made flesh, men may be "partakers of the Divine nature, escaping the corruption that is in the world through lust." Reason, blind and anxious, may still have its difficulties, and toil and grind in its prison-house, "bound in affliction and iron"; but Faith marches right over them as if they were not; nay, she takes wings and leaves them out of her sight. What we want, *that* our Gospel gives. While Reason is puzzling herself about the mystery, Faith is turning it into her daily bread, and feeding on it thankfully in her heart of hearts. While Reason is applying the tests of her earthly chemistry, threatening to dissolve the very cross of Calvary in her crucibles, Faith has quietly set the holy doctrine to the music of her joy, and is singing it as her hymn of *Benedictus*, or *Magnificat*, in unquestioning peace. The doctrine may crucify the proud, but it crowns the meek with salvation.

We cannot separate, then, fellow Christians, the two main grounds of our Christian rejoicing this day. If reconciliation is by the Lord's sacrifice, so is daily righteousness and sanctification by His life. There could be no Mediator without both; and by both we are saved. If, "being justified by faith, we have peace with God through our Lord Jesus Christ," so in the blessed remembrance of the Divine humanity of that unseen Friend we shall find a power to raise us, day by day, above the weakness, the suffering, and the sinfulness of the mortal flesh. Perhaps some of us will find there what will even comfort us more than the bare thought of an "escape from the wrath to come," viz., a power to help us mightily in this mysterious and constant strife of the flesh with the spirit. We know now that the world of matter and the body is under no malignant deity or demon at war with God; but to the believer even the outer tabernacle is sanctified by Him who took it upon Him; the flesh, too, is redeemed; the "creature itself shall be delivered from the bondage of corruption into the glorious liberty of the children of God"; and, while "the whole creation groaneth and travaileth in pain together," we wait in Christ who hath taken our flesh "for the redemption and resurrection of our body," which is the living image and figure of His Church.

Honor and praise, then, in the Church, with Christmas anthems, with the shepherds, and the sages, and the virgin-mother, and the heavenly host, to our Emmanuel, as the Son of Man! As man He was born. As man He was a servant, was homeless, was weary, was an hungered, and wept. As man He was tempted, and as man He was without sin. As man He endured contradiction, reviling, insult, cruelty, and yet said, "Daughters of Jerusalem, weep not for Me, but weep for yourselves and for your children." As man He was crucified, dead, and buried. As man He rose again, ascended, and reigns. As man He shall come again, to divide, and to judge, and to reign; for "therefore is all judgment committed unto Him, because He is the Son of Man."

So well-grounded is the universal joy of this day's feast. The blessing belonging to it falls not on one day, or on a few rare and separated spots. Its light shines in through all the frost and fruitage of the year. When the star in the east came and stood over where the young child was, and looked in on the Bethlehem stable, it saw the beginning of a reconciliation which should bring rest to the world. When the song of the angels startled the shepherds, keeping watch over their flocks by night, it was the first strain of a harmony in which we bear our unworthy part this morning, to sound on till it is completed, where it was begun,—in heaven. The manger is a cradle for all the anxieties and sorrows and fears of our hearts, where they may sleep in child-like peace. The human nativity of Jesus is the Divine birthday and new creation of the soul.

# FAITH OUTLIVING ITS SPECIAL OCCASIONS.

*Sunday after Christmas.*

"AND it came to pass, as the angels were gone away from them into Heaven, the shepherds said one to another, Let us now go even unto Bethlehem, and see this thing which is come to pass, which the Lord hath made known unto us."—*St. Luke* ii. 15.

THE trial of men's faith comes after God's awakening angels have gone away.

His angels are His messengers. In so sublime a ceremonial as the visible ushering into the world of the Person of its Lord they might well come as winged forms in the sky, heavenly light clothing them, singing a supernatural hymn: the whole appearance a court befitting the glory of the King. When God bringeth His only begotten Son into the world, He "maketh His angels spirits, and His ministers a flame of fire." We call it supernatural, and it is; yet what could be more natural *to Him* than that, when the eternal Son, begotten of His Father before all worlds, becomes a man,—because men could not be thoroughly and inwardly saved but by the sacrifice and sympathy of a Saviour entering into the poverty and suffering of their mortal estate,—those intermediate orders of life which stand between Him and us should attend His advent, and announce the transcendent blessing to the world? It was too high a mystery to be heralded, even in music, from the stained and sinning lips of men.

To us God's favoring messengers are stripped of their miraculous raiment. They take the shape of merciful providences to relieve and comfort us, of Christian ordinances to strengthen us, festivals to reawaken our thanksgiving, and human hearts to enrich the poverty of ours with their affection. The Faith that was born at Bethlehem is ages old; its outer benefits as well as its forms are familiar. While they are present to the senses in the vividness of some special impression it is not very difficult probably for our feelings to move in grateful answer to their ministrations. On the Mount of Transfiguration the three favored disciples cried, "Let us build tabernacles and abide here"; yet scarcely had they stepped down from the splendors of Tabor when they began disputing which follower of the poor stable-born and homeless Redeemer should be greatest. In the fresh mercy of some gracious deliverance, from sadness or pain or accident or threatened sorrow, men cast their thank-offering into the treasury of the Church, and wonder that they should ever be forgetful of God's care. In the stillness of a sanctuary, when all the harmonies of holy times and places seem to shut out temptation, to set open the windows of heaven, and fill the uplifted spirit with hearty praise, men say, "Would to God all days and places were like this; for then faith, and zeal, and charity never would grow cold!" In the warmth of the feast it is easy to be glad. And even when the shadow moves into the house,—for that shadow too is one of God's angels,—the whole family, bending with prayers and whispers above one fevered, wasting child, find it easy to turn to the Saviour, and impossible not to pray. But these hours pass by. The angels are gone away into heaven. The festive lights are put out; the temple-doors are shut; the Winter snow lies white and smooth on the little grave in the burial-ground. The world comes crowding, beseeching, flattering, threatening, almost forcing its way back, with its noise and its guilt, into the unguarded and yielding heart. Then comes the test of the reality, the sincerity, the power, of your Christian principles.

When the song ceased, the first Christmas eve, and the bright host vanished from the sky, the shepherds did not fall asleep again, and so have only a dream to tell the next morning. They verified the vision, like earnest and constant men. They stayed a while, and watched, and resolved: "Let us now go even unto Bethlehem, and see this thing which is come to pass, which the Lord hath made known to us."

Secondly: Such willingness to watch and seek commonly leads, as it does here, to an equal readiness to *believe* when the promise is fulfilled, and they that have sought Christ find Him. It will be easy to imagine in them—and all the easier because there are so many people close at hand that are examples of it,—a state of mind exactly opposite to this simple, believing, and confiding one in the shepherds. They might have said,—and if they had been modern philosophers, conceited critics, or ambitious naturalists, they would have been very sure to say,—to each other, " Beware how you believe: these, to be sure, are extraordinary phenomena; they look very much as miracles are said to look,— brilliant figures plainly seen by many witnesses, nay, by our own eyes, and articulate melodies from their tongues!—but possibly electricity, meteorology, optics, or acoustics may explain them all;—light or sound." And if the legitimate sciences fail, they can at least fall back on necromancy and witchcraft,—the retributive " spiritualism " which often persuades those who would not believe a miracle of truth to believe the miracle of a lie. Anything but simple, straight-forward Christian faith, of Gospel and Church together! They say, "We will look into our books. It is extremely unlikely that nature would interrupt her order, or let in new light by a new channel. Let us take care not to be ridiculed for believing too much." And so, while they turn downward from God to themselves, these Scribes of outward knowledge and Pharisees of the law of nature, as fast bound against all the living power of truth and the liberty in Christ as ever the Scribes and Pharisees of the letter and law of Judaism were, freeze in unbelief. Glories of heaven and earth, grander than telescopes ever pierced among the stars, or hammers ever uncovered in the rocks, pass by, and there is no vision to behold them. Quick minds, but dull affections! Full understandings and empty hearts! Spiritual things not seen for want of spiritual senses! "O fools and slow of heart to believe" all that God's prophets, God's angels, God's Scriptures have spoken!

Around the person of Jesus in the flesh, when the Divine voice was ringing out of Heaven above Him, some said that it thundered, others that an angel spoke to Him. These shepherds were wiser than the sages. God knew whom he was choosing when he opened Heaven on those clear-hearted keepers of simple flocks. They discredited neither messenger nor message,—as true and humble-minded disciples reject neither Christ nor His Church, the Bridegroom nor the Bride. They said, not as our own doubters say, "Let us go somewhere and see whether this thing is come to pass or not"; but, "Let us go and see this thing *which is come to pass*, which the Lord hath made known to us." Everywhere you see men ready to *know*, ready to reason, ready to speculate, ready to stand by their party and their prejudice, ready to dogmatize and denounce those that differ, ready to receive this world's gifts. But when that divinest gift of all comes,—pardon and eternal life; purity and peace; Emmanuel born in a manger; a kingdom coming not with observation; the gift of Christ; a Life that is within life and beyond life, which can come only by believing; are they ready? Not till they are will Christmas Day be really honored, or Jesus really come within us in power.

Thirdly: When Faith is prompt, honest, and manly, like this, it comes out as it does in these brave men, to an open confession. The shepherds said what they said frankly, "*one to another*," and with one consent. It was a confession of Faith as much as the Creed we have said this morning; and, like that, its substance was not an opinion of men, but a Divine Fact which had taken place. So they did not hide their purposes, or play fast and loose with their convictions. They did not arise and go, one by one, in byways of concealment, as if they were ashamed of their errand, or were going only on guesses instead of certainties; they looked each other in the face, as men do who act upon realities, and know what they believe, and expect the same good faith in their fellows. They spoke out their belief. They set up their banner. They came forth from among the unbelieving. They enrolled themselves under their Leader. Would all the men who actually believe with them, and mean not to dishonor their Master, but are kept back by false teaching, unfounded fears, and scruples that no evangelic promise justifies, only *come* with them,—there would be such a rallying of workmen under the cross to-day as would make it almost a new nativity, such a feast as the Church has scarcely kept since Pentecost; enough to make the whole family in heaven and earth sing "Glory to God in the highest," with united acclamation.

But after all these,—after the constancy which outlives the visit of the special privilege, after the willing Faith that accepts without question the offered Saviour, and after the frank and fearless confession of His name before men, comes one sharp criterion more. Will those men who have resolved to go to Bethlehem and see, really arise and go? Many a Christian life falters and fails in every congregation between these two. Will resolve pass on into action, and a good faith confirm and demonstrate itself in good works? Yes, "they came with haste, and found Mary and Joseph, and the Babe lying in a manger. And when they had seen it, they *made known abroad* the saying which was told them concerning the Child."

So complete are the intimations of Christian doctrine in this story of the shepherds. It ends where every Christian life must be lived, in hearty service to Christ and the preaching of His truth. Visions are transient; the festival is but for a day; the angels go away into heaven. But the indwelling Christ abides. *Every day*, amidst ignorance, and wrong, and difficulty, His will is to be done. For us all, the true trial of our faith is in the constancy which clings to the promise of His Word, and the diligence which keeps its vows, and bears His cross.

We have now celebrated the birthday not only of Christ, but of Christendom. Men point sincerely enough to its vast fields, and its centuries of blessing, and call on their fellow-men to receive a religion which yields such fruit. But in that way souls are seldom gained to a living trust, such as either satisfies or sanctifies the heart. We must still return to that old and inspired definition: "Now faith is the substance of things hoped for; the evidence of things not seen." It is not by looking at what has been in the world of the past, it is by feeling the wants of the sinful world within, and by the preparation for the sinless world to come, that we seek and find our Lord. Blessed are they that so hunger and thirst, for they shall be filled! and that so seek, for they shall find!

# NEW AND OLD.

### BEGINNING OF THE YEAR.

*Second Sunday after Christmas.*

"THINGS new and old."— *Matthew* xiii. 52.

INTO these two kinds our Saviour sorts the materials of wise instruction. The doctrines, the spiritual forces, the ways of interesting, influencing, and moulding men for a true service in the Christian life, are of these two classes,—partly new and partly old. This fact is at once an explanation of His own method of teaching, and a direction to His disciples how they should proceed to build up the Church, or to convert and to sanctify any individual heart.

The great Teacher had Himself just spoken to the multitude gathered within the reach of His voice seven striking parables. Four of them,—the parables of the Sower, the Tares growing with the wheat, the Mustard-seed becoming a tree, and of the Leaven penetrating through the woman's measures of wheat,—were doubtless delivered from a fishing-vessel anchored by the shore of the Sea of Galilee, to a multitude of people listening on the banks. The other three,—those of the Treasure hidden in the field, of the Merchant seeking goodly pearls, and of the Draw-net which gathers in its meshes of every kind,—were heard afterward by a smaller group, collected in a dwelling-house that He had entered, not far from the sea-side. All the subjects, you notice, are taken from the agricultural, commercial, maritime, or domestic pursuits of the people He was instructing. Yet there was such novelty in the use made of them, such unexpected arrangement, coloring, and application of these "old" daily doings, that they were at once transfigured before the people into a fascinating glory; they listened under the spell of an indescribable charm; it all seemed "new," as if the things spoken of were just created, and had the dew of the morning on them. So the touch of true genius, in a painting, is never so plain as where the figures and objects represented are common, yet the whole effect is original as a creation. "Things new and old" together make up the mystery and the beauty of the parable and the picture. But more than this,—in what the parables taught, or the hidden meaning that Christ conveyed through them, there was the same mixture of the two elements. As they hearkened to the Lord from heaven these Galilean peasants and fishermen found something that was new, and something that was old. Duties were declared, principles were announced, springs of human feeling and action were touched, which their religious education and the light of their consciences had made as familiar to them as the slopes of the hills about the lake, the curves of the shore, or the trees along the street, under the common sunshine, where they plied their daily calling. This was "old," but this was not all. As the heavenly words came from the lips of this "Son of Man," knowing not only all that is in man but the secrets in the bosom of God, they caught glimpses of something "new," and as grand as it was new. Very faint and inadequate these glimpses were, at first. But the patient Master knew the work He had to do, and led their dull intellects along through this simple path of parable, giving them what they were able to bear, —tempered beams for their weak eyes. What He was seeking to unfold to them was nothing less than the nature of that everlasting and universal kingdom of God, which embraces all other truth, transcends all mortal understanding, and provides redemption for all the nations of our race, and yet sets up its true throne in the unlettered heart of a regenerated child or a penitent slave. Holding fast all that was good in the "old" religion of conscience and Law He was bringing forth to them the "newness" of His Gospel.

"Then said He unto them, Every Scribe which is instructed unto the kingdom of heaven is like unto a man which is an householder, which bringeth forth out of his treasure things new and old." Perhaps, while He was speaking, the table in the house where He was had been hospitably spread for this welcome and beloved Friend, like that of the lover in the Song of Solomon who sings, "At our gates are all manner of fruits, *new and old*, which I have laid up for thee, O my beloved";— and thus Jesus frames another allegory from the ready meal;—"so thoroughly," says Stier, "has He got into the taste for parables, that the festive board becomes a symbol of the nourishment of His Bread of Life." Neander, on the other hand, supposes the "treasure" to be the jewels which Eastern hosts sometimes display to their guests,—"old" heirlooms to recall the past, and "new" gems to signify present prosperity or friendship, both alike precious.

We shall find that the principle the Saviour announces here is too broad to be confined to any one profession, even the most sacred. It appears in the whole providential disposition of our lives, and impresses a particular lesson as we pass, under Christ our Leader, from the things of the old year to the things of the new.

Take notice, first, with what wonderful beneficence, in the mere outward scenery of our mortal life, God has joined these two elements,—the new and the old. A great deal that we hear, see, and experience every day is so familiar that it excites no surprise, and so fixed that we come to rely on its continuance; but intermixed with this there is a great deal besides in every day that we never saw, or heard, or felt before, which keeps up a perpetual entertainment. The "old" supplies a foothold to assure us, props to lean upon, a sense of stability to rest our groping and unsettled faculties, giving to the world about us something of the feeling of a home. The "new" stimulates those faculties, wakes up our dulness, and prevents us from sinking down into a stupid, careless monotony of mechanical routine. Every morning opens upon us with the same well-known elements of earth and water, air and sky. But when some subtle change in the season, the temperature, or the light, puts a new expression on the earth's face, shifts the scenes in the sky, scatters sunshine and shadow with an original pencilling, we seem to wake into a day that never had its exact likeness in any day that went before, and yet it is a day in the same old world. Were everything new, we should be strangers in a homeless dance of accidents, desultory, frivolous, careless, without concentration of purpose, or continuity of affection, or labor. Were everything old, we should rust and harden in lifeless repetitions. So God balances our being mercifully between uniformity and variety, between fixedness and alteration, between habit and experiment, between memory and hope, between endearments and friendships which grow ripe and mellow with time on the one hand, and, on the other, blessings, efforts, enterprises, and discoveries which, as it is written, are a part of the Creator's compassions, "New every morning and fresh every evening." One great part of what makes life precious and sweet we bear on with us in our arms and hearts through all the changes; the other part is like the unexpected openings in the winding road of a traveller, teaching us that the Maker's world is larger than we thought, and that there are not only many mansions in our Father's house, but endless opportunities for gaining knowledge and being useful in all these earthly fields, planted and recovered by His Son.

Enter next a sphere which lies closer to the seats of religious character. All the advances that are made in human society toward the practical realization of the great Christian ideas of justice, order, liberty, and love, are carried forward by the providential balance and interworking of these two principles,—the preservation of the old, and the introduction of the new. Each generation is meant to hand down something to its successor, in experience, in wisdom, in a funded stock of valuable traditional opinions and usages. So is each generation meant to find out something new, by study and endeavor, and to add the result to that funded capital, dropping off and pushing aside what it finds to be false or wrong. It is very rare that there is an institution, or custom, or doctrine, gaining the consent of a considerable number of good men, and holding its place a long time, which is so utterly bad that it requires to be completely blotted out,—and even when that is the case, we still hold on upon the past by some better bond not to be dissolved. Our roots to-day all lie back in the soil of centuries gone by, and we grow out of that,—the old. But there were errors and evils growing there that must have the axe laid at their root, to make room for better and nobler forms of life,—the new John Baptist comes heralding the Christ. Truth itself, speaking strictly, is always old,—eternal as God is. But as we are constantly walking around it, catching different aspects of it, and perhaps hewing away the disfigurements that mistaken men before us have plastered upon that majestic and beautiful countenance, its features *seem* to be new. And here comes the distinction between true and false reformers, in their opposite extremes. Destructionists that are over-bold would cut the present clean off from the past, for the sake of having a future built after their own plan,—like the Spartans that killed their old men because they were in the way, making their reform a beginning and a beginning over and over again, never bringing forth out of their treasure "things old." Conservatives that are over-timid, on the other hand, would never allow an innovation, lest it should disturb the peace; they render reform impossible by the fear of change, like Herod, who slaughtered the Holy Innocents lest there should be a young king among them to dispute his throne,—never bringing forth out of their treasure "things new." But the wise Householder in Heaven overrules both of their one-sided follies, and, by opposing each with the other, bears His human family forward in one unbroken order of gradual and merciful advancement.

Pass to the more sacred ground of God's special revelations in the three successive dispensations through which he has guided His Church. First was the Period of Patriarchs, of which we have the description and history in the Book of Genesis. It was adapted to the childhood of the race; but when the time came for it to give place to a written Law, and an established Ritual, not everything in it was abolished. The grand central doctrine of one God, the duty of religious obedience, the paternal Providence that leads men out and in all their days, the prophetic appointment of sacrifices pointing forward to the Cross of Christ, the promise of the Messiah at the Garden of Eden, the institution of the Sabbath when God blessed the seventh day and hallowed it, the justifying faith of Abraham who believed and trusted God so that it was counted to him for righteousness, the covenant by which children are bound up in the same family-blessing of Faith with their parents, —all these you find in that Book of Genesis, and in that first Biblical dispensation. Were they abolished when Moses came, with the Tables of the Law in his hands at Mount Sinai? Not one of them. Very much in that Mosaic age was new,—statutes, tabernacles, ordinances, and one national seat of the national worship. But much more was old than new,—and of every one of those "old things" that I just mentioned there remains some memorial and some hereditary power even now in our third and Christian age,—Christ promising, even of its final consummation, that His spiritual followers shall be privileged to sit down in the new kingdom above with the old believers and patriarchs, Abraham, Isaac, and Jacob. There is a sublime and majestic unity in these revelations. Moses is, in turn, superseded by Christ; the Law by grace and truth; Jerusalem by the Church universal. Yet not one jot or tittle passes from that old Law till all is fulfilled. The principles that underlie the Ritual and Liturgy of the temple and the synagogue have only a freer and more expanded operation in the worship of Christendom; prophecy is fulfilled; types are followed by their substance; and all the three dispensations of Holy Scripture are one, because within them all is the everlasting Christ,—"the same yesterday, to-day, and forever," "the Alpha and Omega, the Beginning and the End."

These are inspiring and enlarging contemplations. They lift us out of the petty round of our narrow occupations in small cares and selfish calculations, in house and shop, in the poor gossipings, envyings, and competitions of society. They make us feel that the world we are living in is not ours but God's world, and that all its strange, blind ways are, after all, controlled by Him who seeth the end from the beginning.

Yet even over this exalted line of thought I should hardly have invited you to follow me at this solemn time, if I had not been drawing nearer with you, through such an approach, to the very inmost seat of what is most practical and momentous in our individual relations with God and with the judgment to come. There is an "old" life to be "put off," not because it is old, but because it is bad; there is a "new" life to be "put on." Unless every part of the framework and substance of the Gospel is mistaken, every heart that is not willingly renewed to righteousness and true holiness in the image of Christ by God's Holy Spirit is dying the death of sin; then every one of us here who has not consciously and penitently renounced this world as his master for the sake of confessing and serving Christ his Saviour, is lost from God. "That ye put off the old man; that ye put on the new":—this is your Saviour's cry to you again to-day, from this place. Were He to enter here and look in your faces, as He entered and looked round on the old temple just before He suffered, this would be His sermon. Human nature keeps its old weaknesses, and wants, and wickedness

Nothing can cover them up from Him who died to deliver us from them. He would separate you here as He always did on earth, and as He has surely declared He will finally at the last day, into two easily marked and deeply divided classes. The line might not be seen by any outward profession, for men deceive themselves and are deceived. Those on the right side of it are not perfect characters; but that does not put life or hope into the dying hearts of you that are on the wrong side. You all know, or may know by the Word in the New Testament, whether in an honest and good heart you have chosen Christ and followed Him in the regeneration or not. "Now then, as ambassadors for Christ, we beseech you in Christ's stead, be ye reconciled to God."

What are the "old things" that, in such a new revolution, and new confession, and new creation in you, are to be kept and brought forth? Not the old life; that must be rooted out, for self-love, and pleasure-seeking, and pride, and money-getting, and frivolity are the springs and goings forth of it. The old things that are to be kept, when you become a new soul in Christ Jesus, are your old capacities and powers,—the power of choosing, of repenting, of loving, of believing, of working for your Lord, powers which He gave you in an awful trust when He gave your body breath, and your mind the image of Himself. This ground-work of humanity, this *capacity* for conversion, for holiness, and for immortal life is the old element that has not to be given you again. It is there,—a talent buried or used,—and if buried, your Lord is asking, Why have you not yet used it for Him? The Judge standeth at the door.

And for the very reason that He is a merciful Judge, He does not let our life flow on in one even, uninterrupted and continuous stream of time, with no breaks or turns in the current to make us stop and think whither and how fast we are drifting. He breaks it up into days, into years, into periods of infancy, youth, maturity, manhood or womanhood, old age,—shifting the old scene by new employments, new relations, new sorrows, and new blessings. Into every such waymark He puts a voice of warning, making it a solemn minister of His salvation. He says, of infants, to their parents, "Suffer them to come to Me." O child, remember thy Creator in the days of thy youth; O young man, rejoice and let thy heart cheer thee; but remember that for all these things God shall bring thee into judgment. Be strong; overcome the wicked one, and let the Word of God abide in thee. O man and woman, filled and eager with business and pleasure, love not the world, nor the things that are in the world. For all that is in the world, the lust of the flesh, and the lust of the eyes, and the pride of life, is not of the Father. "He that doeth the will of God abideth forever."

Make this a winnowing time, to sift out of the old things in your habits and your desires whatever you do not dare to take with you into the day of your reckoning with God. "Set thy house in order." Make this a "New Year," in a sense so deep, so complete and so blessed, that, like as Christ was raised from the dead, so ye may walk in newness of life!

Take to you the old Gospel, the old promises of God, the old creed of truth, and holding them fast as your imperishable "treasure," move forward with them in the "new" and Living Way!

# THE EPIPHANY GOODNESS.

*First Sunday after Epiphany.*

"Behold my Servant, whom I have chosen; my Beloved, in whom my soul is well-pleased: I will put my Spirit upon Him, and He shall show judgment to the Gentiles. He shall not strive, nor cry; neither shall any man hear His voice in the streets. A bruised reed shall He not break, and smoking flax shall He not quench, till He send forth judgment unto victory. And in His name shall the Gentiles trust."—*St. Matthew* xii. 18-21.

Wherever, in all the world, in any heart of Jew or Gentile, bond or free, formalist or prodigal, there is any movement toward Him, Christ encourages it. Whether it is an outward movement, of travelling feet, an inquiring tongue, the open confession that brings visible offerings, as with the wise men that came out of heathendom to Bethlehem at the Great Epiphany, or whether it is only the inward movement of a secret desire after His holiness, it is never the economy of Heaven to despise it or smother it. It may be very feeble and dull; very awkward and irregular; very much mixed with baser elements, which overlay it with their unsightly deformities and almost kill it. Let them kill it, if you will, God never kills it. It may only smoulder out of sight, like fire in a ball of flax, where nothing but smoke struggles out through the mass of matted fibres, and a little heat warms the hand that feels for it. This does not provoke the mighty Lord to "quench" it.

His hand is patient, and *does* feel for it. He is as long-suffering as He is mighty. By His very name as a Saviour, the business of His ministry, the passion of the "spirit" "put upon Him," is not to destroy the faint flickerings of spiritual life, but to save them. Even the fragments of that poor bread which only nourishes the body He would not waste, but gathered it up in baskets. Much more the broken and dying embers of penitence and faith in the soul will He not quench. He will gather and cherish and watch over and fan them, if He is not hindered, into flames of vigorous and constant ardor.

As with feeble religious affections in men's hearts, so with mistaken opinions in their minds. In almost every false system of belief, whether within or outside the limits of nominal Christianity, there are some traces of truth. Like the seeds of ancient grain that were sometimes wrapped up in the winding-sheets of dead bodies and buried in dusty sepulchres for centuries, which germinate, and send up the green blade, and the full corn, when air and light and soil are given them ages after, so some dry germs of God's early but buried gifts lie lifeless in these dark religions, till Christ, the Light of the world, quickens them. He came into the world on that mission. He came not to create a world, but to seek out, to gather up, to save, something which had been lost *in* the world, and, taking hold of that, to give Himself for it,—to breathe His own life into it, to pour out the blood of His own veins to revive it,—and thus to redeem and recreate the world. Notice how almost every common term that expresses the object of Christ's mediation includes this little particle, which signifies that His work was a second work,—a doing over of what had been done, or a bringing back of what had been thrown away, or a bringing up of what had been buried under iniquity and falsehood,—re-storing, re-generating, re-newing, re-covering, re-forming. To save, to rescue, to deliver, to ransom,—all imply that there is a substance of life remaining to work upon; and that the Great Redeemer's ministry is to seek it out and save it,—in other words, to take these broken, disordered, depraved elements of our humanity out from under their corrupt bandages; to set them free; to cleanse them; to graft them into the Heavenly Vine; to train them up into fruit-bearing branches, as members of His own Life. In doing this His patience and His condescension are wonderful. He despises no virtue because it is frail. He refuses no prayers because they are timid or ignorant. He thrusts away from Him no inquirers because they are yet beclouded with much doubt or superstition. He listens to them. He tells them to come nearer. He makes the way of admission not harder, but as easy as He can. He lays hold, first, of everything in man which is already in sympathy with Him,—the life not utterly gone, the better feelings not completely dead, and by these He strives with this seeking soul to increase its faith, and to recover it altogether. Be it false living, or false doctrine, vice, heresy, heathenism, infidelity, the sin of publicans and harlots,—whatever the transgression, whatever the unbelief, His Divine heart so loves the souls they enslave, and so longs to deliver them, that He comes down into the midst of them; and then, the point at which He begins to save is that last spark of unquenched life which gleams out, brightens, and warms toward Him. This is the central miracle of the Gospel, and the glory of the Cross. It is that "love of Christ which passeth knowledge."

Go with it, this morning, to that grand promise of the gathering in of the nations which now, at Epiphany, stirs the heart and inspires the animating worship of the Church. Look, from under it, at the star in the east, and the adoration of the magi.

After describing how silent and unobtrusive the Saviour's method was, in His teaching and His miracles; how willing He was to wait for the fulfilment of His glorious purposes; how He withdrew Himself from crowds and avoided noisy demonstrations, disappointing the pompous expectations of the people; and how all his Divine patience was only the calm surface of that deep sea of power which was one day to overflow and convert the world,—the Evangelist goes on: "That it might be fulfilled which was spoken by Esaias the Prophet, saying, Behold my Servant, whom I have chosen; my Beloved, in whom my soul is well-pleased: I will put my Spirit upon Him, and He shall show judgment to the Gentiles. He shall not strive, nor cry; neither shall any man hear His voice in the streets. A bruised reed shall He not break, and smoking flax shall He not quench, till He send forth judgment unto victory. And in His name shall the Gentiles trust." That is, these tender traits of His person, these charitable affections of His Gospel, this catholic economy of His kingdom, this patient and comprehensive love of His sacrifice, shall accomplish the gathering in of Gentile nations to His feet. He meets them where they are. His judgment of them, as of us, is first gentle, condescending, and so afterward the more terribly just. His victory over them is on the Cross where He suffers for them. Oh, to *believe* this is to be "justified by faith."

Turn to the wise men, following the star to His birthplace. Think who they were, and why they came. They were from far beyond the bounds of that chosen and favored Israel whose were the covenants, the oracles, the fires of Sinai, the glory of Sion, and the faith of the fathers. They came, doubtless, from Persia, a heathen country. With whatever distinction among their countrymen, they were yet hitherto but princes among pagans, or a priesthood of superstition. Their business was a vain attempt to read the fortunes of empires and of men by watching the changing positions and mutual attractions of the stars. No plainer revelation of God's loving-kindness and wisdom for them stood before their eyes than the cold splendors of the midnight sky. The heavenly commandment and promise they must spell out in the mystic syllables of the constellations, or else grope on in darkness. The sun was the burning eye of an Unknown Deity. With night-long, solemn vigils, they strained their eyes into the heavens; but they saw no "Heaven of heavens," because they saw no Father of forgiveness, and no heart of love, there. Astrology was their pursuit, and astrology was neither a true faith nor a true science. Not Abraham, nor Moses, nor Elijah, nor Daniel, nor Isaiah, nor any of the "glorious company" was their prophet, but Zoroaster,—a mysterious if not quite mythical personage, ever vanishing in the shadows of an uncertain antiquity. These were the men that God was leading to Bethlehem, representatives of that whole pagan world that He would draw to the Saviour.

On the other hand, we must take care not to fall into the popular mistake about these magi. They held the best religion of their time, outside of Judaism. Their sacred books prove them to have been no degraded or sensual idolaters, probably not idolaters at all. When they fed their sacred fires with spices and fragrant wood, it was not the fire they worshipped, but a strange and unseen Light, of which the fire was a symbol. Their Ormuzd was an Infinite Spirit, and the star-spirits were his bright subordinates. They believed in immortality, in judgment, in prayer, in the sacredness of marriage, in obedience, in honesty; they practised carefully most of the virtues of the Christian morality, including that foundation one of truthfulness, which is rare enough in both East and West, and which Christianity has found it so hard to establish in public or in private life, in all its eighteen centuries of discipline. And to this day, when the American traveller or merchant meets among the miserable native communities of the East-Indian cities a citizen more intelligent, more upright, of nobler manners and gentler hospitality than the rest, he is almost sure to find him a Parsee descendant of those Zoroastrian students of the stars: brethren or children of the wise men who offered their gold, frankincense, and myrrh to the infant Messiah in the stable.

Now, from these mixed characteristics of the magi,—the first worshippers our Lord had on earth,—it is easy to learn, I think, just what their place on the pages of Scripture is meant to teach:—practical truth for us all.

First, they teach us this: *that, in the largeness of the plan of His salvation, Christ not only breaks over all the narrow notions of national, family, and social prejudice, but He permits every heart to come to Him, in spite of its imperfections and errors, by the best light and the best feeling it has.* These astrologers were all wrong about the stars presiding over the destinies of men, and foretelling the birth of kings. Yet, condescending to them, taking them up at that low point of their childish superstition, this "testimony of Jesus, which is the spirit of prophecy," made use of their astrological credulity to guide them to Christian knowledge, shaping the miracle even to their mistake, by all means to bring them out into "the truth as it is in Jesus"; saving them finally from their error, in seeming to save them by it.

It is most impressive to see how this patience and condescension, beginning there at the cradle, run through our Lord's personal ministry among men. He always gains persons, just as He gains the world, by going down to them. If fishermen are to be converted, He gets into a boat, or sits down by them as they are mending their nets. If Nicodemus is too cowardly to come to Him in the daytime, He lets him come in the night, and willingly wakes to explain to him the new birth of water and spirit which is the entrance into life. In order to show the proud doctors of the law that all their traditional learning is good for nothing without a simple heart, He goes in among them at the temple, as a child, listens to them, and asks them questions, in the fashion of their Rabbinical schools. When wicked women are to be purified, He allows them to come in the wild earnestness of their impulsive devotion, and lets them wash His feet with tears. Sometimes He reasons with men; sometimes He waits silently for them; sometimes He sends them away only till they need Him more; sometimes He passes quietly out of their reach, to let their passions cool. If the cure of disease, or raising the dead, or stilling the sea, will turn men's hearts to Him, He works the outward wonder for the inward blessing. Indeed, it is probable that the whole system of miracle-working, sublime as it is to us, was rather a condescension of our Lord, and looked to Him as but an inferior ministry, —since He said, "Blessed are they which have not seen and yet have believed," and "If ye will not believe Me, believe the works." When He chose His disciples, He adapted their calling to their capacity,—some to speak, others to work. Because common people are more readily reached by those in their own condition He chose poverty, and sat down to meat with publicans and sinners. So when His Apostle to the Gentiles preached, He addressed the love of eloquence at Athens, the logical understanding at Rome, the versatile imaginations and emotions of the East at Corinth, Ephesus, and Antioch. Everywhere, without abating a whit the strict sanctity of its principles, or the awfulness of its righteous retributions, the Gospel goes forward, becoming all things to all men, taking men as it finds them, suiting the manner and voice of its appeal to their culture, tastes, and aptitudes; feeling after some better quality or longing in them, to lay hold of, by all means, as St. Paul puts it, to "save some." For the present, Christ says He is not come to judge the world, but to save the world—quenching not the smoking flax. When all these merciful and fostering ministries are ended,—*then* cometh the judgment, rendering unto every man according as he has accepted or slighted them.

We see the same gracious economy proceeding about us every day. Every careless, unchristian person is like these wandering Gentiles. Worse than that, he may be living in frivolity, or in pride and self-will. But the Spirit of God is constantly at work, trying and searching him, to see if there is any tender spot in his heart, any sacred memory, any purer attachment, any look toward the stars, any nobler aspiration, or at least any susceptibility to suffering, by which he can be touched and renewed. By that door repentance may enter. So all our personal traits are, one by one, taken in hand by the Spirit, as instruments to awaken and sanctify us, that we may not perish. If pain and sorrow and death are used, it is only because nothing softer would rouse us. There is not one stroke of superfluous agony. Every pulse of anguish is felt by God, as the refiner and purifier of silver watches the furnace, sure to lift the molten metal out, or to cool the fire, when the needed change is wrought. The instant faith's deep discipline is accomplished, Christ stays His hand. The bruised reed will not be broken, nor the smoking flax quenched, till He bring forth judgment unto victory.

Another part of what is taught by the leading of the Gentile wise men to Christ is, *that at every step forward in the Christian life, each disciple's amount of privilege or blessing is generally in proportion to the growth of his faith, up to that time.* We saw, just now, that these Eastern magi were the purest-minded and most spiritual religionists in the heathen world. There can hardly be a doubt that it was for that superior cleanness of heart that they were honored with this heavenly illumination, and promoted to the leadership of the whole Gentile procession in their pilgrimage to the Son of God. I believe the rule of God's dealing is the same with ourselves: that our future advances in the knowledge and obedience of the Gospel are always in the degree of our past endeavors. We are not to carry the doctrine of Christ's condescension to such a pitch of extremity as to hide from view the real differences in men's hearts. Christ seeks for all, invites all, dies for all, that none might perish. But He does not kindle a star for every one, nor make all converts memorable among His saints wherever the Gospel is preached. There are laws in the economy of grace, as in the growth of the body and the mind. Blessings are according to faith. Faith is nothing but the soul's willingness to receive Christ's blessings, and to receive them in Him by whom alone they can come. If, like the wise men, you have been true to the early light; if, like Timothy, you have remembered what a Christian mother,—your mother after the flesh, or your mother in the Spirit, the Christian Church,—has taught you; if conscience has been kept tender and true; if, like Saul of Tarsus, while you were only under the law you were a faithful and scrupulous servant of the law,—then there is a firm and healthy stock on which your new-born Christian grace will thrive. Then the pagan abominations of a godless youth, or the renounced delusions of worldliness, or of a conceited mind dallying with doubt and proud of unbelief, will not hinder and darken your way to Heaven. Spiritual glory will be revealed to spiritual eyes. Character will unfold and strengthen in its heavenly order. According to your faith it will be unto you. Every new year will set you nobly forward toward higher purities of sanctification. Power, patience, consistency, self-control, peace with God, joy in believing, victory over the world,—these and every other grace will grow with your growth. Such a life will be a perpetual journey of honor, with light all the way, and immortality at the end.

Once more, the subject completes itself in the still higher thought that, *after all, wherever the starting-point, whoever the travellers, whatever the gentleness that forbears to quench our feeble life, and however merciful the long-suffering that waits for us, there is an end of the whole way, at the feet of the Lord.* All His patience, His diversities of working, the discipline of life, the dealings of the Spirit; all the gentleness and infinite charity in Christ, are for this end. And if, after all, we are not found there,—hear the Scripture of God,—" there remaineth no more sacrifice for sin, but a certain fearful looking for of judgment."

Judge, then, of yourselves, my friends, whether this is not the unvarying doctrine of God's whole Word, of His Providence in Christ, of the daily discipline of His Spirit. Through these unclean chambers of our hearts, like the earnest woman who swept her littered house for the lost piece of silver, moves this our Blessed Friend,—the same who receives the praises of saints and the adoration of angels,—searching amidst the poor rubbish that the world and the senses have scattered there for some remaining sign of hope, some fire of love not quite gone out, some broken pledge of union with Himself that He may bind together again, and so make us His own, in everlasting comfort. Or, as in another parable, He walks among the stones and thorns and thistles, there searching for stray affections, like the shepherd for the wandering sheep. I have seen a striking picture, by a great artist, of that Shepherd, with the recovered sheep lying weak and famished on His shoulders. The fierce, dark wilderness is behind. A rocky precipice falls steep and rough to the bitter sea below, and up in the wintry sky whirl the disappointed vultures, that had waited for their perishing prey. How can we help crying in thankful faith, O faithful and everlasting Shepherd, find us in our wilderness; let not the adversary have dominion over us; quench not, but rekindle by Thy Spirit, the dying embers of our repentance; bring us home, where the angels rejoice over every wanderer that was lost!

# THE SOUL SOUGHT BY CHRIST AND SEEKING HIM.

*Second Sunday after Epiphany.*

"AGAIN the next day after John stood, and two of his disciples; and looking upon Jesus as He walked, he saith, Behold the Lamb of God! And the two disciples heard him speak, and they followed Jesus. Then Jesus turned, and saw them following, and saith unto them, What seek ye? They said unto Him, Rabbi (which is to say, being interpreted, Master), where dwellest Thou? He saith unto them, Come and see. They came and saw where He dwelt, and abode with Him that day: for it was about the tenth hour. One of the two which heard John speak, and followed Him, was Andrew, Simon Peter's brother. He first findeth his own brother Simon, and saith unto him, We have found the Messias, which is, being interpreted, the Christ. And he brought him to Jesus."—*St. John* i. 35–42.

So the loving biographer, who, by that wisdom which is partly intellectual and partly spiritual, knew so much more of the Master than we know, goes on, telling in to-day's Morning Lesson what was said and done in that group of persons of whom One was the King of heaven and earth. As to the manner of the Divine story, it is in the same artless style that a child would use in telling it to another child. The things told took place under St. John's own eyes; for when he writes here of there being two disciples that were saluted by John the Baptist, and that were so honored as to be received as guests under the Lord's own roof, though he mentions the name of only one of them, it is because the other was himself. This is his modest way throughout his Gospel: he hides himself whenever he can; and when he must refer to himself at all, he leaves out the name. The noblest spirits are the meekest. Those who have most in them that is worth showing are least anxious to show it. This best-beloved apostle is always thinking of his Saviour, not of himself. That is one reason why he *is* the best-beloved. And so, although he is to have all Christendom, in all ages, for his vast and admiring audience, he is altogether unconscious and natural in his narrative, as we all are when we are describing something because of the feeling and impression in ourselves, and not trying to produce an effect *for* ourselves. He tells us what this one said, and that one, —the very words; what day it was, and the hour of the day; who were there, and how they were related to each other; he explains what "Rabbi" and "Messias" mean, for fear some reader not brought up in Judea might be puzzled by a hard word. The strokes are strong because they are true, and they make a very graphic picture. Great orators never do better than this. Nay, it is not a whit the less likely, on this account, but the more certain, that the Evangelist wrote as he was moved by the Holy Spirit.

For the purposes of our instruction this town might be Bethabara, beyond Jordan; America might be Syria; it might be you and I that were looking for Jesus, and finding Him, too, and listening to Him, and leading our friends to Him, instead of Andrew and John and Simon. This House where we are might be that dwelling where He abode, of which He said, "Come and see," and where they "abode with Him."

Among you who are listening it is almost certain there are some hearts that are thus looking for Him, and wishing they might hear His voice: some whose lips may still refuse to utter their wants before men, but who have unsatisfied desires, who are discontented, and sometimes even wretched, to think how they have been so long living,—whose consciences torment them with shame for their sins, who really know that there is something in their lives which separates between them and God. Are not some of you conscious of having had occasional glimpses of a better way and a nobler aim,—hours when, secretly at least, you have said to the watchman on the upper walls, "Saw ye Him whom my soul loveth?" or to Himself, in your prayers, "Tell me where Thou feedest, where Thou makest Thy flock to rest at noon: for why should I be as one that turneth aside by the flocks of Thy companions? Draw me; I will run after Thee." In this you are like the world waiting for Christ before His coming. It wanted Him without knowing clearly what it wanted. Busy as it was with its poor work, eager with its ambitions, mad with its unholy appetites, it was not satisfied; and its finer spirits knew it. Deep down in the heart of humanity somewhere there was a restless longing for a better life. And hence one prophet says, very affectingly, that the "Desire of all nations shall come,"—the Son of Man.

He came. He has been "manifested." I will not believe it possible that all of you can hear that announcement without real feeling. It means too much, too much, for that. You cannot, I am sure you cannot all be unconcerned about the rest of the message which is thus solemnly begun. For you, then, here in this House, this text is recorded. If we take it by its several parts in order, and enter down into its eternal signification, we shall find it represents the soul of man both sought after by its Saviour and seeking after Him.

1. "John stood, and two of his disciples, looking upon Jesus as He walked." As in other historic statements where we have great things to learn, our minds go behind the plain fact stated and inquire how it happens to be, or what lies behind it. Was it by accident, was it a matter of course, was it one of the ordinary "happenings" of history, that the Eternal and Only Begotten of the Father, whose name is the perpetual worship of saints and angels, and who had dwelt from before all worlds with the Father, should be walking there, in a little province of this planet, a world full of trouble and evil at the best? They were "looking upon Jesus as He walked." He was walking to find them, who had it now for the infinite joy of their life that they were found of Him. They had not gone to bring Him; like all of us, they were too blind and weak for that, and would not have known what kind of a Christ to look for. They had not persuaded Him to come; He came of the great "love wherewith He loved them." They had not arranged the arrival of the Traveller, "travelling in the greatness of His strength." That was the miraculous hospitality which brightened the skies over Bethlehem with the new star, and set the glory of God in the face of the new-born Child. No needy and sinning heart ever has to furnish or obtain its Christ. Before it begins to seek, to inquire, to beg, He is already walking near. The very first word is encouragement for you. Christ is waiting for you. God in man, Emmanuel, is never far from where man is. He may be unseen. Our best possessions are always unseen; those we love best may be long absent, but friendship has other than the bodily eyes. All the possibilities of a pure and holy life are within your reach. Heaven itself is "brought nigh." The

blessed Incarnation that takes millions of souls from death to life is accomplished. Prophecy is fulfilled. The Epiphany is a fact.

2. How do men treat it? "And the two disciples heard John speak, and they followed Jesus." Now begins man's part in the great reconciliation. It is an act that decides for every man what manner of man he is, what he lives for, and, when he dies, whether it is the agony of an eternal death or the transient struggle that ends in the triumph of a life imperishable. Not every one, like St. Andrew (whose name means *man*), is to be an apostle; an apostle is one "sent," commissioned for a special service. All are to be disciples; a disciple is one who learns, for a service that is common. But whether apostle or disciple each must first "follow"; and finally each, by following, learning, and seeing, will be lifted into likeness to the Master and enter into the priesthood and kingship of Christian character. With the gifts and powers necessary for that in His hand the Son of God appears, offering them to you. The choice is with you. Will you look on *a little while*, at the sound of a new voice, from curiosity, from momentary impulse, as long as the Church service lasts, as long as the sympathies of the social meeting keep you entertained, as long as the sober recollection of your sorrow or your sickness lies upon you, and then turn and go the other way, where Christ does not lead you; and so will you lose the sight of Him? Or will you, cheerfully, thankfully, steadily, take His Cross up and go after Him whithersoever He goeth?

3. It is not certain whether the first impulse to follow will prove a constant religious principle. "What seek ye?" He asks them. Rather a chilling and forbidding

question, as it stands: love does not take that tone, unless it is such profound and holy love as is willing to be misconstrued for a moment for the sake of ensuring to the beloved some unseen good. We cannot know the manner of Christ's saying it, or how the tone and look went to interpret and temper the severity. But we know His object, because we know *Him*. One spirit ruled all His speech. He saw that at just that point the *motives* of these ardent converts must be lifted into the light and laid open to themselves. You may say, it is the Lord you are seeking, and that so long as you can say that, you are safe. But words that are only words are no better for being the highest and holiest we can speak. "Coming to Christ," "following Christ," "experiencing religion," "getting a new hope," these are all great phrases if they mean religiously just what they mean literally. But Christ himself comes and searches them out. "What seek ye?" What do you *really* seek, when you seem to be seeking the Saviour? Is it for His sake, or only for your own sake, that you seek Him? Is it only to make sure of a self-indulgent heaven? Is it for the complacent feeling of belonging to a safe set of people? Is it only to furnish a counter-excitement to ease the sting of some trouble, following a law of emotional reaction that has no grace in it, or a sentimental fancy for the excitements of religion, or for its externals? It is a good test for every Christian to apply to his own heart, whether he is just awakened to his duty or further on at any stage of his life. God applies it by many touchstones. Time is one of them; at the mere wearing out of novelty, the repetition of the same homely duties, the love of many grows cold. The candid Scripture tells us of them: they "went back." Worldly examples and associates are another: "Demas hath forsaken me, having loved this present world." Spiritual disappointment is another: results are not so striking as their promise; it is small harvesting, and tame drudging; the same old conflict and vexation every day. *What*, then, are you seeking? Is it truth? Is it goodness? Is it self-denying virtue? Christ wants uncalculating love, loyal love, disinterested love, and love that works gladly, by faith, for His poorest and meanest people, in His name. There is no lack of tenderness in this question.

4. Now, then, comes the place for a deeper exercise of that faith, and the rising by it into a higher life. Will the disciple *bear* the proof? Will he evade the question, and simply follow along, on the level of the old decency, —going with the multitude, saying careless prayers, paying church taxes enough to escape social scandal, and presuming that where the Bible speaks of mounting up with wings as eagles, of going from grace to grace, of being more than conquerors, of the joy of believing, and of having one's life hid with Christ in God, it only means worrying on through week-day cares and Sunday ceremonies, half under the law, and half under the pitiless stare of public opinion, with Sinai for our Calvary, with experiments instead of covenants, with preaching platforms for the Ark of the Fold, with a mere suspicion that all will come out well enough in the end, instead of the assurance of a present salvation: with a system of interesting doctrinal suggestions suited to the times, which may be true and may be not, instead of the promises that are "yea and amen" in the Gospel of Him who is above all "times," "the same yesterday, to-day, and forever"? Notice the spiritual beauty in the answer of the two disciples. They call Him "Master"; but not now in the old sense of the common form of

salutation. They find a new and tenderer meaning in that lordly title,—the same that the holy George Herbert found:

> "How sweetly doth My Master sound! My Master!
> As ambergris leaves a rich scent
> Unto the taster,
> So do these words a sweet content,
> An Oriental fragrancy,—My Master."

Calling Him Master, they said, "Where dwellest Thou?" This is the least ostentatious and yet directest possible confession of a desire for a closer personal communion. It is precisely the growth of that feeling in a man which marks an ascent into a purer and more positive type of spiritual character. It is a confession of ignorance, a renunciation of intellectual conceit, a penitential prayer for a hiding-place in a peaceful pavilion. It is the question of one whose brain is weary of subtle contriving, and whose "locks are filled with the drops of the night." To get clear of blind leaders of the blind, to cease confounding speculation with belief, or morbid sensibility with piety,—to come into sympathy with the healthy and unexaggerated earnestness of Him who could at once gather up the fragments of broken bread and lay down His life to save bad men;—yes, to "abide" with Him, to be under the Lord's roof, to sit down and rise up with Him, and to be rooted and grounded in Him,—to cease from self in the holy joy of this celestial fellowship,—that will be the summit, the mountain vision, of a Christian's expectation.

5. Would it be granted, only for the asking? "He saith unto them, Come and see!" Let that stand for the dispelling of all your doubt. There is no description of the house beforehand to excite wrong anticipa-

tions. Find out what the Christian life is by living it. Eye hath not seen, nor ear heard, nor heart conceived, the things that He hath prepared. The feast in the Christian's heart, the antepast of Heaven, is not understood by verbal pictures of it, but only as we ripen spiritually for the relish of it. When the Bridegroom leads His spouse to the banqueting-house, there is no attempted enumeration of the delicacies in store. It is only said, how finely! that "the banner over her is love"; leaving it for a growing faith to learn what He will give His people, whose own meat and drink it is to do His Father's will. "Come and see." "Him that cometh to Me I will in no wise cast out." "Knock, and it shall be opened."

6. "They came and abode with Him." If they had been like some Christians, they would have disbelieved that any so great blessing and honor could be really intended for persons hitherto so insignificant and undeserving; — as if God's favors were *ever* granted because we are deserving! If they had been like some of us, they would have hesitated between resolving and doing, and, having professed a religious interest, they would have stopped short between the word and the deed. With true saints, however, and with all who ever mean to be saints, believing action must be not only the uniform but the immediate follower upon inquiry. Faith takes God at His word.

7. And now, see playing outward the holy power which has been at work in the man's own heart and character. It begins to take the form of active usefulness and to testify for Christ abroad; the operation of the missionary spirit. No sooner is the awakened heart in actual fellowship with Christ, and settled on that centre, than it begins to cast about and ask what it can

do for Him. No matter in what sphere. No time is to be lost in discussing methods, debating difficulties, or wondering whether it is worth while to undertake to do good at all if it can only be done on a small scale or in one's own pattern-way. As some one says, there are two sorts of people: those that go and do the thing, and those that stand and wonder why it was not done after some other fashion. St. Andrew begins at the nearest point; begins in his own household. "He first findeth his own brother Simon." There is no postponement for a complete plan, for the "times," for the weather, for becoming "good enough," for great occasions. His heart is full, and he does what he can. How soon this spirit in all the followers of Christ would bring the world to His feet,—so fearless, so self-forgetful, so hearty. Out the mighty conviction comes,—must come:—let him that hath ears hear, and whosoever will let him come. When thou art converted, strengthen thy brethren, and call them that they *may* be strengthened. And when you are at the door, the Great Shepherd will listen not only for your "Here am I," but for the better plea, "Here are those whom Thou hast given to believe and to come through my life, or my tongue,—children, relatives, friends, neighbors: the living gifts of a new Epiphany."

The subject is completed, dear friends, with two thoughts belonging to it, specially fitted to this day. What the one brother says to another is a joyful recognition of the fulfilment of ancient promises. "We have found the Messias,"—predicted and expected,—Him of whom Moses and the prophets did write. Epiphany, like Advent, is peculiarly sacred to prophecy. The prophets lifted the veil from before the nations sitting in darkness. They should see a "great Light."

Finally, what was it that roused and started these two

disciples on their search, and brought them to their full acceptance before their predicted Lord? "Behold the Lamb of God." They beheld, followed, believed, and lived. This, then, is the message of Christ's witnesses to the world. All preaching of the Gospel must begin and end here. Epiphany and Easter, Advent and Passion, are one. "Behold the Lamb of God!" Not Christ the Pattern only, not Christ the Teacher only, not Christ the Bridegroom or the Shepherd or the King only, but Christ the Sufferer; suffering with us, and for us;—the "Lamb slain." Stand where we will in the annual round of faith's blessed commemorations, never can we forget to say, "Behold the Lamb of God, which taketh away the sin of the world." For through all that round sin walks near us; in ourselves. And there is in us no justification. In the Son of Man we know that God is faithful and just to forgive, and to cleanse us from all unrighteousness.

# THE LAW OF CHRISTIAN ENLARGEMENT.

*Third Sunday after Epiphany.*

"In every nation he that feareth God, and worketh righteousness, is accepted with Him."—*Acts* x. 35.

It has been made an objection to Christianity that it involves a system of religious privileges expressly limited, for some two thousand years, to a single nation. Admitted, it is said, that the New Testament proposes a more catholic plan, and offers its advantages impartially to the whole race, irrespective of national boundaries: still, the New Testament makes itself responsible for the Old; the Gospel for the Judaism on which it was grafted. No intenser national exclusiveness than the Jewish, it is added with truth, was ever known. The feeling of every Hebrew for every foreigner was a mixture of political animosity, religious intolerance, and social contempt; a triple combination of hereditary passions hard to break down. The sacred writings *appear* to encourage it. How is this consistent with the benevolence of a God whose love is wider than the world?

In your minds, Christian believers, this precise form of scepticism may not take a very definite shape. But it is one branch of a difficulty about the Bible of a more general kind, never more common than now. That difficulty is this: an apparent conflict between the clearer moral sentiments and judgments of men with some of the literal records or else with some of the traditional interpretations of Scripture. Men say, "We know something of the character of the Christian's God: it is not compatible with that character that a few Oriental tribes should be segregated and isolated from the rest of the race and made the petted child of heaven." The same conflict may gather about other apparent points of incongruity,—as the Hebrew criminal code, the destruction of the Canaanites, or the standard of moral character in conspicuous Jewish leaders. In other words, you make use of the sharper moral vision and the broader ideas for which you are actually indebted to the Gospel as a revelation, and as an educating power, to criticise and fault the Gospel.

The Church must not shrink from this criticism. If it is fair, it must be met. If it is unfair, it can be shown to be.

I mention three answers.

First stands the recorded fact that long before this separation and isolation of Israel took place, God declared that it was not the permanent law or normal method of His Divine purpose with His children: it was rather a special and provisional economy brought in to meet a peculiar and temporary emergency occasioned by the wrong choice of men. At the very moment when the special selection began to be made, an explicit and reiterated prediction was carefully annexed to it that it was to be used only for a required end, and would then be expanded into a grand Brotherhood of the world, of equal advantages, lying four-square and open to all the quarters of the earth, and which should be no respecter either of nationalities or of persons. The man in whom the special calling began was Abraham. And he was the very man to whom the Lord broke apart the august silence of the midnight sky, and spoke from beyond the stars, to say, that among his descendants there should be a "seed," a certain wonderful Son, in whom not one country or people only, but all the nations of the earth, should be blessed. That mysterious Shepherd-king of the whole human flock was to have a human mother, and that mother a Hebrew:—"born of a woman and born under the law," so as to connect the special preparation with the universal blessing:—but that He might, on the other side, be free of every possible human restriction, His Father was to be the Father of all that live, and His Life begotten from eternity. There is therefore no mistake, no concealment, no reconsideration or suspense in the plan. The promise in Genesis is as broad and as catholic as the preaching of St. Peter in the text from the Acts.

Secondly, is there anything in the method itself, the selection of the Hebrew tribes and the Jewish Church, that makes a reasonable justification of it to the highest moral instincts,—suppose we must be judges of God's way? When a Christian missionary goes into a population of barbarians, why does he gather in a score or two of children, out of hundreds, into a school, leaving the rest for the time untaught? When an intelligent American merchant, doing business in a pagan seaport, wants to benefit that paganism, why does he choose out one or two native youths of bright parts and send them to America or England for an education, instead of spending the same amount of money in scattering spelling-books among the heathen houses? When you want to introduce into a manufacturing interest an original and improved kind of machinery, why do you send a single student to the best engineering school in the United States or Europe, instead of issuing an exhortation some morning to all the agents and masters of the mills to improve themselves in that department of science? The principle appears to be pretty plain in these practical undertakings:—it is the principle of selection and concentration, for the sake of an ulterior benefit that is to become general, a result that is to be wide-spread. Such is the nature of the human mind and of human society that practically this is the better and shorter way. Do for one mind, thoroughly, first, what you want the whole to do afterward. Now, in the world, when Moses was lying all unconscious of it in the little rush-basket in the Nile, the great problem was how to stop the race from going any further wrong, into stark savagery and idolatry, and how to turn it about, and get it ready for the setting up of a Divine order upon it, and for the reconciling and renovating of it with the heavenly communion it had lost. This was the thing to be done. And it was to be done, suppose, not by the thrusting in of an arbitrary revolution, a stupendous miracle of mechanism which would simply set the outward works all right, but would leave the springs of spiritual life,—love, choice, energy, faith,—all untouched and unchanged. The very thing wanted was to bring in and set up these grand interior holy forces in the soul. "The world by wisdom knew not God." God only could make it know Him; and, being what He is, He could do it only by preserving man's freedom, and respecting every law wrought into his nature. He took, therefore, what we call the practical way; He used the principles of selection, concentration, and adaptation. He did it gradually. He did it by human instruments. He limited the scene and the numbers. He took this child out of the rush-basket, bearing in his veins the finer blood of that Hebrew pastoral people that God had led with His own hand and voice before, over the hills and pastures of Mesopotamia and Canaan,—the most reverent and conscientious on the earth. He trained that child in the best scientific school of the time, —" in all the wisdom of the Egyptians," and then He set him at the head of a commonwealth. He selected a priesthood. He made elders. He organized a State. He arranged a ritual. He chose a limited territory in the right spot. And then He put this crude and childish nation down,—not in liberty yet,—they were not ripe for that,—but under discipline and regulation; not in the Gospel yet,—for they would abuse and waste it if they had it,—but in the Law. This was the school and the scholar. In a word God did,—only better and more gloriously, and with some sublime signals of miraculous justice and mercy breaking through all along to turn to it the eyes of mankind and the reverent memory of the generations forever,—just what wisdom must do. He chose out one nation, and sent it to school to learn the prophetic rudiments of Christianity and to make ready a people prepared for the Lord. The Old Testament is simply the narrative of that training school for Christ and for men. Some parts are more obscure than others; for the time was a great way back, and the materials of knowledge were scanty, and, above all, the Infinite and Inscrutable One, whose ways are often past our finding out, was the Master. But this is the key to the scheme. Was not the plan magnificent? Can the best critic or the shrewdest objector suggest a wiser way to save and lift to heavenly places enervated, sensual, vulgar, wretched humanity? And when we take a view of the whole Old Testament history wide and deep and rational as this,—with all its strange incidents, its erring heroes, and faulty saints, intermingled with its splendid virtues, its sublime loyalty, its eloquence and poetry unequalled in all the literature of the world, and its supernatural prophecies,—all intense and bright with hallowed fire, because it is the school of God,—is it not a very poor thing indeed to carp at an unexplained passage here and there, or to sneer and cavil at some half-veiled feature in the majestic working out of the design?

And all this while the original intention, disclosed to the patriarch far back on the plains, under the stars, was never forgotten, or dropped, or suffered to fail. We were reading, the other morning, a piece of fiery logic from one of St. Paul's Epistles, to prove that no temporary narrowing of the system under the law, for a special object, would disannul or alter the older and broader and more catholic revelation to Abraham, four hundred and fifty years before,—a covenant having in it by promise the largeness of the Gospel and the universality of Christ. When the Jew should have been drilled and taught, the Gentiles would be gathered in. No siderial motion in astronomy, no regularity in celestial cycles and orbits will be more sure than the rising, in the due and foretold time, of the Epiphany star. The Saviour will fulfil both the parts of the great plan:— "A light to lighten the Gentiles, and the glory of My people Israel."

There is a third explanation to relieve the alleged narrowness of the Jewish religion,—and that is its constant progress as it goes on into a larger and larger breadth and liberty, more and more like the breadth and liberty of the great world-embracing Church and Gospel in which it is finally merged, as the winding river is lost in the sea.

We have only to study the Hebrew prophets, and to study them with some system, in the order of their living and writing, with this clew in hand,—the progressive enlarging of their conceptions of God's goodness to the whole Gentile world,—to find ample demonstrations that the Divine tuition they were under was doing its work. Instead of over-coloring this evangelistic element in Old Testament prophecy, I doubt whether the Christian pulpit or Christian writers have ever adequately represented it. With a hostility in their blood to everything foreign, intenser than any people on earth, probably, has ever felt; with an intolerance, arrogance, and superciliousness all the more tenacious and unsparing because bound up with their religious scruples, there was yet never a national mind at all approaching theirs in the frequency, earnestness, solemnity, pathos, of the expectation and hope of the breaking down of all international walls, and the gathering in of all the families and kingdoms of the continents and islands to an equal share with themselves in the peace and glory of the Messiah's dominion. To be sure the gathering was to be *unto* Zion; Israel was still to be central and somehow parental; yet there was to be equality. And the beauty and splendor of the fore-visions of that homeward march of the Gentiles, as we have them in all the Epiphany chapters, have no match in any book. Should any nation on earth instantly drop all that is selfish in its policy, and all that is exclusive in its patriotism, and proclaim an economy of the universal and impartial opening of every door of privilege to all lands, the moral spectacle would really be less striking than the Hebrew predictions of Gentile conversion under Christ. The strain grows louder and more confident all along:—till, in Malachi, we have it resounding in that sentence at the opening of our service, to which the famous saying of the great orator, where the morning drum-beat of the

British Empire circles the earth, is but a feeble figure: "From the rising of the sun, even unto the going down of the same, My name shall be great among the Gentiles; and in every place incense shall be offered unto My name, and a pure offering: for My name shall be great among the heathen, saith the Lord of hosts."

Give a few moments now to a use of St. Peter's words which will bring them down to ourselves. "In every nation he that feareth God, and worketh righteousness, is accepted with Him."

The sense here is not theological, but popular; so that they are wide of the mark who suppose that the Apostle means to take back all that he preached, up and down the world, and wrote in his Epistles, of every man's need of true repentance, and of the faith in Christ as a Redeemer, and of our reaching a spiritual and eternal life only through that faith. That would be to unsay all the burning confessions, and quench all the noble enthusiasms, of his Christian life and apostleship. Why, then, should he be preaching Christ, and the Cross, as the "only way," to Cornelius, and to every Jew and Gentile that he can reach? No. He means by "fearing God and working righteousness" this:—In every nation, now that Jesus Christ has come, there is an equal access to the open door for every tongue and tribe and people. Under this new and heavenly reign of light and love which has been set up, all are free citizens. Partition-walls are levelled. Caste, rank, prescription, arbitrary terms of admission, are done with. The Pentecostal signs mean nothing less. Circumcision, miracles, Jew and Gentile, Barbarian, Scythian, bond, and free, are without difference at Bethlehem and Calvary, at baptism, at the Christian communion, everywhere in the Church, and at the resurrection. There are no external disqualifications. There are no internal incapabilities for being saved. You can all be saved if you will: you will live forever, if you will let the life of the Spirit in Christ enter in. "Fearing God and working righteousness" is the universal ground of acceptance, not meritoriously, into heaven, but into the gracious privileges and helps of the Church and family of Christ in this world, as the school for heaven. All this St. Peter had just found out in a peculiar way,—the vision of the four-cornered sheet three times let down from heaven, to show him that the ceremonial distinctions of things to be lawfully eaten,—symbols of all other natural disqualifications,—were abolished. The Gentile world which God has now liberated from its long neglect, "call not thou common." But go to it, preach to it, respect and love human nature in Cesarea just as much as in Jerusalem or Bethany: there is no difference. The Gospel is no respecter of persons. Christ died for all. The Church is Catholic. The Christian is tolerant and friendly to all souls, for his Lord's sake. And while St. Peter spoke after that gracious fashion, "on the Gentiles also was poured out the gift of the Holy Ghost."

So the Word and Spirit of Christ go on constantly filling out our small measures of charity and hope,—breaking up our petty and jealous judgments, enlarging our sympathies for all classes and conditions of men. This is certainly one great and very beautiful teaching of this season. We have a great many personal and private limitations; each has his own. We all live inside several concentric circles, self being the centre-point; and unless we watch and pray, and deny ourselves, and give away a great deal, these are constantly narrowing in and cramping us into smaller and meaner souls. First, there is the circle of our own purely personal interests,—in physical ease and comfort, in property, in dress, in eating, in mawkish sentiments and a self-indulgent giving way to them, to the inconvenience or injury of others. Christ, by the Cross of His sacrifice, makes His whole ministry among men, and His Gospel, a constant remonstrance against this; and unless we catch that spirit, and give up self for service, and for one another, we can be none of His. Next is the circle of the family, of kindred. This is a little wider, but often *only* a little. Because family fastidiousness, family pride, and family resentments, are all very belittling and unchristian feelings. We may only see ourselves, and love ourselves, reflected in our children, or other kindred that are specially necessary to our comfort. Then there is an unchristian fondness for them while they live, and an unchristian, unsubmissive sorrow for them when they die. The Epiphany doctrine requires us to look into these luxurious gratifications, to see whether our absorption in our own domestic pleasures restricts our sympathies for strangers, for neighbors, for the poor, and so stops our growth in the Lord's likeness. Then there is the circle of our own social set,—a very dangerous as well as subtle enemy to true spirituality, as well as to true nobleness and largeness of character. The very selectness of the associations gives a charm to them. All the mutually admiring and complacent members just reflect each other's prejudices, study to please each other's whims, listen to each other, ridicule or satirize the rest of society, and so, of course, must stop growing in all that constitutes greatness of heart. Then there is the circle of business engagements, where the confinement of attention and the engrossment of concern at last become a passion, or a habit, that looks like necessity,—and the slave of mercantile ambition, or routine, sacrifices home and church, his higher life, his spiritual culture, his communion with his Lord, for the poverty that is thus starving him in all the generous and lofty desires of his manhood. Beyond these still lies the circle of patriotic attachments, or devotion to country. And scarcely yet, —Christian as we claim to be,—has the idea of the brotherhood of nations in one family and Church of God entered into the statesmanship, much less into the politics and legislation, of even civilized man.

We are not to suppose that Epiphany signifies to us a mere sending out, in a lifeless and formal sort of way, of a few missionaries here or there to foreign countries. Done earnestly and heartily, that is worth doing, and, in proportion as we really appreciate what Christ is to the world and to ourselves, we shall probably do it, or give for it, more and more, the more Christianlike we become. Men may say they prefer to give their missionary money nearer home, where they see what becomes of it. But remember that it is by setting up standards and beacons, getting hold of a few here and there and Christianizing them, even when results look small, that a great testimony to Christ is finally given. Make the Gospel "witness to all nations," before the end comes. The Apostles travelled and sailed, casting their bread upon the waters, not too anxious to count up visible results. The great commission was, "Go, preach the Gospel to all nations." There is no knowing where the fruit will spring.

But, above all, it is not to be forgotten that there is a kind of heathendom within ourselves to be yet converted. Surely we are alike in this. Self, in disguised shapes, behind masks, and with cunning weapons, still fights bitterly against the large love and the generous righteousness of the true disciple. We ourselves are the Gentiles for whom these glorious prophecies were written, and the Epiphany light was sent, and the sacrifice was made. What a miserable failure it will be, if, after all, looking, as He surely does, into our hearts, God sees there no true reflection of the light of His glory in the face of Jesus Christ!

# THE SAVIOUR IN THE SHIP.

*Fourth Sunday after Epiphany.*

"THE ship was covered with the waves."—*Matthew* viii. 24.

THE quieting or peace-making power of Christ, overcoming all disorder, is what we feel most in the account of the stilling of the storm in this morning's Gospel. There was a short voyage across Gennesaret, after a fatiguing day spent by Jesus in preaching to multitudes of people in the open air on the shore of the lake. Everything as we read is very real. Only suppose the whole scene transferred to waters that we are acquainted with,—bring it down to our own day,—let it be known that one of the cloudy tempests that sweep through our sky had been stayed instantly and dissolved into calm sunshine at the command of a living voice,—and you will feel in a measure how distance and time are apt to dull our sense even to the grandest realities. When we look more carefully at the account, there are touching and beautiful traits of a natural order, making us conscious that we are in the presence of actual events, and not reading a fiction. The little fishing-vessel laboring in the waves that make a clean breach over her deck; the human frame of Jesus asleep in the midst of all this trouble, with bodily weariness and mental peace; the disciples, who are themselves the ship's company, toiling and tacking as long as they can, reluctant to disturb that revered and beloved sleeper, but driven to it at last by sheer terror and desperation; when they come to their "wits' end," the Master's serenity and authority at waking, and then the most natural transition in their minds, when the deliverance is over, from the escape itself to the mystery and marvel of the rescue. These are very impressive introductory aspects of the miracle, predisposing us to treat it with the same intellectual honesty and religious reverence that we find in the story itself, and leading us along into a deeper opening of its spiritual sense.

Let us try to touch this spiritual sense now only at three principal points, showing how they are connected with each other, and how much they suggest of personal assistance in the practical difficulties of a faithful following of Christ.

1. First, then, we do not need to be literally at sea, or to feel waves literally breaking over our heads, to find out what absolute helplessness is. Most men will allow that,—because by far the greater number of us, at some time in our lives, have known what it was to touch the last limit of our strength. You have desired something, supremely perhaps, and having put out all your ingenuity, all your persuasions with other minds, all your energies, you have been obliged to say, "That is the bound of my ability; if the desired thing comes now, it is well, but if it refuses to come I cannot compel it, for my power is spent." You have dreaded something, and for the time that fear excluded every other evil from your view, just as in the perspective of natural objects a small shrub close to your eyes will hide from you broad meadows of sunlight, with shining streams and hills of defence beyond; but every possible *resistance* you could bring to bear, of mind and body, has been tried, and

you stood dismayed at the thought that after all, in spite of this struggle, the terrible calamity might come. One of the commonest forms of this exhaustion of human strength is in the struggle with disease or death, approaching yourself or some one you love like a part of yourself. Regimen, travel, medicine and surgery, the finest skill, have all been tried; and lying there, weak and wasting, or watching over the dear form that you want to clasp and hold back from the grave, you acknowledge that, come what will, your part in the issue is done. The most determined characters some time or other reach this end. Affection, ambition, vanity, accumulation, the mere imitative passion, the longing of worldly men to live on because they know there is nothing for them afterward — all are spent. The powers that overmatch us, tire us out, and run us down, are various, — time, hereditary maladies, sudden sickness, the superior strength of other people serving their own interests against us, that formless enemy, never so seen as to be struck, but often "preventing" us, — that we call "bad luck"; everything that hedges about our inclinations, thwarts our plans, baffles the brain and the will, and brings us up where we wish *not to be.* Most plainly it is a part of God's scheme of mercy to lead us, in our self-confidence and self-will, every one of us, to *just that point*, so that when we are obliged to stop trusting or calculating for ourselves we shall come *willingly* to Him. Humiliating as the fact is, it is, with the great majority of us, only when we are pushed on to that sense of impotence that either reason or faith so wakes up in us that we begin to cry, as we ought to have cried, in thankful confidence and devout dependence all along, to our Lord. God's love is too loving to let us alone. We would not begin right, or come right, in prosperity and health and youth; we set our best parts against the Providence of Life, and are conquered. We would not grow up Christians in the Fold, under the Shepherd's hands, and hence the Shepherd lets us run on the sharp stones, the barren ledges and thorns of the mountains, till we are quite certain we are lost, before He comes after us; but then He is sure to come. Hence, as we see in all the working of this Divine discipline with our perversity, whatever the kind of storm it is that makes us confess we can do nothing more for ourselves, but are empty and forlorn and lost,— it is just *that confession* that our Lord wants of us. We say we are full, satisfied, and sufficient to ourselves, and that we have some better way than God's way; and so long we sail straight to shipwreck. No matter what the shape or color of the cloud from which the tempest breaks,— it is the searching and awful sense of the desolation of sin at last,— it is the distress of a conscience afraid to think of God except through the mediation and pardon of the Cross; it is the startled and overwhelming conviction of a man's conversion hour; it is the simple and blessed turning from the sinking ship of nature, that the storm is sent to create. David felt it in the burning agony of retribution for his transgressions when he cried, "All Thy billows have gone over me; deliver me out of the deep waters." Every Christian believer that has had a new heart and a right spirit created in him has come to it and tasted of it. The ship is covered with the waves; nothing left underneath for a foothold,— nothing seen overhead to steer by or to hold by,— only a loose, fickle, slippery, fatal element all around, and gaining on us. The heart, with all its external, traditional, or formal knowledge of the Saviour, may hold Him as if He were asleep in its own dark chamber. He wakes, *to us*, whenever we go to Him and call upon Him. And they are the reckless mariners on a deeper sea who put the waking off, on one pretense or another, till the ship is covered with the waves.

2. Observe that when, at last, the voyager comes sincerely and anxiously to that, and utters the prayer, Christ does not refuse him because he did not call sooner, or because when he prayed his prayer was not the purest and loftiest of prayers. Hardly any heart's prayer is *that*, when it is first agitated under the flashing conviction that it is all wrong. While its deep disorder is first discovered it can think only of being delivered. The Gospel constantly informs us of waking unbelievers that they ask, "What shall I do to be saved? What shall I do to inherit eternal life?" just like these half-spiritualized sailors of Galilee; "Lord, save us, we perish." And the Gospel approves and blesses their asking. When they have gone deeper into the real motives of this disinterested religion, and have drunk more deeply of the Spirit of Christ himself, their petitions will rise to loftier ranges of spiritual desire; they will pray for inward purity and power, for more perfect sanctification, for the increase of faith, hope, and charity, for others' welfare, and for the speeding and enlarging of Christ's kingdom. At present this patient Intercessor and Redeemer accepts the crudest supplication, so only it comes out of a penitent, contrite heart, and is directed to Him. This is enough. He wakes. His sleep is not like other sleep. He implies that during that physical slumber an Almighty security surrounded Him and went out from Him, so that no harm befell the ship, even though she was under the waves, till His "hour" was come. Why else should He reprove the disciples at all? The fault was that there was so much alarm mingled with

their belief in Him, and that they did not rest contentedly in the trust that wherever *He* was *they* would be safe. He saw this weakness; He called it a "little faith." But He does not denounce it as no faith at all; nor does He disdain it because it is but little. Take courage from that, you that are conscious of having turned to your Saviour, and yet are very distrustful whether you have so turned as to be accepted of Him. He says, "Why are ye fearful." But He does not say, "Ye shall sink and perish *because* ye are fearful." The whole dealing of Christ with the new young life in believing hearts goes on this gracious, encouraging principle. He fosters the faintest glow of faith. He cherishes the nascent, half-formed purpose of obedience. The life of God in the soul of man, He teaches, is always a growing thing, and so by necessity must be imperfect at the beginning. Christians full grown at their Christian birth are as rare as full grown scholars or philosphers or athletes or soldiers at the natural birth, or corn at the planting. The germ of the holy life actually lodged and alive in the soul is the essential requirement and test of a disciple. Is the prayer earnest? Does it come, even though it stammers, out of unfeigned lips? If it does, then the Lord is never so in slumber as not to hear it, or so unyielding and unpitying as to turn it back. Christ is not a critic on the soul's frail steps, as it comes tottering home to Him, a prodigal from the far country or a penitent from the sinful ways of the city. Every promise of His Gospel is a pledge to accept sinners, *not after they have ceased to be sinners,*—for when would that be?—but while yet they are sinners. This is the glory of the Cross. The dying is for the ungodly. The Physician is for the sick. The scarred shoulders of the Shepherd are for the sheep that was lost. That candle of the Lord that is lit in the dark house of the world is to find the "lost" piece of silver. He saves unto the uttermost. Every one that asketh receiveth more than he asketh. None of us know what to pray for as we ought. To him that crieth only in fear, and because the weather of this troublesome world is too much for him, the sea is smoothed. And whosoever so cometh, provided only it is to the Lord that he directs his supplication, shall in no wise be cast out.

3. But we should miss the full breadth of Gospel teaching in this miracle of the quieted tempest if we saw nothing more in it than a mere figure or likeness of what goes on in an individual heart. The whole strain of the New Testament teaches us a profounder doctrine than this of the connection between the visible world of nature and the invisible world of God's spiritual kingdom. We needed to know what the Pagan, the Jew even, and many a student of science born and bred in Christendom has never really comprehended, that the Person of Jesus, Son of God and Son of Man, is the actual bond of a living unity between both these two great realms of God's creation; that He mediates between them and reconciles them. Scholars will never explore nature thoroughly, or right wisely, till they see this religious signification of every law, every force, and every particle of mattter, and explore it by the light of faith. God is in everything or in nothing,—in lumps of common clay, as Ruskin says, and in drops of water, as in the kindling of the day-star, and in the lifting of the pillars of Heaven. The naturalists of antiquity were quite as original and acute, in the purely intellectual quality, as the moderns. But none of them, of any nation, ever really grasped this doctrine of creation till Christ revealed it. It is the Christian conception of nature,—even

though many men who have the knowledge are too blind or bigoted in their theories of nature to admit it. The miracles of Jesus in Judea, as attestations that the elements of nature were plastic in His hands, are really a new key to the grandest scientific principle in the universe,—which is that God lives and moves and acts in all of nature, every instant, and that the whole creation is formed and guided in the interest of the spiritual man, *i. e.*, of the kingdom of heaven on the earth. This world is a place for the training of souls in a Christian immortality. All its laws are yet to serve that end. Its evils, sufferings, disorders; its blights and tempests and agonies, are somehow in it,—we know not how, and shall not know at present, because it is the residence of a wrong-choosing, falling, and sinning race. When Jesus of Nazareth took our flesh, which is one with the dust of the earth, He entered on the stupendous and transcendent work of redeeming not men only, but the earth itself. Man's body is not a temporary accident. Everything material, visible and tangible, answers to something, expresses something, symbolizes something, in the soul and its spiritual life, as it is hereafter to be developed. Hence Christ must be Lord of life and death, of seas and storms, of diseases and demons, of every mystery and might and secret of created things. "The winds and the sea obey Him." The whole creation, now groaning and travailing in pain together, waits for the redemption, the manifestation of the sons of God. The estrangements even of dumb creatures, as the prophets say, in some remote Christian age are to partake in the general reconciliation,—the wolf lying down with the lamb, and the young lion and the fatling together, and a little child leading them in peaceful harmony. This individual soul of yours, when it is aroused to holy life because the waters have gone over it, and cries for help, and is forgiven, is not left a solitary thing, struggling alone to swim against the tide. It is in the ship with the Master. It is one of an innumerable company. It is surrounded with the praises of the Church of the First-born. It belongs to a Christ who has all power in heaven and in earth, and whom all the angels of God worship.

4. Incomplete still would this enlarging view of the miracle be, if it did not further disclose to us the true practical use both of the Gospel miracles themselves, and of every other gift and blessing of Heaven, in leading us up in affectionate gratitude to Him who stands as the central figure among all these visible wonders, the impersonation of all spiritual beauty, the heart of all holy love, and the originator of all the peace-making powers which tranquillize and reconcile the turbulences of the world. Whatever other and more abstract or general truths of the spiritual creation these supernatural works of the New Testament may express, it is plainest and most precious of all, that they draw believing and thankful hearts to the Saviour himself. The disciples, you see, did not selfishly congratulate *themselves* on their escape, or, with the impoverished spirit, the thin blood, and niggardly honor of modern rationalism, refer their relief to the laws of nature, or to peculiarities of climate, and so, proud of their sagacity, make for the port. Their reverent minds, quickened by faith, travelled fast from the wonder to the wonder-worker. "The men marvelled, saying, What manner of man is this!" It was not the mercy to men's imperilled or sick bodies that Christ had first in view when He loosened the bodily ordinances and let the streams of Divine energy flow in on mortal sufferers. "That ye might believe in me,"— this is the continual explanation,—we might almost say

the excuse, He offered for deeds that must necessarily be exceptional and temporary. I have heard Christians with the doubting temperament of St. Thomas, slow but desirous to believe, avow their wish that miracles could come to confirm and satisfy them now; and I have heard others, easier to believe, express their expectation that they would come again, in some new supernatural cycle of the Church. All that miraculous treasure of Christ is ours, not only by certified history, as undeniable fact, but because in having Him we have all the benefit and blessing of His supernatural life included. The wonders fulfilled their office when they gained men's ears and hearts for their Redeemer. He living in our hearts by faith, we can dispense with the rest as but the transient vehicle of His grace. Feeding on Him, dying with Him, at liberty with His freedom, walking daily in His light, forgiven through His mediation, enriched and sanctified by His intercession,—what can the brave and true Christian need more? The tranquillity will be like that of the sea when the storm had been subdued,—not a dead or stagnant " calm," but, as the same original word signifies in Homer's Epic Greek, the rippling calm that laughs, because it moves and makes music and catches all the light of heaven. If the Saviour of us from our sins into everlasting life "giveth peace, who then can make trouble?"

Augustine, of the fourth century, who knew as well as most men what the storms of temptation are, and better than most men what the deliverance is, and by Whom the victory comes, often in his writings refers to this passage of the evangelist, and those psalms, like the forty-sixth and ninety-third and one hundred and seventh, where we almost seem to hear the roaring of the waters and the voice of God above them. In one of these he sums up the practical application of the miracle in language that cannot be bettered : " We are sailing in this life as through a sea, and the wind rises, and storms of temptation are not wanting. Whence is this, save because Jesus is sleeping in thee? If He were not sleeping in thee thou wouldst have calm within. But what means this, that Jesus is sleeping in thee, save that thy faith, which is from Jesus, is slumbering in thine heart? What shalt thou do to be delivered? Arouse Him and say, Master, we perish. He will awaken; that is, thy faith will return to thee and abide with thee always. When Christ is awakened, though the tempest *beat into* yet it will not *fill* thy ship; thy faith will now command the winds and the waves, and the danger will be over."

# TWO AND TWO BEFORE HIS FACE.

*Fifth Sunday after Epiphany.*

"AFTER these things the Lord appointed other seventy also, and sent them two and two before His face into every city and place, whither He himself would come."—*St. Luke* x. 1.

It is remarkable how little stress has been laid on this statement. There have been a few conjectures, among scholars, that one or another of the historic men whose early confession of the Faith gave their names a place in the Christian records was among these "seventy." But we really are told about any of them only two things,— their errand, and the fact that they were held worthy, through their prompt and obedient discipleship to the Master, to be made forerunners of His own ministry. From Jerusalem eastward beyond Jordan, and so up to Bethsaida,—from Nazareth west to the coasts of Tyre and across through Samaria,—might be seen these pairs of pilgrims, bound on a mysterious march, eager, solemn, urgent, as if the spell of another world was on their spirits;—this is all we know.

Yet questions of high interest immediately arise. Why should there *be* any forerunners? What were they sent to do? How were they received by their countrymen where they came? And what were the after fortunes of their lives? Silent as the narrative is on points like these, there are indicated in the single sentence which mentions the incident two or three principles of the Christian life, in the world and in man, of great practical power. He "sent them two and two before His face into every place whither He himself would come."

In order to the full personal influence and reign of Christ anywhere, there is a law of necessary preparation. Very impressive it is to see that God, when He has any great gift to communicate, proceeds by prearrangement. He never bursts into His family with thunders of revelation too sudden or loud for them to bear. Take the one signal event which stands in the centre of all history,—the personal coming of the Son of God on the earth. In one sense, to be sure, His birth was a surprise; the dull mind of the lodgers at the Bethlehem tavern, and of the peasants at Nazareth, was not looking for Him in the place and fashion of His actual appearance. But Simeon and Anna in the Temple were ready for Him. The prophetic spirit of His nation had been looking out for Him, as nightly watchers on Mount Moriah looked out for the dawn toward Hebron, two thousand years. A group of magi from the far East, without Bible or Hebrew tradition or Mosaic monuments, were expecting Him, earnestly enough to travel a long way by a strange road to find Him. Herod was not surprised,—foreknowing Him by that presentiment of alarm with which unrighteous kings always dread prophets. Every student who reads below the surface of the letter understands that the whole course of Eastern empire and emigration, from the patriarchs, as much as the literal predictions of Jacob or Isaiah, was a *making ready* for just that spiritual revolution which came embodied in the Galilean carpenter, the Desire of all nations, the Everlasting King. From the very beginning He was sending out, along the highways of ages, voices, two and two, of herald and psalm, of priesthood and commandments, of awakened conscience and struggling faith, of failing virtue and falling thrones, into the places whither He himself would come.

There is a wider view of history, and of God's majestic purposes in it, still. To narrow and jealous interpreters it used to appear to be somehow a slight upon the Scriptures to suppose that the Almighty took other nations besides the Jews into His design, or that He illuminated Gentile seers and sages to catch any glimpses of the Gospel. But Scripture itself is bound by no such exclusive rule. It sees religion beyond the bounds of Judea. It honors Melchisedec's devotion and Balaam's vision of the Christian Star rising out of Jacob, and celebrates the adoration of the wise men, and welcomes the ships of Tarshish, the dromedaries of Midian and Ephah, the outstretched hands of Ethiopia. Christian scholarship in later years, rising to loftier conceptions of the Christly providence and the Divine philosophy in history, discovers proofs that, long before Mary took her way to the feast, or laid Jesus in the manger, there were great converging lines of thought and life pointing to that wonderful nativity. On the purer pages of both Greek and Latin literature there are guesses of an Evangelic future; there are ideas working out from men's minds under the breath of the all-inspiring Spirit, preparing the way for the reconciliation of Calvary, for the brotherhood of the race, for the Sermon on the Mount, for the parable of the Good Samaritan, for the missionary journeys of St. Paul. Over the plains of Syria, along the sea-coasts of the Mediterranean, in the northern forests, tribes and their captains were moving, thrones were put down and set up, armies were gathered and dispersed,—the mighty leaders themselves not conscious for what King of kings they were opening a path, but all shaping the face of the earth for His kingdom. Literally, Caesar's legions were building roads out from Italy to every quarter of the compass, not more for the Pretorian eagles to pass than for the apostles and witnesses of the Cross. Alexandria laid the keels and spread the sails of her galleys for a better freight than she knew,—for the message of love on earth, good will to East and West, and glory to God in the highest, out to the Pillars of Hercules. The Athenians, through period after period, in the exquisite culture of their perfect tongue, were producing a language for the truth as it is in Jesus to proclaim its glad tidings in, from the Ganges to the Danube. Roman jurisprudence, by its skilful statutes and admirable discipline, quite as much as military conquests, was familiarizing courts and senates and thinkers with the idea of universal law. In fact, to eyes that see the divinity in the Saviour's face at all it is not difficult to discern, all along those earlier ages, heralds like " the other seventy also," going before that Face into the places whither He himself was afterward to come.

Now, on that great scale of time and space we have a picture, in colossal proportions, of what goes on in every one of our own breasts. Conscious of it or not, agencies are at work in us to make ready, if we only will, for the entrance of the Lord of the heart into His home and dwelling-place there. Having created us for Christian service, as the true end and real glory of our being, our Father takes pains to fit and to fashion us for that destiny, with all its honor and all its joy. By secret influences, untraceable as the wind that bloweth where it listeth, silently pressing on the springs of feeling and principle within us; by strange sorrows and misgivings there; by hours of uneasiness not explained; by sharp twinges of conscience; by open providences, prosperous or painful, so plain that he who runs, in the busiest habits, can read their meaning, and even the wayfaring fool can hardly miss it; by letting us have what we want, to encourage or to shame us; by taking away what we love too well, or love falsely, that we may become wise and strong and pure in our grief,—this process of personal preparation is in continual operation. The heralds are out, sent by Him who is coming after them. The "other seventy" are proceeding on their errand. We ourselves are the cities and places whither He would come. He wants us, and He would have us want Him. He has named us, one by one, to the messengers. He has marked each heart, as He did the chamber in the city by the man bearing a pitcher of water where He would have the disciples "make ready the passover." This is the Divine reality of our human life, and it throws over its common things one of their tenderest and most earnest aspects. Nothing is separate from this blessed plan; and so nothing is insignificant. Even the commonplaces, in God's view, however it may be with ours, are parts of the formation of character. They are always teaching what manner of persons we ought to be. The voice of the wilderness rings through them,—"Prepare ye the Lord's way." He knows of each one whether the door is open or shut. And by one touch or another He will open it, unless we would rather die than live.

All our approaches to full religious truth, to spiritual power, or holiness, or peace, are gradual. The best are not *best at once*, any more than the very bad are worst at once. The towns and cottages of Palestine must hear a little about the Messiah before they saw Him, and get used at least to His name. "Is not this He that should come?" Not Elias, not one of the old prophets,—but everybody's Friend, the Saviour of publicans and laboring men, of sinning women, and of the little child. Were our ears open, we should hear about Him in other voices than those of sermons. Childish instruction is one of them, including all the little morsels of Christian knowledge that are scattered in the houses of the people. Many of them are but crude and broken bits; the information is scanty and one-sided; it is mixed with false theories and mistaken impressions; but there it is,—some precept about prayer, some fragment of the New Testament narrative, some text committed to memory, some names of saints, some verses of a hymn. Even in households not very religious, or in streets, or in secular schools, these crumbs of the sacred Bread of Life are dropped; and they help to prepare the way. The children cry in the market-place, "Hosanna to the Son of David!" and they may be the more glad to greet Him and sit at His feet afterward. Sunday-school teaching, imperfect as it is, goes before the face of Christ, and that is a reason why it ought to be more carefully and thoroughly done. If there is too little of Christ himself there, there are at least His promises, His gifts, His praises from young lips, and knees bent to Him. All habits of daily devotion are a preparation for Christ. He may not be faithfully received, or confessed, or followed; yet the practice of saying something often to God, "through Jesus Christ our Lord," keeps a private by-path where His holy feet may walk at any time, in some season of penitence, or agony, or under the shadow of a cross. So it is with morality. It is not always Christian morality. The flavor of the passion-flower, the sweetness of humility, the strength and sanctity of faith, may not be in it.

There is a morality that is hard, proud, bitter, self-approving. Men may do right from wrong motives,—be honest from policy, or amiable for favor, or liberal for popularity, and even austerely just in a kind of haughty ambition to do as well without religion as Christians do with it. But, generally, right living is akin to righteous living. Zaccheus was the better pupil to Jesus for his obedience. The stern moralists of antiquity, Marcus Aurelius, Seneca, Socrates, would doubtless have welcomed the Son of Man from Galilee if they had seen Him. And therefore, along with a right education goes a correct ordering of conduct, the two casting up a causeway, through miry grounds, for the spiritual sovereign of the soul.

Again, it appears from the Lord's sending of the seventy that all personal efforts and public movements for extending truth and increasing righteousness in the world are really parts of His work, and are dependent on His spiritual power. Christendom everywhere is full of beneficent activities. They are philanthropic, educational, sanitary, reformatory, missionary. Sometimes they scarcely recognize, and oftener they fail to praise, with explicit and conscious gratitude, the Great Fountain from which they spring, and the ever-present Leader who inspires and sends them. So much the worse for their vitality and their honor if they do. But none the less are they the merciful emanations of the one great central, mighty, and missionary Heart which has brought the love of heaven into the dwellings of men. No matter where you find them, or what human agents started them, or what particular form of good they aim at, they are none the less, in their first origin, products of the one great healing and loving plan,—just as the million shapes of organization in the forests and flora of vegetable nature spring and bloom and bear fruit from a single living principle at the heart of the universe. The grandest result of modern scientific discovery and scholarly thought is the growing conviction of a unification of forces:—all the infinite variety of shape and color and odor, of leaf and blossom and stalk, flowing from one Head, in one shoreless stream, under one all-including Law. The spiritual creation is not less orderly, or less at unity in itself, than the material. "Master, we saw one casting out devils in Thy name, and he followeth not us; and we forbad him." But Jesus said, "Forbid him not, for there is no man which shall do a miracle in My name that can lightly speak evil of Me. For he that is not against us is on our part." "Whosoever receiveth a child in My name, receiveth Me": and the ignorant and the heathen and the poor are children. "Whosoever shall give you a cup to drink in My name shall not lose his reward": and healthy tenements, or temperance, or bathing-houses, or schools, or hospital care, or flower-missions in cities, are cups of water. "Wisdom is justified of *all* her children." "He that keepeth My commandments, he it is that loveth Me." "All souls are Mine." The benefactions of this late age, half-blind though they may be, or forgetful of their Author, were born at Bethlehem, and grew in stature at Nazareth, and conquered their enemies,—selfishness and pride and wrath,—at Calvary, and went out among the nations with the apostles. If we had seen one of the seventy walking in some by-way of Jericho or Bethany, we might have seen no badge of Christ upon him, and wondered at his eager gait or absorbed expression. But he was going where the Master sent him, and the Master's mantle was on him, and the Master's secret in his soul. Thither, after him, the Master himself would come,—to reaffirm and fulfil His words,—to deepen, sanction, complete His work. Large or small, these forerunners run over the earth,—from Zion to Damascus and to Spain, from London to Cape Town and Japan, from the New York Bible House to Mexico and Oregon. One Sender sends them. One Reaper and Ingatherer and Finisher follows them. He is the Alpha, beginning them,—the Omega who will end them. They began in His charity. They will end in His righteousness His grace conceived them—every one. His mediation holds them up. His glory will crown them, in His own good time. The many-handed Church Missionary Society of Great Britain, with its million dollars a year, and the little "auxiliary" of a few quiet women in a rural parish, are branches of one tree, drawing their life from one root, yielding for that patient Planter who will come "seeking fruit."

And on Him they all depend. Underneath their roots, and filling every pore with the sweet stream that nourishes each fibre, He is *over* them as well, watching and tending and watering, and lifting the boughs into air and light. Without Him they can do nothing, as without His creation they could not have been. Unless they cut themselves off,—severing the secret channels by unbelief, by headstrong self-will, by a quarrelsome and alien temper, by the bitterness of a radical rejection of Him,—He feeds their springs. That is the wonder and the beauty of the love. So much does He care for the whole flock, that He will let shepherds almost as simple as the sheep go after them,—to lead some, to drive others. So much does He long to draw souls in, that He opens gates in all the walls, on the four sides of the city, which lies four-square to all the points of the compass,—the city of holiness and rest. He never shuts them. If they ever seem "strait," and the way to them "narrow," it is only because, without obedience and a likeness to the self-denying Lord of the place, they that enter would not be at home there, but uneasy prisoners at the court of a goodness which judges them. His heavenly economy is not to bar out but to invite in. He suffers ten thousand stammering tongues, of scanty wisdom, to teach and preach Him, if only they will heartily repeat His name. If there are not ordained and official hands to baptize new-born children into His family, they shall not be left outasts and homeless for want of outward and inward water, and a welcome. "The Son of Man is not come to destroy men's lives, but to save them."

How plain it is, then, that all our exertions to do good to our fellow-men, or to ourselves, are strong and effective exactly in proportion as we keep them in direct connection with Christ. Do you inquire how? By our inward feeling; by the outward confession, and the continual thanksgiving, and the sacramental memorial; by carrying requests to Him; by marking the signs of His guiding will and following them, though they cross interests or break up projects of our own; by managing and deliberating and administering, working alone or working in societies, in His Spirit; by thinking of Him in our work, reverently and affectionately. Wherever they went, in mountain passes, or river jungles, or lonely deserts, among robbers, among Pharisees, among serpents, do you suppose the seventy ever forgot the voice, the face, or the blessing of Him who said to them, "Go ye, *before Me*"? Their knees would have trembled, their hearts would have sunk in them, many a time, if they had. Whether we try to convert the heathen, or to Christianize our western barbarians, or to build churches, or to reclaim in our Christian communities "such as neglect so great salvation," or to train the young, or to nurse the sick, or to employ the idle, or to house and clothe orphanage and old age,—it is *not only* true that "without Him we can do nothing"; it is just as true that in the degree of our conscious and willing and loving memory of Him we prosper and prevail. As we are in communion with Him, He strengthens us. As His name and creed are on our lips, His mark on our foreheads, our knees bent to Him, we prepare His way. He comes after us, and comes up with us, and we walk with Him, and the bread is broken, and our eyes are opened to the vision of Him, and we feast with Him, and with His Father, who is *our* Father, and They with us. His kingdom comes *in* Him, *from* Him, and round about Him, and abides with Him wherever He is.

This leads on to the final truth. When the spiritual life unfolds into its real freedom and practical energy, the character it presents is a Christlike character. The moment we see it, we see not only its beauty and usefulness but its *source*. The stamp of its authorship is upon it. However rude, imperfect, immature the earlier forms of religious life may be, as surely as they grow and ripen there comes out in them the likeness of the perfect Pattern of them all. Many failures and rough outlines at first; not much else but sincere longings, penitent resolves, half-discouraged struggles to worry through the daily fight and break down the old selfish or sensual habit. Amendment is slow; the record only a little better to-day than yesterday; some backslidings, very likely; timid faith asking "where is the promise of His coming"; Peter sinking in the waves as the wind rises; and half-pagan Christian neighbors looking on with little hope and less cheer. But what then?

Always the herald must be less than the king. Preparation is not perfection, nor is seed-time the harvest, nor is John calling down fire on Samaritans the John on the Lord's breast at the Last Supper. First the blade; then the ear; after that the full corn in the ear. Only make sure that the seed-corn is the genuine grain; that the tillage goes on; that the blade is nurtured, and the weeds are killed. Then the full corn will be Christ's life again. Is the true quality here in the germ,—the baptism of the Spirit,—the new creature's breath and blood,—the love and longing for God, however feeble or faint? Then take care of it. Your business is to water and feed it,—and, if need be, to fight for it. The Church's business is to train it; she is its nursing-mother; the entire system of her ministrations is a divine arrangement and provision for it; her christening *Christ*ens it; her confirmation confirms it; her adoring prayers hold it up to the light of the Lord's countenance; her teaching gives it body and soundness; her Church work makes sinew and nerve and hardness for it; her Eucharist satisfies and renews it; her hymns invigorate its aspiration, making it rise like the wings of the eagle. But, in all Christ must be, or there is nothing. To Him it must all tend and work in the heart, or it works to vanity. Christ begins and finishes its glorious circle of seven-fold light and grace in personal lives. When we speak of the kingdom, it is only the society of Christ's men, the complete and brotherly body of living souls, alive in Him. That only is the Church that rises, and makes Gentiles see the brightness of its rising, and brings sons from far, and nurses daughters at its side, and gathers gold and incense from east and west, and doves of the air to its windows,—its gates not shut day nor night, and glorified with the glory of the Holy One.

Who He is you know. All better things, of desire and purpose, in the heart point to Him and prophesy Him. Seventy times seven messengers, in these Christian ages, go before Him. Our repentance is comforted by His forgiveness. Every step is made safe and steady by His hand. The whole course and order look to Him,—" Path, motive, guide, original, and end."

Men of our time think they see a grander future in store for the people, and for the world. They are right, if they look for an age of greater nearness to the Son of Man. The heralds go out. Commerce, science, discovery, education, nature interpreted, sea and sky and land comprehended, humanity awakened, the universe explored, every law traced,—these are messengers that will not only foresee but help bring in the millennium they predict, if they labor and move together in the faith of the great reconciliation, for the righteousness and peace, for the love and purity of God. For then these are manifestations of the kingdom of His Son. Is that kingdom within you?

# INSTANT OBEDIENCE.

*Sixth Sunday after Epiphany.*

"His mother saith unto the servants, Whatsoever He saith unto you, do it."—*St. John* ii. 5.

The right path into the meaning of this saying, found in one of the Epiphany "Gospels," lies through the scene where it was spoken, or rather it is found in an interior view of the three states of mind represented in the little group at the wedding:—that of Mary, who speaks; of the servants, to whom she speaks; and of the Saviour, for whose decisive word she and they are waiting.

On the part of Mary, the mother of the Lord, there was evidently a mixture of perplexity, impatience, reverence, and trust. The impatience, betrayed a moment before, in her anxiety that her Son should interfere to relieve the embarrassed host,—who is conjectured to have been a relative of her own family,—an anxiety heightened very probably by a little natural pride in the indications of extraordinary wisdom and authority already apparent in Jesus,—had been sufficiently reproved and restrained. His "Woman, what have I to do with thee?" (more exactly rendered, What is there in common between Me and thee?) had produced the intended effect: dispelling her rising complacency, and placing her on that level of ordinary human dependence where, with all the loveliness and beauty of her character and the sanctity of her maternal relation to the human nature in Christ, she must ever remain. Nothing but an utterly baseless superstition would ever presume to remove her from it into a semi-adorable divinity. As St. Augustine says on the passage, it is as if Christ had replied to her, "That in Me which works miracles was not born of thee." See the deep distinction between the mere filial feeling, always so tender and strong in the Redeemer, up to the last moment when He commended her to St. John's faithful care on the cross, and, on the other hand, that loftier and more august life of God within Him by which He must pursue His solemn work of miracle and sacrifice all alone. Even you, my mother, —He seems to answer her,—must now keep silence and wait. Dismiss that natural complacency and vain ambition of display for Me. Let Me, from this time forth, release and disengage Myself, not indeed from a son's affection, but from all dependence and deference, that I may go on without hindrance or interruption to this solitary and separate office of mediatorship and propitiation. Henceforth be the holy woman, the meek follower, the redeemed though not sinless disciple,—and nothing more than that, whatever erring men may pretend. But for Me, the Son of God, whom the Father hath sanctified and sent into the world,—not an act in My merciful ministry can be either hurried forward or kept back for an instant; it must be done only when "Mine hour" for it "is come."

All this would be a direct appeal to faith, and a call for increased faith. For thirty years Mary had carried in the solemn silence of her soul the memory of the strange events which signalized His birth, childhood, and youth at Bethlehem and the Temple. Probably the remarkable words He had shortly before uttered to Nathaniel, written just at the close of the previous chapter, had been repeated to her, "Hereafter ye shall see the angels of God ascending and descending upon the Son of Man." As yet He had given no supernatural sign; for we are expressly told that this was the "beginning" of His miracles, manifesting forth His glory. If He had really come with a celestial commission,—greater than Moses and Elias,—was it not almost time, almost the "hour," for some token of it to appear? Moses fed the hungry people with heavenly bread in the wilderness, and, when they thirsted, opened springs of water in the rock; Elias multiplied the widow's oil and flour. Why should not this greater Prophet, to whom all the prophets gave witness, fill the six stone water-pots before Him with wine, and gladden the frugal wedding with bounty by His hand? Yet when she adventured on that so reasonable suggestion, she was rebuffed.

Just at this point of uncertainty, then, she stood. The dull servants, knowing nothing of this mystery, ready to take their order, were at hand. She only looked at Jesus, and all doubts fled, all impatience gave way, all fears and marvels sank to rest in one blessed resolution of simple, trusting obedience. "Whatsoever He saith unto you, do it." This was the complete confession of her faith. It was the grand triumph in her of the very spirit of the Lord. And I shall go on to lay it open before you now as a condensed and blessed commandment of love for us Christians of to-day. Let me do this by drawing out three contrasts, implied in the text.

"Whatsoever *He* saith unto you." One voice is singled out, and we are told of it, here and in every part of the

Word of Life,—that voice alone has supreme authority. There are other voices, a whole Babel of them, clamoring to be heard. It has been said, with a great deal of truth, that the difference between one man and another is in their choice of their masters. Some master every human being has, and none are in so complete a bondage as those who fancy themselves to be absolutely independent. We never call the service that we like a slavery; the neighbor who looks on and sees the toil, but has no sympathy with the motive, may call it so. To the indolent voluptuary the business man's unremitting application is a bondage; but this busy worker, with far more reason, gives the same name to the voluptuary's indolence. A mother's incessant care of her children seems a slavery to those who have no sense of maternal affection. Each of the trades, professions, callings, to observers who have no feeling of the spring from which it is done, and no aptitude or relish for it, bears in its routine this servile aspect. There is always liberty in doing what we love to do. There are as many masters as there are interests, appetites, tastes, passions, and pursuits,—of the body and the mind. There are people who scorn the idea of working at all, who yet work harder, put up with more humiliations, and part with more real liberty, for vanity, for fashion, for a certain standing in society or a certain amount of prosperity, or a sensual pleasure, than the serf that is bought and sold and whipped. So it appears that men are always choosing their masters. And, however it may be with the outward employments, when we come to their moral life, *i. e.*, the region of their motives, men are at liberty to choose as they will. It is there, on that ground of their moral freedom, that the Gospel meets them. The freedom of this choice, and its responsibility, keep on with them, and follow them up, till they die. Hence the mercy of God keeps the message of salvation sounding through the world. He has turned your feet in here to hear it once more to-day; and He only knows whether it is the last time you will hear it before judgment begins. Choose now this day *whom you will serve.* Were there any interference with your choice, any compulsion, the whole state of the case would be changed; preaching to you would be an impertinence; and your hearing would be in vain. But there is no interference and no compulsion: the most frivolous and careless sinner knows that. Temptation, in all its degrees,—opportunity, temperament, example, education, perversions of the truth, bad custom, —these are fearful forces; but never, anywhere, do they for a moment annihilate responsibility, or quench the light lighting every man that cometh into the world. The liberty to choose your master clings to your soul. Choose Christ, and live forever; choose otherwise, any other master, and forever die. And you do choose. Not only have we the liberty to choose *if we will*, but we use the liberty. Every heart chooses. Every life is the result of that choice. We may go on choosing and choosing again, trying *many* masters; falsehood is never consistent with itself, and sin loves change. Every passion and appetite and interest may take its turn in playing master. We may fancy we make some progress, *because* we change, when really the selfish principle, the root of all the evil, is just as vital, and as bitter and poisonous in its vitality as ever, under all the refinements of culture and manners. The external habits may become more orderly and decent; the tastes less gross; the results of labor more useful to others. But God is not mocked, and we must not deceive ourselves. Changing our masters is of no avail till we exchange every other for God. Hence it is that the Bible always treats the false masters of the soul as altogether but one;—"He that is not for Christ is against Him," it says. So it presents but one alternative. "No man can serve two masters." The order of the mother of Jesus at the feast expands and reaffirms itself, you see, into a searching, universal, and unrepealable command for every soul that would live. "Whatsoever *He* saith unto you, do it." We are servants, all. Listen to no other leader. One voice, only one, is supreme. Till we have found the perfectly holy, the all-wise, and almighty One, we shift our masters to no purpose. Christ alone can turn the water into wine; the old life into the new.

Advance to the truth that, as there is but one voice of supreme authority, so there is, on our part, but one great principle of Christian duty, and that so comprehensive as to include all particular directions and settle all open questions, viz., instant, active obedience. "Whatever He saith unto you, *do it.*"

Try to consider, my friends, how many of our failures and miseries in Christian living creep in between the clear hearing of God's command, and the doing of it,— or even the resolute, determined, hearty *attempting* to do it. I say *miseries*, because to earnest people failures are miseries. I believe a careful analysis, a sifting to the bottom of the religious unhappiness and dissatisfaction so often complained of, would show that it springs very commonly from mistaking speculative for practical truth; from putting matters of feeling and opinion in place of matters of obedient action, or doing God's will; in other words, from postponing an unquestioning acceptance of God's plain word to a questioning which puts the soul out of the line and attitude of simple obedience altogether. Some impenetrable problem of God's providence, never meant for man to comprehend, is conjured up and brooded over, as if man had a right to fathom it, or, still worse, had a right to keep his faith and repentance waiting till he can fathom it. Some obscure dogma, which, in the regular order of Christian progress, should be left to clear itself up to the mind at some later and more advanced stage of the process of sanctification,— under the law that he who doeth the will shall finally know doctrines,—is torn from its spiritual relations, and set up as a stumbling-block to piety, the young disciple imagining he is justified in serving some other master than Christ because he is not made a master himself! There are other kindred impediments to true, straightforward Christian obedience and the joy of believing: moods of depression and discontent; sorrowful misgivings of having backslidden and grown cold; queryings whether the plan of life is right, whether time is properly divided between the conflicting claims of friends, neighbors, family, or between the active and contemplative elements of religion; there are discouragements and griefs at the unbelief and unconcern of those so much beloved, that the thought of their having no faith darkens the daylight of all the days; there are strange, nerveless, inert seasons, when it seems as if our hands were tied and could not be loosened, our feet paralyzed as in a nightmare, all the horizon of usefulness narrowing in, and pinching us into spiritual dwarfs or cripples. What is to be said of all these drawbacks on the liberty and growth of a joyous discipleship, and what the Bible does say repeatedly is this: that they are to be cast off and left behind, not by more thinking over them, or more spasmodic efforts to pump up or manufacture mere *feeling*, but by a more prompt, unremitting, unambitious doing of Christ's will; a willingness to do it with just what strength and wisdom God has lent you, and no more; with just that degree of success, or celebrity, or comfort, or honor, that God allows, and no more. "Jesus saith unto them, Fill the water-pots with water; and they filled them up to the brim." We are servants under Him, nothing more, and must drink of all the cup of obedience that He drinks of in doing His Father's will, and be baptized with all the baptism that He is baptized with,—in suffering, weeping, being sorrowful, and living in a sinful world. Here is the Master's way. Doubts, fears, depressions, break up and dissolve under it. The homely opportunities that stand all round us in our everyday business, in the houses and the familiar workshops of the world, are our six water-pots of stone. Fill them; fill them ungrudgingly and unhesitatingly; fill them with such water as you have, and up *to the brim*. There is but one thing to be done: "Whatever He saith unto you, do it." Whether the water shall be made wine is for Him, the Master, to decide; not for us. We can settle but few difficult points, and puzzle out but few knotted problems. We are like Mary in her perplexity; very often confessing silently, "Well, all this is strange, inexplicable; we should not have expected it so; but one thing is certainly safe and clear; one blessed path lies open; that will bring all out well and right at last: Whatever He saith unto you, do it." There is no doom or danger in that. Be about the Master's business. Go to the nearest duty. Take up the first cross. Count no costs too great. Go forward to confession of Christ and His ordinances. Feed upon Him in faith. Do all manner of kindnesses and charities to the least of His people as unto Him. Esteem a small house large enough to be an entrance-way to heaven. If the poor season of this mortal life and this commonplace world is ever to be turned, by the miracle of grace, into a wedding-feast for the eternal Bridegroom and the Church His Bride, it must be by this working of love in Christians to fill the water-pots with water,—preparing the way for the wisdom that transforms our weak and watery offerings into the wine of the new kingdom.

There is another kind of difficulty that is cured by the same obedient and prompt doing of the will,—I mean indecision as to *beginning* to follow Christ. There, too, with most persons born and bred in a land of sanctuaries and scriptures, the obstacle is in a want of religious action, a lack of the practical link that joins a sight of duty with the doing of it, or a longing desire for Christ's acceptance with the practical effort to obtain it. There must be some persons now listening here that have not so decided and begun. I ask them to go back into their past lives, and say if they cannot recall some time gone by when they were almost persuaded, heard the Spirit pleading, saw the gate open, and then let this world draw them back. What was it that closed the way to God's right hand? It was the not walking at once *in* that way. It was no mystical or metaphysical or external impediment; it was the moral chasm between hearing the command and minding it. It is not till our part,—the servants' part,—is done, and the firkins are filled, that the supernatural energy will change the nature of the heart into the new creature in Christ Jesus. Believe; faith is the power; but the proof and fruit of faith is not separated from it: "Arise, and wash away thy sins; bring forth fruit meet for repentance; bear witness to the Redeemer; and have charity for one another. So shall all men know that ye are My disciples."

One other word completes the scope of this lesson: the first word of the text,—"Whatever." "Whatever

He saith unto you, do it." What it should be that He would say His mother did not know; the servants did not know. It turned out, with them, to be no very heavy or difficult task; it *might* have been to travel to the Kedron or the Jordan; but it certainly was a trial of their faith, and a greater trial than many of those are that we call so. How was the pouring into the jars of mere colorless and tasteless water to remedy the want of wine? Very much so it looks to us, in respect to many of the simple and commanded *acts* of faith, which are required of us nevertheless. How are our money offerings to convert souls to Christ? How are our prayers to move the everlasting arm, stay sickness or sin, and turn back the currents of evil? How shall bread and wine feed the heart? How shall any of the miracles of Christ's power and compassion be wrought? We are slow to learn the irrelevancy and vanity of those inquiries; yet learn it we must, or never be wise enough to take our blessing and live forever.

And then there are trials, not for all of us, but for some, which need this broad "whatever" to cover them. When you find yourself beginning to calculate the consequences of your obedience, and measuring out your sacrifices by your prospects of reward; when your flesh and blood cry out that the sacrifice hurts, and the wicked world seems happier than they that suffer affliction with the people of God; when you must give up more than you ever gave before, and more than your neighbors do, —you will want this "whatever,"—"Whatever He saith to you, do it." You will want the wide faith it expresses and requires; and you can have it. Nay, you will want *Him* who is the author and finisher of it, and who said beforehand, "In the world ye shall have tribulation; but be of good cheer, I have overcome the world."

And what a life of holy power and beauty and beneficence this will yield in our dwellings! He who began His wonders at the marriage in Cana will continue to manifest His glory and diffuse His joy in every place where this blessed and trusting spirit has consecrated the family, and ordered its occupation. Draw out now, and bear unto every guest in the Father's house. As in every miracle of His the Lord never proceeded without regard to some natural and ordinary substance to be acted on, never created things anew out of nothing, but always changed, healed, transformed, or *made better* something existing in *disorder* before Him, so it is in the glorious operation of His Divine power on the character, heart, and life of men. He takes these old and common water-pots of our mortal relationships, our household affairs, our every-day dispositions and employments, and then, if only we are ready with our obedience, fills them with that new wine to which He himself so often compares His gift of life. When the new man is put on, "old things pass away, and all things become new," but the identity is not lost. The effect is new; the life is new; but you are yourself still, only transformed, and the new life is your own.

# THE FOREMOST DESIRE.

*Septuagesima Sunday.*

"SEEK ye first the kingdom of God, and His righteousness."—
*St. Matthew* vi. 33.

TO-DAY the Church turns its thoughts from the beginnings of our Lord's ministry toward its close. We have been occupied with His coming, birth, and manifestation: we now move toward His cross.

The spirit of the text is the spirit of the Epistle. There is one "race" to be run; one "prize" to be gained. Everything else is less than the "incorruptible crown." The cross lies on the way to that. Put all else aside; count all else immaterial; do all, bear all, for that. Seek it "first."

The command carries the whole weight and compass of its meaning clearly written on its face. "Seek ye first the kingdom of God, and His righteousness." The impression it conveys directly to every soul is the true one. I doubt whether in this congregation there is a person really listening to it that has not said silently, "That is a high call; that must come out of the very Spirit and throne of God; it sounds like the voice of One who speaks with an authority that it would be vain to question; the words have the ring of eternal truth, reason, and right in them." It is an explicit requirement,—positive, comprehensive, intelligible. It stands there in the midst of that Divine sermon, which begins with beatitudes and ends with a warning, like the mount on which it was delivered in the scenery around it, the summit of an ascending grade of many heavenward-leading invitations. It sounds out a rallying cry for the waking minute-men of the army of the Great King. "Seek ye first the kingdom of God, and His righteousness."

Sometimes when men are called so to rouse and enrol themselves under Christ's cross they are ready *in the main*, they acknowledge the general duty; but they want to ask particular questions and to receive particular explanations. Such states of mind, if they are honest, and are fairly met, may end in faithful service on the Saviour's side. Seeking, they find. But Christ knew that there are other postures of men's minds, terribly common, where a life with Him amid the realities of the spiritual world are not set at all into this foremost place; *indifference* is the first and fatal danger. There is not concern enough to raise particular inquiries. There are no questions to be asked about the methods, the conditions, the preparations, the way of the eternal life with Christ, because the treasure lies too far away. Sometimes, when you, men of business, are invited to embark in a new enterprise, you see and acknowledge its eminent importance, and only delay for an intelligent investigation. In other cases, you say at once that it has no attraction for you; you are interested in other matters; and, before he has opened his portfolio or unrolled his scheme, you dismiss the applicant from your door. It is to this last class of dealers with His heavenly benefit that the Saviour is here speaking,—*the unconcerned*. To use His own language, which is always the best, " the cares of this world," " the deceitfulness of riches," " the pride of life," "what shall we eat?" "wherewithal shall we be clothed?" "how shall more goods be got and laid up for many years," or spent, or shown?—these are the real interests; they are supreme. Why not frankly confess it, you man or woman of the world? Why do you go round about the matter with ingenious circumlocutions, with your apologetic postponements, your half-way assent, or your heartless confessions? If these "be thy gods," why not acknowledge and stand by them? Why add an unmanly pretension to an ungodly preference, and crown your faithlessness to Christ with an acted lie to your fellow-men? Why buy your unopened Bible, and pay the tax on your reluctantly occupied pew, and repeat compliments to a public Christianity, and send for the minister to bury your dead, if your life and heart have another master, another worship, and another heaven? Natural honor must admire Elijah's straightforward and clear-dividing doctrine: "If the Lord be God, follow Him; but if Baal, then follow him." Only one kingdom can be *first*.

"The kingdom of God, and His righteousness." Can there be any ambiguity about the object? It is plainly of two parts: one social and outward,—God's "kingdom"; the other personal and inward,—"His righteousness"; and these two are so fitted together, and so partake of each other, that each alone is incomplete; both are one in the fulfilment of the Christian obligation. And the Saviour's command is not kept till both are sought. Yet, in seeking them, there is no dividing of the attention, no doubling of the purpose, and no divergence in the road. After all it is but *one thing*, one object, one seeking, one choice and act, one eternal blessing. How is it with the prodigal? Up to a certain time he has no particular destination, no plan, as he has no faith. He only intends to wander on, and get the most selfish enjoyment out of the world that it can be made to yield him. The one bad determining act was done where he set up his own headstrong will, took the means of self-gratification into his hands, and made the world's great sensual saloon his only home. But the prodigal was no extraordinary monster. This Christian community has thousands of men in it that are doing the same thing in kind every day, and doing it reputably enough. The one characteristic fact about him was that his back was turned to his father and his father's house. He sought another kingdom *first*. Precisely how far he had gone, or into what company, was not the *first* consideration; but which way he was moving. His father let him have his portion of the property, to try his unfilial and dismal experiment with; and so Providence lets irreligious and unchristian men have money and prosperity, for the same purpose, here. There is something unspeakably pathetic, sad, in the sight of a man, with a heart in his breast which God made, getting worldly success, nothing else, and working this experiment out. The badges of fortune that He hangs out about him, and about his family, are only the mockeries of his mistake. How he is to discover it is only a question of time; and this is partly the sadness of it. You look at him as one after another of his purposes is accomplished, as one token after another of his rising and flourishing condition is put forth in his establishment, and you wonder when and how it will be that the hunger in his heart is to discover itself to him. What will be the mysterious influence,—whose infidelity, whose treachery, what disorder, what miscalculation,— that will turn all these splendors into husks, and these apples into ashes? On which child's bloom will the blight settle? In what night will the alarm come, that is the beginning of the end, saying, "Thy soul is required of thee"? Fulness of the intellect, fulness of the body, fulness of the estate, will not keep the sense of hunger away,—and the sense of it is the reality of it.

When "he comes to himself," you find one thing presenting itself to this man's empty heart. It is that one thing that makes all the difference between a bad and a good son, a self-alienated, wretched child and a filial one, an obstinate and a repenting sinner. The whole change is wrought *immediately* within him. But what change? Not a change of place; he has done nothing yet but think and feel. Not a change in his outer man. Neither time nor miracle has repaired the waste of dissipation in his body. Not a complete revolution yet, in all the courses and tendencies of his thoughts and desires,—for it takes time to swing all these round, in the new-born man, so that they shall play spontaneously and harmoniously with the motions of the Spirit in the "new creature." But, *a change in his relations to his Father and his Father's house*. In that point, which is the decisive point in every character, the change is entire. Before, every longing, impulse, passion, from intellectual curiosity down to fleshly lust, looked for its indulgence *away* from home, which means away from God; and obeying that choice, every step bore him literally "away." Place is not essential at first; but destination is essential. Distance is not the principal thing; direction is. Does the heart turn loyally and yearn faithfully to God? And now, what is the first sign and proof of the inward transformation? It is in the character of the "first" thought and the "first" desire. Before, it was to get away from the Father and forget Him; now, it is to get home and abide with Him. And here you find just those two parts of the new life which the text requires; the new *place* and the new *heart;* the seat at the family board, and the reconciled feeling; the open and visible return, as well as the secret repentance; the Father's house, or Church, as well as the Father's favor and forgiveness;—indeed, where else shall the favor and forgiveness be found but there, on the appointed spot, at the threshold of the old house-door, where childhood and baptism once left him? Yes, "the *kingdom* of God, and the *righteousness* thereof." It will not do to stay back among the husks of the far country, no matter whether they are the dissolute husks of sensual pleasure, or the sordid husks of a thrifty and elegant worldly-mindedness, or the frost-bitten husks of intellectual pride;—not the least matter. It is your Father's house that claims you. Men will ask, and they have a right to ask, "Under which king? *Whose* art thou?" Much goods may have been laid up for many years, or you may have failed to get them, or may have squandered them. These are not differences in the sight of Him who says, "Seek *first* the kingdom of God, and His righteousness." To Him the only difference is between those that are seeking and those that are not. "This night thy soul shall be required of thee." *Whose* is that soul?

"Seek ye." But there are two different kinds of seeking. One is the seeking of those who do not know, while they seek, whether they shall find or not; the other of those who know,—because they believe, and know in whom they believe,—that by seeking they *shall* find. This seems to some of you, perhaps, a not very important difference; or else so very plain a one that everybody must see it. You would not think so, any of you, if you saw how many people there are in every assembly as large as this who can say sincerely that they wish they were Christ's disciples, and yet are not, and do not know how to be, or whether in fact they can be. What is this but seeking without knowing whether they shall find "the kingdom of God, and His righteousness"? They seek, if peradventure they *may* find. Some do,—they say,—and some fail; they are not sure whether there is some antecedent, fatal, foreordained objection in the mind of God;—they are not sure whether the message the King has sent them is all true, and the offer of His love is as large as it seems; they are not sure whether there are not difficulties in themselves, of constitution, or habit, a temper or a tongue so unpromising as to shut out all probability of their ever making strong Christians; they are not sure whether they shall have any helps after they begin seeking, or enough to carry them through; they are not sure but there are some mystical conditions, or incomprehensible doctrines, which are laid down at the door of the kingdom, which they are expected to comprehend, or be kept away. It is easy to see what irresolute, ineffectual seeking this will be. It is not that seeking of faith which the Saviour tries in so many ways to create, —by showing us Himself, by assuring us of the tenderness of the Father's compassion, by comparing earthly things with spiritual, and the temporal with the eternal, telling us that all our outward wealth is but the grass that tomorrow is cast into the oven; by solemn repetitions of the promise that He *will* keep those who once, in a good confession, commit themselves to Him; by declaring that no one shall pluck them out of His hand; by miracles that open the kingdom of God to our very eyes; by the parable of the great supper for "the lame, the halt, and the blind"; and by dying in the depth and boundlessness of His love, that "whosoever will" may come. Yes: "the kingdom of God" is there, and is open; the "righteousness" of God is real and waiting. It is not a venture, a possibility, a haphazard seeking,—like that before the dreary and unbelieving mind of Rabelais, when he felt himself dying, and said, in melancholy acquiescence, "I go to seek the great Perhaps." How unlike St. Paul's "I have finished my course, henceforth there is laid up for me a crown of righteousness which the Lord will give me," or St. Stephen's "Lord Jesus, receive my spirit," with his face already like the face of an angel! Yes, there must be *some* faith, to begin the seeking; faith enough to be sure of God; faith enough to be certain that, whatever we may do or be, Christ means what He says when He declares "The kingdom of God has come nigh unto you," "Ask, and ye shall receive," "Seek, and ye shall find."

Seek it first:—first in time, now, before anything else is sought or done; first in importance, never letting any other interest crowd this aside, or other engagements take precedence of the appointed means and ordinances that lead to this; first in earnestness, cheerfully sacrificing society, business, income, admiration, just *so far* as they hinder or interfere with this; first in affection, so that you can sincerely say, with St. Paul, "I am persuaded that neither life nor death, nor things present nor things to come, nor high things nor low things, nor any other creature, shall be able to separate me from the love of God which is in Christ Jesus my Lord." Why, if this were the manner and the spirit of all our seeking,—intense and sober and confident,—if all the world's business were so done, and its pleasure so moderated and purified, as to be in all points made secondary and tributary to this,—I hardly know whether the greater change would pass over the world or over the Church;—over those that profess and call themselves Christians, yet make their religion wait for their traffic and their entertainment, or over the surrounding multitudes that do not believe the faith of Christ to be a reality at all only because they do not see avowed Christians treating it and presenting it as the "first" thing. Yet this is perfectly compatible with a diligent business life, with doing vigorously the daily work that your hand finds to do, with public spirit, with learning, with patriotism, with all the refinements and culture of a high-bred tone of civilization. Nay, everything other than this,—everything that inverts this Divine order, or subordinates Christ's kingdom and righteousness to the kingdom of this world, and seeks material or merely intellectual glory *first*, is *not* a high-bred civilization; but the seeds of weakness and vulgarity and extravagance and hollow scepticism, and a foetid barbarism are in it, till the curses of God light upon it, and you have the old spectacle of commonwealths revolting from their heavenly King, and perishing in dishonor. To make spiritual interests foremost and supreme is not fanaticism or asceticism. Christ takes all truth into His Gospel, and remembers our whole condition. When He says, "Seek ye first the kingdom of God, and His righteousness," what follows? "all other things shall be added unto you." "Godliness is profitable for the life that now is, as well as for that which is to come"; for both lie within the Father's keeping, and over both His empire extends.

There was living, not long ago, a thoroughly consecrated Christian merchant, now among God's saints no doubt in paradise, who began and finished his whole prosperous career as a steward seeking "first" Christ's kingdom,—and giving of his income, to the glory of that kingdom, first a tenth, then a half, and finally the whole. When this man found himself prostrated by disease, and not very likely to recover, his conversation was as cheerful and manly as ever. If the Master should call him, he was ready. But it would be a severe disappointment, he said, if he should be long inactive and unprofitable. There was the balance, in him, of the *believing* and the *working* faculties. "You can understand this state of feeling," he said to his clergyman, "because you are interested in your own work for the Master, and would regard your separation from it as a calamity. Not," he continued, "that I would compare money-making in importance with the preaching of Christ, but I think I can say, as in the sight of God, that my *aim* in making money is the same as that of every true minister of Christ in preaching the Gospel." That candid and confidential statement, with eternity in plain sight, disclosed the real secret of the energy of his business life. It is just as possible for such a man to seek first God's kingdom and righteousness in the regulated and sanctified activity which yet never takes him from his place in the Lord's service, as if he waked and slept in a cloister.

I recall another eminent merchant, up to the close of his last day of health working indefatigably, as he had worked for many years, not to add more to a great fortune, but to serve and set forward, with what he already had, and with every capacity of his capacious nature, this kingdom, and the glory of its King. The few final months he gave especially to the relief and evangelization of the freedmen at the South. On one of the bitterest days of the Winter, as if some solemn preintimation told him his hour was at hand, he refused to leave his counting-house, where he was laboring from morning till night in this work of mercy. Feeling a strange pain in his head, he bandaged it with water and worked on. As the night came on, he rose from that desk, where he had earned a dignity which gives him a place, it seems to me, with the missionaries and soldiers of the cross, with statesmen and scholars, and turning to his clerk said, as his last words,—sublime in their simplicity as almost any of the dying expressions of saints on record,—"Now,—have I left anything undone?" Before he had reached his home, the cloud fell over his mind; and, after a few half-articulate syllables, showing that his thought was still reaching back to the poor creatures that leaned upon him, breathing that charity which "never faileth," about midnight he fell asleep. Why is it, O men of strength, young men, or men in whom the fire of youth is cooling,—why is it that we do not see the true glory of our lives, and round them out, and end them, oftener, in such holy grandeur as this?—"Have I left anything undone?" for Christ and His kingdom? It matters very little how soon the night shuts in, or the Master calls, if all our days ended with that. The kingdom would go forward, though men die; the race would be emancipated and regenerated by the living power and witness of the Holy Spirit, the Comforter.

Would to God, dear friends, that all the air about us were quick with that spirit! that the life kindled and glowed, with healthful fire, along all our sluggish congregations and our worldly highways! Have no fears that faith and prayer will open the windows of heaven too wide, or that our staid Lents and reverential Pentecosts will be too refreshing! Spiritual interests *are* foremost and supreme. Eternity *is* close at hand. The Judge *does* stand at the door. The time *is* short. Wisdom does utter her voice in these streets, "Unto you, O men, I call." Jesus of Nazareth, as the Gospel says, is passing by. This Church is opening her gate for the yearly ingathering. No man can serve two masters. Seek ye *first* the kingdom of God, and His righteousness,—first in time, first in concern, first in earnestness, first in affection.

> " Awake, thou Spirit who of old, in love and truth,
> Didst fire the watchmen of the Church's youth,
> Whose voices through the world are ringing still,
> And bringing hearts to know and do Thy will.
>
> " Would there were help within our walls!
>   Oh let the promised Spirit come again
> Before whom every barrier falls,
>   And, ere the night, shine forth as then!
> Rend Thou the heavens, and make Thy presence felt;
> These chains that bind us at Thy touch would melt.
>
> " Oh that thy fire were kindled soon!
>   That swift from land to land its flame might leap!
> Lord, give us but this priceless boon
>   Of faithful servants, fit, for Thee, to reap,—
> And let them all the earth for Thee reclaim
> To *be* Thy kingdom, and to know Thy name !"

# SONS AND DAUGHTERS IN THE FAMILY OF CHRIST.

*Sexagesima Sunday.*

"WHEREFORE come out from among them, and be ye separate, saith the Lord, and touch not the unclean thing; and I will receive you, and will be a Father unto you, and ye shall be my sons and daughters, saith the Lord Almighty."—*II. Corinthians* vi. 17, 18.

Two elements, you perceive, enter into the substance of this majestic sentence: a precept and a promise. The strength of the apostle's thought seems to accumulate from period to period, through the preceding passage, till the gathered force of his argument, like a great wave striking the shore, breaks over into a flood of feeling. Having glanced from the earthly tabernacle to the "House not made with hands, eternal in the heavens," from the "light affliction" befalling the "outward" man that faints and perishes, to the "eternal weight of glory" yet invisible, showing how, in every soul that is new-created in Christ Jesus, "mortality is swallowed up of life," because that "inward man is renewed day by day," and then setting forth the mighty *motive* to that conversion, viz., that "God was in Christ reconciling the world unto Himself," He comes at last to that close point in the process, where he defines the essential contradiction between the spiritual and the earthly man. By a succession of quick, sharp questions, the sword of his doctrine cuts asunder the sophistry which would mix up worldly self-will with Christian consecration, and shows the world to be made up of two sorts of persons. "What fellowship hath righteousness with unrighteousness? What communion hath light with darkness? What concord hath Christ with Belial? What part hath he that believeth with an infidel? What agreement hath the temple of God with idols?" And then, the crowning conclusion: "*Wherefore* come out from among them, and be ye separate, and touch not the unclean thing, saith the Lord";—for it is this "*Thus saith the Lord*" that seals the promise. "And I will be a Father unto you, and ye shall be my sons and daughters, saith the Lord Almighty."

1. There is a precept. In order to a Christian position there must be a special act; an act so personal, positive, and comprehensive, that it determines on which side of one fixed line the rest of our actions shall stand. You may call it by whatever name bears most significance to your own mind; the Scriptures furnish as great a variety as you can desire: "renewal of the mind"; "conversion"; "believing on the Lord Jesus Christ"; "getting a new heart and spirit"; "putting off the works of darkness and putting on the armor of light"; "forsaking idols"; "coming out and being separate"; these are the Biblical terms for a single fact; and if you can find a term more descriptive of that fact than either of these, Scripture nowhere forbids you to use it, provided you are sure to retain the substance of the thing meant. What is essential is that conscious choice of the soul by which it gathers up its powers, and resolves,— God's grace helping it, as He ever will help,—to be on Christ's side, in this fronting of armies and this awful battle of our life.

Furthermore, this act of choice is the same deep necessity now that it was when Corinth was corrupting the whole East, and the citizens were wasting their manhood with Oriental luxuries and sensuality, and this brave apostle was warning them. The human heart is the same, as to its depravity, and its immortality. The same temptations, with only slight variations in their form, beset men now as then. The same two armies face each other; believers standing up for Christ Jesus, and unconverted men standing up for themselves; and there is also the same cowardly company on the margin, trying to be neutral, and trying in vain; flattering themselves that they can be not exactly *for* Christ without being exactly *against* Him, and with just the same success; fancying that they can carry the credit of being good men without carrying the cross for it; that they can blur over that eternal dividing line which runs down from the throne of God, where there is a right hand and a left, through every nation, and every city, and congregation, and company, and sometimes between the two that walk arm in arm, or sit in the church side by side. The same two adversaries play their old game for the soul of man. The stake is the same. The strategy and snares, the deceptions and disguises, are the same. We Americans sail swifter ships, and over wider waters, than were steered from the double-port of that "mistress of the keys of the Peloponnesus" into the Ionian and Egean Seas; but the practices that make all traffic Christian or unchristian are not far different. Our civil constitution and relations are not those of a colonial dependence on a distant throne; but the inducements to political fraud, and the robberies perpetrated by parties on the nation, and by selfishness on the State, are little altered by time. Social frivolity may here be less stimulated by climate, and convivial excess may flow through a less public apparatus; but this only aggravates the shame of those women here that prepare and patronize the frivolity, and those men that encourage the excess. The fires of appetite have not been quenched by our colder skies, or burnt out through eighteen centuries of burning. Tell us, men who are sitting at the heads of these pews, has the love of money, that root of evil, rotted in our northern soil? or been weeded out? Every age brings its new brood of vices and adds to the funded stock; but very few that have once got a foothold die out. History hardly tells of one extinct species in the flora of guilt. If civilization multiplies the refinements of culture, so does it the refinements of iniquity. Pride remains as obstinate; self-love as subtle; envy as adroit; avarice as grasping; ambition as unscrupulous; self-satisfied indifference as stupid; and worldly enterprise as often "without God in the world." Nay, and going behind all the moralities of life into the evangelic test lying at the heart of the Gospel, men are just as eager to climb up some other way, instead of entering by the lowly door of "repentance toward God and faith in our Lord Jesus Christ." And therefore, what it most concerns us to remember, the responsibility of choice is just as pressing. It is as impossible to evade it and slip into any third way. On one side *we must be*,—Christ's or Belial's. Righteousness refuses fellowship with unrighteousness. Light offers no hospitality to darkness. If idols have our hearts' secret worship, the true temple of God shuts its doors upon us. We must touch and handle the unclean thing, or let it alone. We do assort with the unbelievers, or come out from among them and be separate; and the Judge knows which we do.

It need not be forgotten that the Church has sometimes made a mistaken use of this truth. It has done so whenever it has sought to exaggerate the distinction between the world's people and Christ's people, for purposes of self-complacency or self-applause. It has done so whenever it has drawn itself up in phylacteries, and stood, a Pharisee, aloof from the throng of humanity, saying scornfully, "I am holier than thou." It has done so whenever it has made dress, badge, ritual, feeling, professions, the line of distinction, rather than a principle ruling the life. The right way for the Church to distinguish itself from the world is, as its Head distinguished Himself from His countrymen after the flesh, by a purer holiness, and a warmer zeal to help and *save* the world. Perpetuating its Lord's divine ministry and spirit, it should be as anxious as His own pitying heart was to rescue the lost, to call prodigals home, to redeem publicans and sinners, to undo heavy burdens, to sanctify children from their childhood, to preach and spread on earth the kingdom of heaven. Christian men should be known from men not Christian by every nobler disposition, every more honorable and lovelier trait, every holier affection and deed. Their peculiar badge ought to be a superior righteousness. Their presence in any company or any market ought to be a presence of calmer temper, of firmer resistance against wrong, of greater loyalty to every principle that lends stability to society, —a presence of kinder forbearance and sweeter compassion, of manlier patience under suffering and of clearer testimony to the suffering that redeemed us on the cross. That is the way the Church,—which is nothing else than the united and organized fellowship of Christian souls,—ought to "come out and be separate." Nevertheless, it will be true,—nay, all the more manifestly will it be true for so glorious a contrast,—that *there is a distinction*, or a "coming out";—that mankind *are* of two armies, under two leaders; that outward decency cannot be taken for inward renewal, self-cultivation for the upward-looking faith which works by love and through Christ receives the Spirit.

Till each individual soul, in the deliberation of a solemn election, has chosen to clear itself of all entangling alliances with the one of these two opposing forces, and pledged itself to the other,—so passing out of the natural life into the spiritual,—how can it imagine it is safe? If God is almighty, His will perfect, and His word true, it cannot be safe.

Both a beginning, then, and a continuing; both a revolution and a habit; both a new principle and a new life, is this great decisive act of the Christian. A *coming out* from irreligious associations is one part; it implies energy of purpose kindled by faith. Being *separate* implies the maintenance of the ground thus taken against all opponents, whether they frown or laugh, sneer or slight, reason or threaten. "Come out" from the bonds of vicious compliance and ungodly habit is a call to the courage and faith of the awakened heart. "Be separate" from sin is a command to the persevering will. "Touch not" the renounced pollution is an adjuration to the sanctified conscience. And these are the three daily heroisms in the discipline of the soldier of Jesus Christ.

2. But we are not left with the severity of the commandment. To the sternness of the law is added afterwards the tenderness of grace. If man will do his part, God does His. Already, in the renewing, God has done more than man. For it is God that worketh *within His work*, as much "to will as to do,"—prompting the holy desires, and stirring the stagnant fountain. "No

man can come to Me,"—can begin to come, can so much as desire or resolve to "come out,"—"except the Father who hath sent Me draw him." But now the soul, having turned its face heavenward, has got light enough to grow conscious of this in-working Spirit. When that dinner of husks is fairly ended, and the prodigal's penitence has directed his feet towards home,—the first form his lifted eyes see is his father's—meeting him "while yet a great way off." For the wanderer that went out sullen and rebellious, there is a home and forgiveness there. An infinite benediction falls on the returning child; you feel the power of the promise: "I will receive you, and will be a Father unto you, and ye shall be My sons and daughters, saith the Lord Almighty."

This is that fulness of acceptance which is reserved for the favored hours of the true believer. Do not be ignorant, brethren, that it is possible, that it is reasonable, that it is according to every law of our spiritual nature and the high expectations of the Gospel: never to be sought as a provision of mere comfort; not to cast any heart into dejection or despair because God's time for giving it, or yours for knowing how to use it, has not yet fully come, but a *real state* when the character is ripened for it, and the providential conditions are fulfilled. Whensoever that solemn choice we have been contemplating has not only been taken; when the deliberate consecration has not only lifted the soul out from under the poor servitude to its improvident passions; but when that entire submission has been reached which bows to the Lord's will, not for the sake of any rewards, but for *His own* sake, and because the heart has enough in having Him,—then does enter this peace which passes understanding, and which the world otherwise knows nothing of. Then the Christian life does grow cheerful and affectionate,—cheerful, without losing anything of its earnestness,—affectionate, without losing anything of its reverence. So actually wrote a consecrated child of pain, whom I knew, who had been lying on a bed, and in one position on it, more than twenty years, most of that time in keen distress, and there rising into a victory of faith where she could say, "God must have loved me very much, or He would not have brought me to this life of suffering." Then God does veritably speak, and the voice is, "I will be a Father unto you, and ye shall be My sons and daughters, saith the Lord Almighty."

Sons and daughters! What a power of personal endearment is lodged in that particularity of speech! Not "children," merely, losing individual consolation in the generality of the family! God uses names that come nearer to personal affection, and meet a personal want. He calleth His own by name. Every individual man, struggling under his own load, combatting his own hardships, can say, "My God, thou art *my* Father." Every woman, suffering under her own untold trial, and praying for rest out of a sensitive heart full of misery, is suffered to hear God promising, "Thou shalt be My daughter." And so I have known of such an one, stricken with the long sorrow of a dreadful bereavement, and bowed down for years in that darkness which can behold no pardon and no heaven, from which she could in no wise lift up herself, at last, on hearing these strong and tender syllables of the text, suddenly to be called back again to the light, and to be comforted thenceforth. "Is it so?" said the mourner; "has God, the unchangeably True, said it? and shall I not believe His word? Shall it not comfort me? Shall I not give all to Him, and *be* His daughter?" So the doctrine becomes a doctrine for the heart. Every affection becomes God's cheerful servant. The whole soul is the filial instrument of that Father Almighty.

"Almighty." Mark the special pledge, secured, too, in that word. It is added now, as if so boundless an offer might be distrusted. And whereas it was the Lord that said "Come," it is the Lord *Almighty*, with His Omnipotence the guaranty of His promise, that says, "Ye shall be My sons and my daughters." Of the spiritual power of a communion so tender and so holy, consciously established between any soul and God, there must be distinct, practical results upon character,—confirming, supporting, quickening.

1. Confirming;—and chiefly by fostering in the heart a keener abhorrence of sin. Under the witnessing of that Divine Guest, impurity, selfishness, uncharitableness, grow insupportably hateful. If the heart is ever recommitted to its old mastery, in any moment of surprise or weakness, it rebounds with disgust to its duty, saying with St. Paul, "It is no more I that did it," but "the former sin" clinging to me and shaming me. Sharper-sighted sentinels are set to guard the secret avenues whereby passion used to storm the conscience. Watchmen are appointed to keep the unclean thing off so far from the desires that the fingers cannot reach it if they would. A son, harboring vile companions during the visits of the Infinite, Parental Purity, which finds stains on spotless skies! A daughter, insulting the Father of Eternal Truth, who has become *her* Father, by vanities and deceits!—the offence feels too monstrous now. With every fresh backsliding, a bolder resistance is offered, till victory begins to lift its banners into the morning sky.

> "Then every tempting form of sin,
>   Awed by Thy presence, disappears,
> And all the glowing, raptured soul,
>   The likeness it contemplates wears."

2. Supporting;—by supplying heavenly arms under the agitations of sorrow. If God, who holds the waters of all afflictions, like the oceans that swing their waves from continent to continent, in the hollow of His hand, who hears every cry wherewith deep calls to deep in that unsounded sea, the heart of man,—if this God, whose pity enfolds the suffering universe, and whose Spirit is the Comforter, calls me *His son*, what are the terrors that can harm me? On the bosom of Everlasting Help shall not grief itself feel safe? And even if the present agonizing discords, or desolating separations, make patience tremble, will not this indwelling Father show His sons and daughters what one of them, he who wrote the "Holy Living and Dying," saw by the vision of faith, —"glories standing behind the curtain, to which they cannot come but by passing through the cloud, and being wet by the dew of heaven and the waters of affliction;— days without night, joys without sorrow, society without envying, possession without fear, charity without stain, sanctity without sin"? All consolations for the bereaved are gathered into this one: "I will receive you, and will be a Father unto you, and ye shall be My sons and daughters, saith the Lord Almighty."

3. Quickening;—by fresh spiritual communications out of His own fulness, giving to your growing holiness an increasing power of life. Let all pretensions to piety be brought to that unerring test. Let all hypocrisy be sifted by that fan in the hands of the Searcher of hearts. Let all sincerity be vindicated and honored by that noblest witness to a living faith,—holiness of life. No

sacramental professions, no imposition of official hands, no temple ceremonies, no repetition of a creed, can bring a vintage from the bramble-bush. It is said that there is a pagan people in the East who trample on the cross, in resentment for the unchristian cruelties and robberies of nominal Christians. Every willing inconsistency in a disciple wrongs the faith of the Church, and so tramples on the cross. Think not to recommend your religion by bending it to the low maxims, or accommodating it to the doubtful practices, of an unbelieving world. Rather come out and be separate. Be content to drink of your Master's cup, and to be baptized with His baptism. Abide in Him! And may He abide in you!

> "That mystic word of Thine, O Sovereign Lord!
> Is all too pure, too high, too deep, for me.
> Weary with striving, and with longing faint,
> We breathe it back again in prayer to Thee!
> Abide in us! O'ershadow, by Thy love,
> Each half-formed purpose, each dark thought of sin.
> Quench, ere it rise, each selfish, low desire,
> And cleanse our souls with Thy refining fire!
> Touch Thou, and tune each heart, O Hand Divine!
> Till every note and string shall answer Thine."

# ONE WEAK SPOT.

*Quinquagesima Sunday.*

"Yet lackest thou one thing."—*St. Luke* xviii. 22.

The power of Christian truth is proved by the thoroughness of its action rather than by the extent of surface over which its action spreads. It regards completeness, in its spiritual conquests, rather than width of territory. Christian influence is essentially concentrative, as well as essentially diffusive. It acts downward, *into* society, as well as abroad, *over* it.

First of all, it demands absolute control where it enters; and when it moves, it moves always with the full weight of its command; condensing the whole strength of its blessing on every point of occupation, and accepting none but unconditional submission. One parable it is true compares it to leaven,—a symbol of diffusiveness; but then leaven operates by changing or converting the whole mass, through a new element reaching every particle in the lump. Another parable likens it to a tree, or mustard,—the symbol of growth; but then vegetable growth implies the presence of one characteristic vital principle, one vivifying sap, which penetrates every fibre, streams from root to leaf, and regulates, by its own special law, each step of the process, from germination to maturity.

Connect this general truth with the particular train

of suggestions opened by those words of Jesus,—" Yet lackest thou one thing." He says to the complacent man who has come to Him with such a handsome catalogue of his virtues, "All these are very well; excellent traits; you cannot spare one of them. You have kept, you say, these important commandments from your youth. But it so happens, in the complicated state of your character, that neither one of these good qualities, nor even their sum total, decides that you are a right-hearted man, or fit to be My disciple. That question will be settled by another requirement which will try you in a more decisive point. These other good qualities you have claimed fail to furnish such a test; they happen to be easy *to you*. So, now, I shall reach down deeper into the secrets of your soul, into your motives, your hidden life. I shall select just that one thing which will put your obedience to God and your selfishness into a balance. Sell what you have and give the proceeds to the poor. This will tell where your heart is. If your devotion to Me will stand that strain, you are worthy to take up My self-denying cause,—to bear My cross, to be called by My name, to be a member of My Church." Need it be argued before you, my friends, that precisely what Christ says to this Hebrew youth, He says to you and to me, and to each several soul of us all? He wants no divided empire. He desires no friendship that would shut Him out from that portion of our life which most concerns our affections. He would bless us with a universal joy, giving vigor to every faculty, help, light, freedom, and victory, to every step of the way, and every effort to overcome the world. "God is love." And therefore it is that He requires the surrender of every unyielding passion.

When Jesus tells us that we cannot be His disciples

so long as we lack one thing,—does He mean that we must have supplied every moral defect, must have attained every grace, must have vanquished every spiritual enemy, and, in fact, have ceased to sin,—before we can be His disciples? That would be simply saying that none of us can hope to be a Christian unless he is morally perfect; and that, of course, involves the converse, that every true Christian *is* thus morally perfect. The shock this statement gives to our common-sense, and its manifest contradiction of the whole drift of the New Testament, at once drives us from any such interpretation. We find a consistent meaning, I suppose, if we understand Him as declaring that no heart is really Christianized, or converted, so long as there is any *one conscious, deliberate, or intentional reservation from entire obedience to the Divine will.* So that if I say, Here is one particular sin which I must continue to practise; all the rest of my conduct I freely conform to God's law, but this known wrong I must continue to do;—then I am no Christian. If you single out some one chosen indulgence, however secret,—a dubious custom in business, a fault of the tongue or temper, —and placing your hand over that reply to the all-searching commandment of the Most High,—" This I cannot let go; this is too sweet to me, or too profitable to me, or too tightly interwoven with my constitutional predilections, or too hard to be put off,"—then the quality of a disciple is not in you. There is a portion of your being which you do not mean, or try, to consecrate to Heaven. And that single persistent offence vitiates the whole character. It keeps you, as a man, as a whole man, on the *self*-side or *world*-side, and away from Christ's side. For it not only shuts off righteousness from one district of your nature, and so abridges the *quantity* of your life, but it inflicts the much more radical damage of denying the supremacy of the law of righteousness, and thus corrupts the *quality*. It practically rejects the heavenly rule, when that rule crosses the private inclination. And that is the essence of rebellion. The test-case is decided the wrong way. Any common intelligence can see the distinction between a moral state like this, and one where the intention, the aim, the endeavor, are all *towards* a perfect obedience, because the heart is right, where the inmost love aspires Christward,—though the performance still comes mournfully short, through the infirmities of a mortal nature and the lingering mischiefs of a repented and disowned habit. That is the state of which St. Paul speaks so graphically,—"The evil that I would not, that I do." "It is no more I that do it, but sin that dwelleth in me." In the one case, the shortcoming is deplored and disowned the instant it is seen. In the other, it is designed and provided for beforehand. One is the *falling below the mark* of a heart that has turned in faith to the Master and taken its standard from Him; the other is determinate transgression. One is a loyal follower's error; the other is disloyalty itself. One comes of weakness, the other of wilfulness. One is the mistake of a right minded subject; the other is the defiance of a rebel.

We shall have the distinction illustrated,—if it needs illustration,—by imagining a kingdom under a good king, whose subjects really love him at heart, and mean to obey his laws, but fail sometimes through enticements; and then the same kingdom with a tribe lodged in the fastnesses of its mountains owning no allegiance in critical emergencies, obeying only when it suits the fancy, disputing orders at will, and formidable enough to nullify all organized national defence when the country is assailed from abroad. In one case you will say there is a strong and consolidated government, safe because sound. In the other there is anarchy,—the form of subordination without the power thereof.

Be careful to remember that this fatal retention of the single nullifying sin is not necessarily brought to a public proclamation. It is much more likely to nestle and hide itself as far from the house-top as possible. Open avowals of it are extremely rare, for *they* belong only to hardened and desperate offenders. All that is essential to the state supposed is that it should be evident to consciousness. Its expression is commonly in that inarticulate but most practical profession, the life.

The principle of the distinction I have been aiming to make plain will help us greatly in understanding several other passages in the Bible, which, for want of an understanding, have sounded either insupportably awful or else unreasonable, and so have driven some to despair and others to unbelief. It will be sufficient to instance the most unqualified and most appalling of them all. St. James says in his epistle: " For whosoever shall keep the whole law, and yet offend in one point, he is guilty of all." That is, whosoever shall conform his conduct to God's express commandment in every other particular, and yet willingly reserve some one district of his life for sin,—some one habit, appetite, indulgence, which he knows that Divine command condemns as much as the rest, saying secretly to himself, "I will keep *all but this*,"—he, because of that one wicked reservation, affronts the Law-giver, who is the author of one command just as much as another; shows himself to have a heart radically wrong,—unreconciled at the test-point,—and therefore is in a radically wrong state, or is " guilty of," amenable, answerable for, all. The heart being impious at the centre-point, the whole state, the whole man, is disordered, out of harmony with Heaven,—irreligious. This is certainly a very different thing from the desolating doctrine that a single moral failure, in a consecrated soul, condemns it to perdition.

Light is thrown on this day's collect. Its subject is charity, or love. Because love is the universal Christian principle, pervading all righteousness, "the fulfilling of the law," "the very bond of all virtues," therefore to be without it damages and diseases everything: "All our doings are nothing worth"; and even he who liveth is "counted dead."

When Jesus spoke thus of one thing fatally lacking to the Jewish ruler, He spoke to us all. But with this difference: that one subtle passion which spoils the whole character for us may not be his passion. With him it seems to have been avarice; he could not bear to turn his private property into public charity. *His* religion broke down just there; in other respects he had done admirably; he had kept other commandments to the letter,—aye, to the *letter;* not perhaps in the spirit, for all true obedience has one spirit. But so far his literal, formal obedience came, and there gave out. Now, with us, this "one thing lacking" *may be* just that,—the inordinate love of money, or if you please, the lack of a willingness to sacrifice it for higher interests, for the heathen's conversion, for the Church of God, for humanity, for spiritual advancement. In commercial communities probably this is likely to be, in the greater number of cases, the one fixed impiety; nor are rural districts clear of it. Wherever it is, remember nothing will attest the complete sway of the Gospel short of a spirit *willing* to meet that sweeping requisition, "Go, sell all that thou hast, and give to the poor, and thou shalt have treasure in heaven." Better enter into immortal life in penniless poverty than, having houses or bank-stock, to be cast down, a shrivelled and shamed soul, into hell. But then you may happen to be so constituted that such an abandonment of wealth would be a very small sacrifice,—one of the least that could be required of you; you are not naturally sordid; you are more inclined to be prodigal; and so this would not be a test-point with you. But there is a test-point about you somewhere. Perhaps it is pride; you cannot bear an affront; you will not confess a fault. Perhaps it is personal vanity, ready to sacrifice everything to display. Perhaps it is a sharp tongue. Perhaps it is some sensual appetite, bent on its unclean gratification. Then you are to gather up *your* moral forces just here, and till that darling sin is brought under the practical law of Christ, you are shut out from Christ's kingdom. I have no right to love anything so well that I cannot give it up for God. Christ does not literally require every one of us to give his possessions to the poor. If there are some with whom doing that would be a glorious and acceptable submission to the heavenly rule, there are others with whom it would be a much sharper trial, and therefore the needed trial, to abandon a chosen course of action or study at the command of Providence, or to lay a beloved friend in a grave. God knows where the trial must be applied. And we are to know that *wherever* it is applied, there is the one thing lacking unless we can say "Thy will be done," and bear it. It may happen that nothing in the whole range of Christian character is so difficult for me as to manage an irritable temper, to keep down petulant and hasty impulses. That, then, is the test-point of *my* Christianity. I suppose that the entire character of a man may depend on his giving up the selfishness which makes him regard his home as a place meant only for his own accommodation, so that he expects everything to be done for his own comfort, frets if the whole household does not wait on his convenience, and yields nothing, plans nothing, for the simple and cheerful entertainment of the rest; putting them off with a treatment which, if God were to transfer it to him, would grind his groaning heart with agonies. So exceeding broad is the Divine commandment that even such an unconsidered shortcoming as this may be the one thing lacking that separates us from Christ.

It is a curious illustration of human infirmity, how we try to wink out of our own view, and crowd out of other people's, this one dangerous and characteristic offence that stands between us and salvation, instead of frankly confessing it, and, with God's help, resolutely fighting it down. Sometimes we attempt to conceal it, by multiplying our activity and concern in other directions, as if to draw off attention by bustling works of supererogation in that quarter, in order to cover the chasm in this. But there is no such law of moral equilibrium in the Divine statics as that. We cannot hire the liberty to persevere in a favorite transgression by paying a *bonus* of easy virtues. Sometimes persons conscious of this one weak spot, and sensitive when it is touched, parry the salutary censure by plunging into a general and not very sincere self-upbraiding. "Oh yes; they are *always* wrong; they never do anything well; they are horribly depraved; and they will never be able to do better." They submerge their *actual* fault in a flood of unmeaning and angry deprecations,—all of which signify simply that you have touched an actual disease, —and that they would like to push the surgery aside by a flutter of extravagant confessions. But none the less does the calm searching eye of the Judge, undeceived, look in on your real shortcoming, and say to you, "Yet lackest thou one thing."

We are told of the young man that came to Jesus and found his single sin so uncompromisingly exposed and rebuked, that he went away sorrowful. An eminent preacher has proposed a different explanation of this sorrow from that which our doctrine requires. His notion is, that while the young man had really fulfilled the perfect scheme of duty, and longed for some loftier satisfaction to his affections, he was merely referred back to the stale and customary round of moral habits. He had exhausted the demands of conscience, and Christ offered him nothing beyond. But besides that this forced hypothesis is not hinted at in the record, while the opposite is affirmed, it treats the Saviour with irreverence, as if there were some heights of experience, or some junctures of spiritual perplexity, which He has not resources to satisfy. The truth is, there was, in this young man's character, though generally so unexceptionable,—fair and lovely in all besides,—one unyielding passion clinging yet, which preferred mammon to God,— "much goods," or a successful business, to Christ's self-denying service and everlasting glory. There was one reserved territory of disobedience where he had not the courage to apply the holy principles of faith—one enemy that he did not love Jesus well enough to conquer. Are any of us partakers in his cowardice?

It is a truth which cannot be too thoroughly preached, that a mere outward conformity with the moral law cannot satisfy the soul; first because the faith of the heart is the indispensable fountain of all spiritual life, or true righteousness, and secondly because a perfect keeping of a perfect law is impossible, so that the law condemns us all alike, and there is no hope for any of us except in a Gospel of grace, or the forgiveness in Christ. But nobody has a right to expect "favor" till he has tried with all his might to honor the law—till he has at least confessed its authority, owned that he ought never to cease trying to keep it, and holds nothing knowingly back. When a man in good faith has acknowledged himself a subject of the law, and done his best unreservedly to obey it, then he is ready to come under Gospel grace. He has failed; but that does not ruin him if he repents of his failure. "There is forgiveness with Thee,—that Thou mayest be feared." But for a man who has persistently allowed himself in one known iniquity,—one unrighteous practice,—refusing to give it up because it brings him gain or pleasure,—to say "I expect grace; I look for pardon; I want to be under Gospel, not law"; this would be the sophistry of a Pharisee. It obliterates Christ's holy commandments; it blasphemes the Holy Ghost. Christ has no encouragement for a faithless temper like this The Gospel does not propose itself as an easy system,—easy in the sense of excusing from duty. It blessedly redeems the earnest souls who have tried to do their duty, and, failing, have cried for pity, for pardon, and for peace.

Were we not right then, in the ground taken at the outset, that the power of Christianity over the character is proved by the thoroughness of its action rather than by the extent of surface over which its action spreads? It displays its heavenly energy in dislodging the one cherished sin, in breaking down the one entrenched fortress that disputes its sway. At the battle of Borodino Napoleon saw that there was no such thing as victory till he had carried the great central redoubt on the

Russian line. Two hundred guns and the choicest of his battalions were poured against that single point,—and when the plumes of his veterans gleamed through the smoke on the highest embrasures of that volcano of shot, he knew the field was won. It matters very little that we do a great many things morally irreproachable, so long as there is one ugly disposition that hangs obstinately back. It is only when we come to a point of real resistance that we know the victory of faith overcoming the world.

Finally, our renewing and redeeming Religion delights to reach down to the roots of the sin that curses us, and spread its healing efficacy there. It yearns to yield us the fulness of its blessing; and this it knows it cannot do till it brings the heart under the completeness of its gentle captivity to Christ. Submission first; then peace, and joy, and love. "Jesus beholding him, loved him"; yet sent him away sorrowing. How tender, and yet how true! tender in the sad affection,—true to the stern, unbending sacrifice of the Cross! It is because He would have us completely happy that He requires a complete submission. "One thing" must not be left lacking. Whosoever would enter into the full strength and joy of a disciple must throw his whole heart upon the altar.

# THE YOKE AND BURDEN ALREADY EASY AND LIGHT.

### *Ash - Wednesday.*

"COME unto Me, . . . for My yoke is easy, and My burden is light."—*St. Matthew* xi. 28, 30.

IT is in the actual life of most of those who do "come" just as it is in this startling figure of our Lord's invitation:—there is a conflict of opposite forces. Contending elements of hardship and ease, of endurance and relief, are strangely intermingled. There is a "yoke." And yet there is such a thing as a certain inward posture, the Saviour says, and some of you no doubt have found it true,—a Divine adjustment or fashioning of the neck to that yoke, which makes it "easy." There is a "burden": every sufferer, that is every soul whose life has been crippled by its conditions, every soul whose love has lost its object or found no answer, every soul whose day's poor performance has shamed its morning vow, or in which the law of the members has warred triumphantly against the law of the mind,—knows something of the meaning of that word "burden"; and yet He who knows tells us this weight can be somehow so carried that the very quality of burdensomeness is cast off from it. Things do not remain what they were when One Hand comes and touches them. Their very nature is changed by a wonder-working energy of grace. So that these words not only convey to us a promise, but they become, in themselves, a kind of type or picture of a believer's conflict and victory, day by day.

There are, therefore, two things to be regarded:—an apparent contradiction, and a secret reconciliation.

Look a moment at the apparent contradiction. Look into yourselves. The very beginning of a Christian consciousness, or life in the soul, is the beginning of a contest of desires. One combatant is already on the field, entrenched there by a hereditary but yet usurping pretension. "The heathen are gone up, O Lord, into Thine inheritance,"—the sacred land in the heart of childhood; and when the Israel of your new life comes up by Sinai, thundered at by the commandment, through a penitential desert, and enters in, it does not take possession of the promise without a siege and many battles. Like the recovery of a man almost dead, the recall of the living pulse and breath is more distressful than the passive process of dying was. Freezing and drowning men find it harder to come back to life than to die. Neither in the second birth nor in the first can the boon of life be had but by anguish. It is a blessing to be born; but the blessing is costly. It comes in under a "burden." For a time the waking will halts, very likely, in a misgiving whether the cost is not too great for the blessing, and the burden intolerable. Hence occur many relapses. You hear the despairing cry: "Let us alone; leave us among the devils; why come to torment us before the time?" Every nearer approach to the likeness of Christ is attended with a deeper *sense* of unworthiness,—which is its "burden." Every quickening of sensibility renders the hurt of sin more painful. As the spiritual eye grows keen, the spots on ourselves grow plainer. The cross requires more and more sacrifice,

—more of the world's dislike, its privations, its crucial nails and thorns. The yoke must be put on again and again. The blessing justifies it, it is true: glory, honor, immortality,—an incorruptible crown; but it does not take away the torture. As you know and feel Christ's truth and love more profoundly, they will ask larger offerings, of time, of property, of ease. How, then, is the " yoke " " easy " ?

Some men say,—and they even say it in Christian pulpits,—"It is easy only as it is to be taken off; it can be borne because death will break it; we are to expect ease hereafter as the offset for this endurance; heaven will be received in reversion; our wages will be paid at last." In this place, however, Christ does not say that, or mean that. He always means exactly according to His words, in every promise He makes. And *here* what he tells the whole sorrowing and sinning and seeking world is *not* that His yoke is to be taken off, or broken, or that the burden is to be made up for by a future compensation. His doctrine is more immediate, and goes deeper. The yoke is to lie there; it *must* be there in order to be an "easy" yoke. The burden is *not* to be taken away, but is to be felt as a "light" burden. We have here the doctrine of a present blessing in Christ;—what He does for His disciple in this life. A relief, a strength, a peace is possible here, in the very midst of the sufferings. Peace enters the heart while the hurt is on. "*Now* are we the sons of God." Doubtless there is a "Rest ($\sigma\alpha\beta\beta\bar{\alpha}\tau\iota\sigma\mu\acute{o}\varsigma$) which *remains—tarries*—for the people of God." But remember also, "He that *hath* the Son *hath* life," already, and if we dwell in Him and He in us we have passed from the real death into that real life, sin having no more dominion over us. See the connections of the Lord's language. It is not, "Stand and look for a salvation afar off; expect your immortality hereafter; live and work as you can gloomily on earth, and only hope for a postponed union with your living Head by and by." But it is, " Come unto Me *now*, just because you have to labor and are heavy laden now. Here I am, at your side; I have left the glory I had, and taken up your aching flesh upon me for another glory, and to this very end, that I might be where you are, and offer you a present salvation. I do not say there is no added yoke in coming; for most men there is; take the yoke up nevertheless; I do not say there is no burden to bear; plausible adventurers hunting proselytes might tell you that. I am "lowly,"—lowly enough to *confess* the yoke, and lowly enough to bear the burden *with* you, *for* you; and therefore your " rest " shall be found *in coming*,—" rest unto your souls." As soon as you begin to turn your feet you will feel the cross, but as soon as you feel the cross you will feel that it is eased for you. Pain will not vanish, but become a privilege. Self-denial will not be annihilated, but will be welcome. A new power will come. The giving up of *property* for your Redeemer's kingdom will demand an effort at first; even the tenth that belongs to Him will seem a great deal; but you will take joyfully, with the saints, that "spoiling of your goods." Cold manners and changed countenances or stinging satires in worldly people will not be pleasant; but you will feel somehow safer and stronger for them on the spot. Come to Me, then, from wherever you are, Matthews from the market-place, sons of Zebedee from the sea, Sauls from the schools, impetuous Peters, and cool, moral Jameses, and contemplative Johns; come, Marys of meditation and Marthas of busy action, come, not for the sake of being exempt from discipline or care; but come expressly to learn of Me how to bear and use them, and how they shall be transformed into holy helpers, as you walk at their side."

"It is difficult," said an old thinker in the things of faith, "and yet not difficult, to be a Christian; only be in earnest, and take not up the Gospel as a *trivial* thing, but upon *both thy shoulders*. Make not light of thy load for Christ, and Christ will make it light for thee."

Just before, our Lord shows us how this wonderful comfort is apprehended;—by simple faith,—never by the dogmatic understanding,—only childlike hearts being clear-sighted enough to read the glorious assurance through the elaborate superscriptions of human learning and ambition: "I thank Thee, O Father, because Thou hast hid these things from the wise and prudent, and hast revealed them unto babes." The knowing men, who may be only fools, the clever calculators that never learned to count beyond ninety years, are outwitted by the youngest scholars in this school of Christ. "In quietness and confidence shall be your strength. In returning and rest," O new-born and illuminated hearts, "shall ye be saved."

In other words,—to generalize the great Gospel-thought,—our faith is for the life that now is, or else it is no faith to fit us for the life to come; and it works out its hallowed alleviations for all the disquietude of these laboring and heavy laden hearts, not by transforming the conditions of their lot, but, while leaving these just as they are, by bringing the inner man into such oneness of life with the Master, that He, the great burden-bearer of all our humanity, shall be their perpetual Passover and their Peace.

In this view, the signification of the text becomes both

more comprehensive and more striking when we enter in and observe that the terms "yoke" and "burden" do not follow one another by any careless accident, but each relates and answers to the two forgoing terms "labor" and "heavy laden." "Come unto Me, all ye that labor and are heavy laden." "Yoke" means labor. "Burden" means suffering. A "yoke" is a symbol of active, tiresome toil. A "burden" is that which hinders strength and drags it down. Take these two thoughts to the two great Biblical dispensations of Law and Love. Each personal history among us reflects that solemn order of Sinai and Gethsemane. Sum up the evils of your old life which formed the "yoke" which hurt you, and their name is self-will,—the *active* principle of anti-Christ. This was the matter of our Lord's first temptation. Sum up the materials of that dull "burden" which sinks the soul the more the more it accumulates, and its name is hopeless sorrow. This was the darkness about the garden and the cross. See now what a spiritual Saviour does for those,—the wide world over and in every house,—who are weary of the yoke and heavy laden under the burden. Christ's "yoke" is submission to *His will*, ceasing from our own; Christ's burden is simply forgetting all else in Him, or rather holding all else as cheap and transient compared with Him. The whole strain of the truth falls, therefore, on that word "My." *Whose* yoke, *whose* burden, is the only question. It is because it is Christ's that it is easy or light. What is borne for Him is not like other pains or losses. The sons and daughters of His afflicting, who come bending unto Him, are the privileged spirits who take their sufferings as love-tokens that He remembers them still, has not left them to their folly, but means by all means to number them with His saints in glory everlasting. The child you lost; the life plan that failed; the fortune that dissolved; the invalid years in a sick chamber; the hidden thorn that stung your side while your *face* smiled from pride or shame,—was a sign that Christ would not leave you to yourself, but knew better than you did how to bring you to the deeper blessedness and nobler freedom of the souls that suffering makes perfect. You will seek no further, but unto Him alone. The legal bondage did hurt; the angel of the Lord took you from your flesh-pots and your fetters together; and Achor, the valley of your trouble, became your avenue to liberty and your "Door of Hope." So exclaims great St. Bernard, "What can be lighter than a burden which takes our burdens away; and a yoke which bears up the bearer himself?"

There is a fine passage, in the uninspired Hebrew writings called the Sohar, which, like a kind of side-light, sets this metaphor of the yoke into singular spiritual beauty. There too the "yoke" of the heavenly kingdom is referred to, and, as if in a prophetic figure of the evangelic truth, the "Thephillim," which are "the fringes of the garments of prayer," are represented as the yoke by which God binds Israel to Himself. "How beautiful," says this Rabbinical Scripture, "is their neck who bear the yoke-robe of Jehovah's precepts!" "Garments of praise for the spirit of heaviness."

No Scripture teaches us that this easing and lightening of the Christian life shall be completed *at once*. The learners in that often sad but blessed school, even though sitting solitary, with pale faces, nerveless limbs, and tears in their eyes, will find "rest" flowing in, not in violent floods, but as the dawn trembles into the sky, by gradual and almost imperceptible increments and risings of the light. Gradually, but steadily, a tranquil faith sets up its unseen pillars of power beneath and within those hanging heads and feeble knees, till the whole body of character is built up, by this edifying submission, a spiritual house. Gradually, but steadily, the blood streams back into the veins; and it is not nature's blood, but is redder and richer and sweeter blood than that, as if the very sweetness and life of the " precious blood " were in it, out of the heart of Jesus, King at once and Lamb, who is the Life of every Christian that lives.

Another Ash-Wednesday has come. It speaks of yoke and burden, of ashes and shadows, of the cross. To some of those who will keep Lent outwardly it will, no doubt, be yoke and burden both, and nothing more,—unwelcome, unrelieved. I need not tell you who they are. Others will find the added service and the unusual restraint easy and light, because through them they will gain the help they need, the deliverance, the purifying, the closer likeness to their Lord, the spiritual liberty they long for. Even these cost something. Self-examination and penitence and crucifixion of the flesh are not joyous exercises, are not meant to be. All our noblest enlargements of power and of peace are sacrificial: there is something hard to do, or hard to bear,—human nature being what it is. We need voluntary acts of self-denial, whether to bring down and humble pride, to chasten fleshly propensities, to clear the soul for prayer, to provide larger charities for Christ's missions and His poor, or to honor God by a simple act of obedience to His word. The particular shape, the needed yoke, may not be the same for us all, and it is not defined. One form of it, the Bible certainly declares, is fasting, and that is to be used. How many need to lay a cross on their lips,—to " fast from strife and debate," from slander, idle words, backbiting! Here are the ashes we are to sprinkle, and the sackcloth we are to wear. The world about you calls this a weariness, and a disagreeable burden; it will even despise and ridicule your scruples if it can. Christ, your Saviour, with the cross on His own shoulders, meets you just here, and faces the world with you. He says, encouragingly and comfortingly, "Yes; here is a yoke, and here is a burden. At first, they will look and feel to you somewhat as they do to the world's people, but not always. As soon as you feel them to be *My* yoke and *My* burden, they will grow lighter and easier every day."

In the Greek word of the evangelist for "easy" there is a concealed sense of "useful." The yoke is eased if by it you help other men. Lent is for human kindnesses, neighborly sympathy, family tenderness. Learn in it to love the brotherhood, to visit the poor, though they are filthy and ungrateful, as your Master did. Hate nothing so much as hatred,—dropping every grudge and every revenge, every bitter or cruel vestige of the old satanic life, out of your heart, forgiving even them that will not forgive. Live fairly and generously with men. Submission, or piety, to God is never perfect without integrity to your neighbor. The Eastern water-carriers bear the burden of the bucket most easily and safely, they say, when they walk uprightly. God makes the path of obedience to Himself to be the path of honesty and sweet temper and loving-kindness to His children. Let thine eyes look right on, and thine eyelids straight before thee. Then it will prove that you are blessed children of the Father. You walk at large, like sons of God. The road of duty will still be narrow, but, travelling in it, you will breathe the immortal air, and every deepening breath will be an inspiration of the

Life eternal. Your daily landscape will be the scenery of both worlds,—all things yours, because ye are Christ's, and Christ is God's.

"Behold, I will allure her, and bring her into the wilderness, and speak comfortably unto her. And I will give her vineyards from thence, and the valley of Achor for a door of hope; and she shall sing there, as in the days of her youth, and as in the day when she came up out of the land of Egypt."

# THE THRONG AND THE TOUCH.

*First Sunday in Lent.*

"Stand in the gate of the Lord's house, and proclaim there this word, and say, Hear the word of the Lord, all ye of Judah, that enter in at these gates to worship the Lord. Thus saith the Lord of hosts, the God of Israel, Amend your ways and your doings, and I will cause you to dwell in this place. Trust ye not in lying words, saying, The temple of the Lord, The temple of the Lord, The temple of the Lord, are these. For if ye thoroughly amend your ways and your doings; if ye thoroughly execute judgment between a man and his neighbor; if ye oppress not the stranger, the fatherless, and the widow, and shed not innocent blood in this place, neither walk after other gods to your hurt: then will I cause you to dwell in this place, in the land that I gave to your fathers, forever and ever."—*Jeremiah* vii. 2-7.

"And Jesus said, Who touched Me? When all denied, Peter and they that were with Him said, Master, the multitude throng thee and press Thee, and sayest Thou, Who touched Me? And Jesus said, Somebody hath touched Me: for I perceive that virtue is gone out of Me."—*St. Luke* viii. 45, 46.

There is a common truth belonging to both these two passages which are so different in the language, and are taken from parts of Scripture so far apart. I believe that the placing of them together will help give that great doctrine more distinctness, put emphasis upon it, and make it easier to remember.

In the first passage, occuring in this morning's first lesson, under a vivid picture of a scene at the door of the old temple, the prophet searches out a moral danger that is apt to accompany all public religious observances. The Spirit of God, acquainted with these perils, and determined to break them up, puts him there, and inspires him with the clear-sightedness and courage to strike straight home at the popular delusion. Standing at the gate he sees a multitude of men crowding in to go through the forms of worship. He knows that they have just come from the selfish practice, in their markets, fields, streets and houses, of injustice, cruelty to the weak, overreaching "the stranger, the fatherless and the widow," of every kind of social, commercial, political, and ecclesiastical falsehood,—for he goes on to specify all these,—and what is a great deal worse, that they are privately intending to go back to the same kinds of meanness and outrage after the prayers and sacrifices are over. He also sees that the moment their want of integrity is pointed out, they will, after the Pharisaic fashion, undertake to throw over it the screen of a religious profession. They will answer, at every rebuke of their immorality, "The temple of the Lord, The temple of the Lord, The temple of the Lord," as if they would make up, by the threefold repetition and noise of their zeal, for their hollow-heartedness. And so, having it for his business as a prophet of God to denounce such corruption everywhere, without apology for his Divine commission, without arguing the matter, without any round-about or imbecile phraseology, he goes to the point at once, and begins, "Trust ye not in lying words: amend your ways and your doings."

The great instructive fact on which attention is to be fixed is this: that out of the multitude of persons who enter the sanctuary, many have only a formal, external, and ostensible, not a substantial, sympathy, or actual concern, with the holy REALITY which is there embodied and presented. They imagine that, in some strange way, the temple-roof is to shield or excuse their allowed neglect of practical obedience to God's commandment. They throng the visible courts, press the material building, but without touching, in living faith, the sacred Presence, the life-giving hand of the Holy One who inhabits it.

Turn now to the other passage. It is a distant scene;—distant in place, for it is up in one of the open highways of Galilee, instead of at the temple in the old Zion;—"a greater than the temple is here," the living and incarnate Christ of whom the tabernacle of the desert and the former and latter house at Jerusalem, in their bravest glory, and all the prophets themselves, were but dim prefigurations. It is distant in time six hundred years. A different tone and color run through the narrative. There is more tenderness, more personal feeling, a plainer working of the power of faith, as befits the healing and gracious spirit of the new dispensation of love. And yet the same old human elements, the same two sorts of persons, with the same sharp line between them, are all there; for neither human nature nor its temptations are among the things that are much altered by time. Here too a multitude throng and press a sacred spot. It is the spot where Jesus of Nazareth stands, and it is made sacred by His blessed feet. So many are the people that when Jesus, perceiving by His quick, mysterious inward sense that one among them has come with an entirely different heart from the rest, inquired, "Who touched Me?" Peter and others wondered at Him, saying, "Master, the multitude throng Thee and press Thee, and sayest Thou, Who touched Me?" The answer of Christ draws again the deep and sharp discrimination between those that are only outwardly and formally with Him, and those that in a wholly different sense are *of* Him. "Somebody hath touched Me." That answer divides one person there from all the indifferent crowd following on, as an idle crowd always will, after any new wonder, from curiosity or self-interest; and it sets her all apart by herself,—half trembling at her detection, half rejoicing that she is not wholly overlooked. Here was a living creature whose life was wasting in her veins. My friends, there is a deeper signification in our Lord's miracles on human bodies than a mere remedy for physical disorder. They mean much more than the quieting of a little aching flesh, or the lengthening out of a few mortal years. The maladies the Saviour healed on earth were images and symbols. His wonders of restoration were only types of the diviner cures He wrought on paralytic consciences, on leprous sensibilities, on the halting purpose, the blind faith, the lame will, the consumptive charity. It will go to the very heart of the matter, then, if we can see just what it was in the woman that made the religious difference between her and the multitude around her. That difference is of vital moment to every soul. Peter said, " The multitude throng Thee and press Thee"; "Jesus said, Somebody hath *touched* Me." What is it merely to come near, and what is it to "touch" the Giver of eternal life? Among us, men and women of this day, what is the act on our part that will carry us over the separating space between the outward presence and the real fellowship or participation with Him?

The woman reached out her hand and touched the Saviour's garment. What was it that *moved her hand?* She believed. But in what did she believe? Not in herself, not in the motion of her arm, not that she was doing anything that was an equivalent for the cure, or would purchase it; nor yet did she believe that by standing aloof and *waiting* awhile till she was partly restored, made stronger or more presentable, by some skill of her own, she should be more likely to get the benefit desired; nor had she any theory whatever about the method in which the curative power was to take effect. You do not find in her clear and urgent sense of need that strange inverting of all reason that we so often see in men when they hesitate about coming to seek heavenly grace in Christ's Church, pleading that they are "not good enough," not strong enough, healthful enough, to be blessed by it. The soldier after the battle, wounded and sick, bloodstained and feverish, creeps along the hot and dusty road, longing only to die under the old home-tree, and under the breath of a mother's lips. He comes to a hospital, and sees it written over the door, "Whosoever will, let him come." Does He creep back, pleading that He is not well enough to go in and be healed? What then *did* the woman believe? She believed that she was to *receive* something, a real blessing, from Christ. This was what distinguished her, in her humility and obscurity, from the sentimental crowd around her. This was that in her which was not in them. They all travelled on in the highway together, talked about Christ, were interested in Him in various ways, discussed His origin and nature, hoped that some good would come of Him to the nation. They thought it prudent to be in the company of a miraculous power, able to feed or heal them, in case there should be occasion for His help; and so they took some pains to keep Him in sight. Word for word, brethren, these phrases describe what uncounted multitudes now are ready to do, when the Gospel and Church of Christ call to them. But the woman *believed that she should personally receive new life from Him.*

She knew she needed it; she knew she had nothing to buy it with,—for she had spent all her living on physicians, and could not be healed of any, but rather grew worse. Most graphic history of how many hearts! She believed that she could have that new life by a touch. The reaching out of her hand was an expression of that faith. Another signal might probably have done just as well. In other cases a prayer was as effectual. But there *must* have been two things: the faith that she should receive the benefit, and some act to embody that faith and bring the benefit home. With faith, action.

It is an almost equally significant part of the interview that her faith, instead of being perfect yet, had some intellectual mistakes clinging to it. Thus she evidently supposed she could obtain the cure without Christ's knowing of her application, or putting forth any conscious exercise of His will. She meant to keep herself hid, probably from so respectable a motive as natural diffidence. It was no intention of hers,—as it never can be of any true confessing Christian,—to distinguish herself from the rest. She was not forward to make "a profession of religion." Would that our Church language might exchange that ostentatious phrase for the better one,—*the confession of Christ!* Probably her idea was,—like what has often been held as one of the elements of superstition, especially in the East,—that a kind of magical charm charged with some sanative efficacy encircled this miraculous person; that the border of His garment was the channel of the healing energy, and hence that she had only to put her finger on it to be made whole. She was wrong as to the mode. But did this intellectual misconception, as to the mere vehicle by which the blessed power was transmitted, spoil her faith, or forfeit the cure? On the contrary, the

Saviour patiently and gently separates the *substance* of the faith from the erroneous fancies impressed upon it by a weak brain or a false education; He takes pains to disabuse her and all about her of the superstitious imagination, by showing them that the cure was not wrought, and could not be, without His conscious and consenting will answering her application,—"I perceive that virtue is gone out of Me,"—and grants her desire. As He always read the thoughts of both Pharisees and penitents alike, as He marked the concealed discipleship in the guileless heart of Nathaniel under the fig-tree, so here He depends on no outward expression to tell Him the soul's prayer, and yet He requires it for the disciple's sake. And in the same goodness now He is ever gathering and drawing saved souls to Himself,—thanks to His great power,—wherever His name is heard, even though there hang about their honest and true trust in Him many a poor shred of misbelief, many a badge of mistaken systems, many a paltry remnant of traditional illusion. It is a comfortable, Catholic encouragement that He gives us,—in the prevalence of so many erratic devices of the theological mind, and so many crude additions to the energetic simplicity of the Truth,—that mistakes of opinion about *methods* of grace do not choke the channels of grace itself, or bar the gate of heaven.

But now there comes forward another aspect of churchly doctrine, bringing with it a new obligation. Why does Christ draw forward this believing follower from her bashful retirement, and insist on her declaring herself in the presence of the multitude? The cure was wrought; the faith had gained its object, and its mistake had been corrected; the receiver of the blessing was creeping away through the crowd, not ungrateful, but unrecognized and unobserved. Why should she not be suffered to retain her humble seclusion? For the reason, doubtless, that her anxiety for herself took just so much from loyalty to her Lord. It is a principle of God's kingdom, and a part of God's command, that a *confession before men* shall accompany the believing of the heart. If anybody could be excused, it would seem that she might be. But there is no exception, none; none for the proudest man, none for the weakest woman. Hitherto her offering is incomplete; she has brought her secret faith, but not herself; and true faith must keep nothing back that the Lord requires. Men cannot say, "My religion is my own affair; it is *only* a thing between myself and my Maker; it is entirely an inward and invisible relation to Him, and so I am satisfied in my private feeling that it is there, no more can be demanded of me." They cannot hold that ground; because the duty of open confession is as clearly enjoined in Scripture as it is illustrated in every sound scriptural example. The fact that there is a faithless multitude, making a merit of formal professions, glossing their worldliness by a pious cant of "The temple of the Lord," and screening their unrighteousness under observances, does not affect a whit the call of sincere believers to acknowledge whose they are and by whom they are healed. "And when the woman saw that she was not hid, she came trembling, and falling down before Him, she declared unto Him, *before all the people* for what cause she had touched Him, and how she was healed immediately." Then the Lord uses for her encouragement a term of endearment he had not spoken before: "Daughter, thy faith hath made thee whole." Her faith had made the occasion,—doing it mediately; His Divine power had made the cure,—doing it directly. Faith is the conditional cause; Christ himself is the efficient, energetic cause. And the acknowledgment of Him is the signal of the final blessing which then falls in a benediction from His lips: "Go in peace."

What you are to make this morning's lesson stamp ineffaceably on your hearts,—shaping it into clear outlines,—is the deep distinction between mere *pressing about* Christ, and touching Him; between resting in the apparatus of salvation, and laying hold of it with your hands; between trusting in the material temple, and clinging with a closeness of heart that neither life nor death can separate to the living Rock. You honor the place of your worship; that is well. But how unreal and shallow it all would be,—how false and foolish we should be with one another,—if this should prove to be all or the chief part of our religion! Why, it would double your condemnation, and mine. Would that the life of every member of the body of Christ were so lifted above the world, so triumphant over it, so visibly given to the Church and so inwardly to Christ, so self-renouncing and so holy, that your completed faithfulness would take the message out of our weak lips and proclaim it in living characters to your neighbor. It oppresses one to remember that here is a reality of infinite majesty and beauty transcending all our conceptions of what is glorious, enough to inspire with enthusiasm every breast that breathes, so grand and lovely in its attraction that it would seem only to need to be held up as it really is to win every heart to the Cross forever,—and yet that so many of us still go on chasing bubbles, fretting with care, scraping together accumulations which if they are not all used for Christ are worth not a particle more than ant-hills on the sand. The very crimes and license of the age, daily published, ought to arouse us, sending us with heartier prayers and more solemn circumspection, in this sacred season, to the altars of God;—nay more, to the hand, to the heart, of Christ. It might appear to you, at times, as if the preacher's chief aim were to persuade you to an outward confession, or a pressing into the gates. But no, that urgency is only because, without that, the higher duties are never done, and the consecration is never complete You may, if you please, do with the text now as Augustine did in his sermon at Carthage, substitute *Ecclesia*—" the Church,"—for Jesus, and write " the body of Christ " for Christ; still it would be true, as he said, " The faith of a few touches it,—the crowd of many (*turba multorum*) only presses against it." The Christian ground is never truly taken till Christ is confessed; but then He may be loudly claimed in the cry, " The temple of the Lord," when no fruits prove the heart to be thoroughly surrendered. Now that many of you are turning your steps more frequently to the solemn assemblies and public ordinances of the Faith, forget not your Lord's imperative command,—let it follow you out into your week-day work: " Amend your ways and your doings." Who is the true Christian? You may suppose the case of a person who from a state of indifference and neglect about religion has been converted to a sense of its real interest and power, and that this person is so placed that the men he meets in his business and in society are not informed of his change. Will they find it out, then, by any manifest change passing over the spirit and manners of his business and social life? Will they find him purer, gentler, better, nobler, holier? Or take the case of two men, one with and the other without the Christian profession. Hold the two aloof awhile from any place or occasion where the profession would be formally shown,—at a churchless trading-port, or in the week-day life of a gay city. Would the world be able to tell which is which? These are the tests. There was an artist in the old times who carved a metal shield, into the bosses of which he so ingeniously and inseparably wrought his own name that it could not be obliterated except by the destruction of the shield itself. Good Christians, you ought to bear the armor of righteousness on the right hand and on the left, and on it that ONE NAME, seen of all men, one image never invisible there, till you take the armor off to go within the veil. That manifestation of the truth in a practical holiness commends the Christian, commends the Church, commends Christ, to every man's conscience in the sight of God. With that inwrought secret of life and immortality in your soul,—a living faith,—though the outward man perish, the inward man is renewed day by day. "Somebody hath touched Me." Are you then touching the temple for your salvation, or Christ for your Saviour? Are you touching Him by your personal faith, or only pressing upon Him with the multitude? Do you only join the popular procession of a nominal Christianity which shouts its heartless hosannas along the highway to Jerusalem, or will you march all the hard road of a holy obedience, with your crucified Master, till he tells you to lay the cross down, when the resurrection morning breaks?

# SUPPLICATION THE CHURCH'S POWER.

*Second Sunday in Lent.*

"AND the whole multitude of the people were praying without at the time of incense."—*St. Luke* i. 10.

BOTH the parents of John, Zacharias and Elizabeth, were of the family of the Hebrew priesthood. For a long time the ministrations of this great sacerdotal order, in the temple service at Jerusalem, had been distributed among twenty-four courses of priests, each course taking its turn for a week, and each having its own leader. At the time when the evangelist's narrative opens, Abia stood at the head of the eighth of these twenty-four courses, and Zacharias, the father of the Baptist, was officiating in his turn in that course. "It came to pass," says St. Luke, "that while he executed the priest's office in the order of his course, his lot was to burn incense when he went into the temple of the Lord. And the whole multitude of the people were praying without at the time of incense. And there appeared unto him an angel of the Lord standing on the right side of the altar of incense."

It moves our veneration,—the majestic continuity of this holy office, the order of its courses reaching from the reign of King David, unbroken save by the short interruptions of captivity, and scarcely even then, for four of the courses returned to Jerusalem to take their places when the exile was over;—the priesthood itself, dating back to the wilderness, reaching over a tract of centuries that saw the rising and falling of many empires,—its ranks very commonly embracing thousands of men. The sublimity of it is only heightened when we recall the nature of that ministry committed to them by God himself. Constant as the morning and evening that daily open and shut their gates on the eyes of men, they waited around that altar which steadfastly prefigured and prophesied the Redeemer; they kept a sleepless watch over the fire on the altar of burnt-offerings, which typified Christ's eternal sacrifice, never letting it go out, day or night; they "fed the golden lamps outside the veil with sacred oil"; they offered the daily sacrifices, morning and evening, at the door of the tabernacle; they were always ready at hand to do the cleansing and comforting offices commanded in the law. And here, in the text, we have a glimpse of them in their lofty work, just as the Gospel fulfilments and spiritual glories broke in on their typical routine in the person of the Son of Man.

From the ministry going on there turn to the place, with its arrangements. Near the entrance of the temple,—the heart of the nation's life,—outside what was properly the sanctuary, advanced as if in token of a freely offered mercy to meet the approaching worshipper, was the large altar of the daily sacrifice. Farther in toward the most holy place, very near to the veil of the covenant, to signify that closer access which the accepted believer has to the Intercessor who is ascended into the true Holy of holies, stood another altar, with its crown of pure gold and its golden rings, on which one of the priests, chosen by lot,—all of them so many that it was a Jewish tradition that the same priest never did it more than once,—offered twice every day the sweet incense, which with its ascending smoke, in the beautiful language of St. John, is as "the prayers of saints." Notice that the fire which lighted this altar was always to be taken fresh from the outer altar, of the sacrifice for sin,—another type of Christian truth,—because the acceptance of Christian prayers depends on their being offered only through a Saviour suffering and crucified.

Another remarkable feature remains. At the moment when the effectual work of propitiation and intercession goes forward *within* the temple,—what is seen without? The whole multitude of the people, bending in silent awe, seconding the priestly office and making it in some sense their own, joining their faith to the sacrifice, and lifting their hearts with the rising incense-cloud, are in supplication before God. This can represent nothing else than the power of the united prayers of the Christian congregation, aiding and supporting the official work of the threefold ministry and the holy offices of the Church, in declaring Christ to the world.

The question before us, then, thrown open in its broadest form, will be this: Are we using the *devotional* power of the Church in due proportion to its other powers? In laying our plans, whether for our private religious regulation and personal growth in holiness, or for the public advancement of Christ's kingdom, are we looking directly enough and constantly enough to God? In shaping and starting new measures, even for the Church's honor and for the saving of men, do we go first, and go most confidently, and go continually, to Him whose presence is our only life, and whose favoring will, in every Christian movement, is the only moving force? In our individual self-discipline, when we are depressed with a sense that it is not going well with us, when some flash of light in these Lenten self-examinations exposes a new weak spot, or when a providence suddenly reveals the wrong direction in which our habits have been gradually and almost imperceptibly deflecting, when the heart seems frozen, the senses leprous, faith sleeping, and we wonder what is the matter, do we take that question straight to the Holy Spirit, as readily as we ask it of ourselves? If in any of our undertakings we fail, there is very little doubt that we fail because we did not expect enough and ask enough of God;—for that expectation is only another name for faith; and that asking is prayer.

Men say, "Religion is a thing between a man and his Maker"; and though it is often said to palliate some inexcusable neglect of an open religious confession before men, yet it is profoundly true. We take you, O men of the world, at your word. Religion *is* a thing between man and his Maker; not between man and himself, not between man and society, not between man and the State. All our relations and duties to these, and theirs to us, come under the law of morality; and though morality, with its practical relations and duties receives inspiration and guidance from the doctrines and ordinances of religion, yet when we rise to religion itself, entering her invisible and heavenly tabernacle, we pass out of all merely moral connections, and are in the presence of God. There are two parties, and only two. The business of religion, therefore, is to bring offerings to Him, and, in answer to our prayers, to take blessings from Him. This, with the sacred sentiments, affections, and actions which belong to that holy intercourse, is the first business of the Church. It sets open the channel of communion, where there is this incessant spiritual passing and repassing between the Infinite Heart of Love which is open there, and these hearts of ours, weak and struggling, uneasy and hungry and sinning, here. By this spiritual interchange, our whole life opens a path into heaven, and the blessed life of heaven opens down upon us. So, Christians, we stand, in this sacred and redeemed creation, always at a temple-door. No doubt there are mysteries. What temple was ever without its suggestions of mystery? Even a very deep and strong human love has its mysteries. But nevertheless, the Light falls down from the Throne. God is there. The door is swung open. We are near to Him; He is near to us. The Mediator and Intercessor is praying there for us. Our prayers are joined with His. The reconciliation is accomplished. It is as if the scene at Jerusalem were reproduced in its Christian and everlasting reality. It is the time of incense. The chief-priest is at the golden altar, with the fire kindled. The whole multitude of the Church below is on its knees, the faithful people supplicating for pardon and peace, entreating that they may perceive and know what things they ought to do, and may have power and grace to fulfil the same,—asking and receiving that their joy may be full.

The next step follows irresistibly. Every movement of religious life among us must get its power and direction from the Spirit of God. Every contrivance of ecclesiastical or parochial wisdom, of energy, even of piety, is nothing but a making ready for this Spirit. We may try other things, as we certainly do, and may try them with the best intentions. We call people together, form societies, write constitutions for them with rules and by-laws, devise and discuss measures, publish statistics, secure an incorporation perhaps, send for the ablest speakers, collect money, and when the institution is thoroughly organized and built, we look at it and watch its working. It is all done in the interest and for the sake of some Christian truth or charity. But the amount of spiritual product is exactly in proportion to the coming into all this apparatus of that living Spirit of God,—the love of the Father, the grace of Christ, the fellowship of the Holy Ghost. And the degree of that coming and power, again, will be exactly in proportion to the fervency and the frequency of prayers that are offered by believers around it. If you would find the true secret of spiritual success, you need not seek for it in the admirableness of the plan, the shrewdness of the management, the numbers that subscribe, or the eloquence of the advocates. You might better seek it in some very obscure chambers, some out-of-the-way corners, some closets with the doors shut, where men or women or children in whose breasts God has a Temple of His own,—never heard of at the public meetings, poor and simple-hearted and of stammering lips,—kneel with their great-hearted and prevailing petitions, not discouraged by the slowness of the answer, trusting not in themselves but only in the Lord Almighty. These are the "multitude praying without." It is they,—be they few or many, known or unknown,—who are the security of your constitutions, the builders of your churches, the senders of your missionaries, the really efficient patrons of your orphan-houses, hospitals, and Christian education societies. The finest and firmest machinery in the world is so much dead material without these prayers. I suppose most of you have seen some elaborate and costly specimen of mechanism, standing still: every little screw and bolt of the complicated system in its place; every post and bar, flange and transom secure; every bright lever and arm, wheel and tooth, tempered and tested;—the whole a splendid embodiment and trophy of intellectual ingenuity and determination,—yet silent and inert as icicles, till some lifted gate or opened valve lets in the mysterious *motive-power* which makes it a sure and mighty servant of a purpose beyond it. So are all our best religious measures, till the breath of the Church's prayers joins them to the Spirit from on High. Throughout all its portions, the Scripture has no other doctrine. "Be strong, all ye people of the Lord, for I am with you, saith the Lord." "Not by might, not by power, but by My Spirit." "Pray ye the Lord of the harvest that He will send forth laborers." "Prove Me if I will not open the windows of heaven, and pour you out a blessing." "O God, we know not what to do, but our eyes are upon Thee." How was it with our blessed Lord himself? It was when He was praying, by the river Jordan, after His baptism, that the heaven was opened and a dove descended; it was when He was praying again, "Father, glorify Thy name," that heaven was opened a second time, and an audible voice spoke. It was when He was praying in the garden of Gethsemane, that it was opened a third time, and an angel was *seen* strengthening Him. " And ye, beloved, praying in the Holy Ghost, keep yourselves in the love of God." "The prayer of a righteous man availeth" for his character, more than his labor; and to those that do not pray there are no promises.

We look into the Bible records of the beginnings and growth of God's kingdom on the earth. On every spot where that kingdom struck root we see a group of men bending in prayer. When the Eastern magi were brought by the star to Bethlehem, all their intellectual strength bowed itself down to a little child; they taught nothing, proposed nothing;—they did not even speak; it was simply an offering; the signification of it was the submission of knowledge to faith. It was worship. From page to page, in the Acts of the Apostles, they are shown to us together looking upward. When an order in the ministry, an apostle, or a missionary, was to be set apart, or sent out, special prayer signalized the ceremony. At the meeting and parting of Christian friends, on their sacred errands, they knelt and prayed. If one of their number was imprisoned, prayer was made for him day and night. When an epistle was written, whatever other words of affectionate salutation there might be, the chief and ever-recurring message ran like this,—" Always, in every prayer of mine, making mention of you all." If another of them touches, in his writing, on such a familiar duty as the harmony of husband and wife, the lofty reason of it he gives is,—" that your prayers be not hindered." If a special ministry of deacons is appointed for the outer cares of charity, it is that the higher office may be more especially reserved for prayer. When the Holy sacrament of the Communion is celebrated, or alms are given, eucharistic prayer accompanies the breaking of bread, and oblation-prayer comes up as a memorial of faith, with the alms, before Christ. What an epoch of prayer was that! So elevated are these ardent and consecrated souls towards heaven, so open towards God's spirit, so conscious that they have only to ask to receive, that devotion seems to have become an instinct, and they pray as they breathe. The whole fiery heart of the Church of Christ was in instant communication with its ascended Head. And what followed? Why, this was the period when the Church grew before men's eyes with such swiftness that a thousand converts were gathered in the time that it takes us to gather ten: in the short lifetime of a single generation the worship of Christ raised itself to power in the chief cities of three continents; the swords of all the Herods and Caesars and their legions could not strike fast enough to cut down one Christian where twenty sprang up; hundreds were baptized in a day; the times of refreshing had come;—the prediction was literally accomplished;—the windows of heaven *were* opened, and the blessing was so poured out that there was not room enough to receive it. If hard questions were encountered, as to discipline, or ritual, or personal preference in the apostleship, they were melted down in these holy fires of common prayer; men could not long strive bitterly with each other who entreated the Lord of unity to pity and bless them together and make them like Himself, every time they looked into each other's faces. *These* were the fruits. How can we fail to connect together the fruit with the seed,—the glorious movement and the motive-power,—the Church pure in doctrine and victorious in converting the world with the multitude of her members not only standing full-clad in all the panoply of the Christian warfare, but praying always, with all prayer and supplication in the Spirit?

All along since the last of the twelve laid down his life, this rule has never had an exception;—the Church has been both strong and pure, victorious abroad and peaceful with itself, just according to its spirit of supplication; according to its devotional nearness to Christ its Head, because that means and carries with it its separation from worldly-mindedness and its indifference to the worldly standards of success. Whenever there has been a great uprising of new missionary power, or a reformation, or a rousing from sleep, as if some immense light had broken on the eyes of the watchers east and west, the one invariable mark of such an age has been a general earnestness and faithfulness in supplication. Men have not been seen running about, till they first went into their sanctuaries and their closets with stronger and heartier cries for the Spirit. They were not looking to each other for help, but to God. They did not undertake first to construct new systems, but they betook themselves first to the mercy-seat by the Church's old and well-worn road. They prayed as they worked, in God's order and appointment. The multitude at Jerusalem had not broken away to worship in their own unbidden and promiscuous fashions, according to their individual fancies, as if new ways would bring new hearts or new blessings. No, they were at the one, right place; at the courts of the Lord's house: bending towards the covenant sign; and it was "at the time of incense." And so the periods of prayer have always been the periods of life. As soon as men imagined they could put schemes, societies, treasuries and buildings in the place of prayer, weakness crept back upon them. The period of power went out as the period of self-reliance or worldly compromise came in. Only by My Spirit can ye be strong, saith the Lord of hosts.

A lingering doubt casts up its faithless suggestion at these words: "Is not the Church constantly praying? Yet where is the fulfilment of the promise?" The answer is found under another word, "*the prayers of faith.*" We may be sure that the measure of the faith *is* the measure of the power of the prayer, and that the measure of such prayer is, sooner or later, the measure of the blessing we receive. We very often mistake the strength of our *desire* for the strength of our faith. Besides, faith is a general quality of the whole soul in all its acts and aspects towards the Saviour, and pertains to its habitual attitude; it is not a mere sudden, special expectation of having some greatly-wanted boon granted. It is, for the most part, a grace of slow, patient, and silent growth. Most of us, in our common moods, scarcely touch the rim of its great depth of meaning, or taste of its incalculable peace. It is true just as it stands,—"According to your faith, in asking, be it unto you." It is true of our private conflicts with the tempter, our struggles with ourselves, our resistance of the sins that most easily beset us, our fight with temper and pride and indolence and luxury, with Satan in his most angelic garment. Spiritual victory and progress will be gained on our knees, by looking up and saying, "Lord, if Thou wilt, Thou canst make me clean. Save me, or I perish." Zacharias saw the vision of the angel, beside the altar of incense, before the veil. To us Christians the veil is rent assunder. The Holy of holies is thrown open. The Saviour whom the types foretold is come. And now, if any man sin, we have an advocate with the Father, Jesus Christ the Righteous, who ever liveth to make intercession for us, the High-priest tempted here as we are, yet sinless, needing not to make sacrifice for His own sins, yet touched with the feeling of our every infirmity, and Himself our sacrifice.

Can we look on any side of us this day and not confess that the great need of Christ's body is this need of Him, of the power which we have seen can come only from Him, and which comes only as we pray for it? The dear Church seems to me to stand, with her holy mysteries, very much as the temple stood that day,—the ark of promise and the altar of incense and of the one eternal sacrifice all safe and sure within. But is the multitude praying as that multitude prayed? Is it that prayer of yearning and earnest and living faith, for new spiritual gifts, which will not be denied? Look every way,—into markets, streets, newspapers, courts, down into the sins of the low places, out into the sins of the high places,—the insubordination of the poor and the extravagance of the rich, the impatience of the weak and the arrogance of the strong, the wrongs of commerce and the impurities of legislation, the selfishness and sensuality tainting the whole structure of the State, and the divisions in the house of the Lord. Seeing that we have no power of ourselves to help ourselves, is it not time to go to Him who alone can show us what things we ought to do, and give us power and grace to fulfil the same? This is not such a world that we can afford to live in it without great nearness to Him who, having died once, liveth evermore. This is not such a life as we should dare to try to live any further without offering the whole of it,—its gold, its incense, and its myrrh,—possessions, prayers, and praises, at the feet of its spiritual King. Light the lamps of faith, then, and watch. Kindle the fire of incense and wait:—not sleeping, but watching unto prayer.

# PURITY AND ITS SAFEGUARDS.

*Third Sunday in Lent.*

"BLESSED are the pure in heart: for they shall see God."—
*St. Matthew* v. 8.

THE warnings of this Sunday are against sins of sensual passion. They are represented as coming by "evil thoughts which assault and hurt the soul." Good men will not be satisfied with escaping the disgrace of public crime. If our minds are set with any reverence towards the right, we shall be asking nothing less than positive purity, or an inward life growing up from a Divine principle, clean from all moral disease, strong with Christian health. Any kind of disease has two effects: it *defiles* the body it belongs to, and *debilitates* it. It pollutes the substance and weakens the energies. Sin is the soul's disease. If the disease is there, then, "from within," out of the foul heart will proceed all the foul things which the Saviour named as defiling the whole man. The question, therefore, is the practical one, how to keep the heart healthy, or clean.

The pure *in heart* are blessed:—not the pure by profession; not those who are pure according to that standard of purity demanded by the prevalent social morality. Christ says of these, knowing just how much and how little they have,—Doubtless they have *their* reward. But it is not the glorious privilege of the pure *in heart.* They and they alone have what the saints of old used to call the "beatific vision." They alone will see that sight which makes any soul completely blessed, —God's full glory in the face of Jesus Christ.

Throughout the appointed Scriptures for Lent, it is very noticeable how prominent and plain-spoken are the Divine rebukes of this one particular kind of transgression, —the sins of the bodily senses. And this is not surprising, for when we look underneath the mere ceremonial surface we see that there must be some deep connection between such a set time of physical self-denial and those special temptations which have their origin in the animal appetites. These appetites, however, remember, are not a separate section of us, lying by itself, cut off from the rest of our nature. They are mysteriously and perilously intertangled with some higher and nobler passions,— like artistic enthusiasm, generous affections, intellectual ambition, and even religious excitement. Apart from the principles of Christian morality, neither what is beautiful in any of the fine arts, nor what is true in science or eloquent in letters, has any effectual restraining power over the sensual propensities,—as is seen by awful demonstration in the ages of Pericles, of the Greek Olympics, of Leo X., and of Louis XIV. This alliance with mental curiosity and aesthetic delight is really the most insidious feature of that species of vice. To the better-born and better-bred classes, such vice, in its coarser shapes, is not tempting, because it is disgusting. Many a young man of natural or cultured refinement is protected from some of the worst forms of immorality simply by their vulgarity. But the fearful flimsiness of that shield is shown the moment the tempter exchanges rags and filth for elegance, accomplishments, and literary luxury. In fact, it is the belief of many thoughtful minds in Christendom that the final manifestation of the power of evil on the earth,—the "man of sin" foretold in the New Testament as to come in "the last time,"—surpassing in his powers of mischief every other embodiment of depravity, terrible in fascination, will be an actual historic character, combining together in this all-surpassing badness the most splendid intellectual abilities with unregenerated, ferocious, fleshly passions,—Milton's ideal Satan, realized in a man.

However this may be, for all of us practically the problem of moral purity is very intimately and subtly connected with this curiosity and eagerness of the mind. An unhallowed knowledge, or the thirst for it, betrays the conscience and seduces the heart. And this is what made St. Paul write to his friend, "I would have you *wise unto that which is good and simple concerning evil.*" An innocent knowledge and a glorious ignorance!

The idea has crept in among our popular theories of social morals, that a knowledge of vice is a safeguard to virtue. We are told that hardy plants are not grown in a conservatory; that our sons and daughters may as well be acquainted with the wickedness of the world's ways first as last; that dissolute fictions and a French stage are a capital discipline for robust principles; in short, that morality is altogether too fragile and insecure a creature to run out-of-doors alone, without a little previous initiation into depravity. Worldly fathers and despairing mothers take what comfort they can from the easy maxim that young people had better have a free range through scenes of temptation, in order that its attractions may not take them by surprise further on, and that they must "see life," to know how to live. If we could lead out in our time the hopeless profligates of a single generation which that plausible philosophy has betrayed, the joyous households, once pure, that it has wrecked and distracted, the sweet, clean hearts it has defiled, the noble natures it has degraded, the men whose honor it has ruined, and the women whose peace it has crushed,—a very long, a very mournful, and a very admonitory procession it would be. At the head of it move the first human pair, marching in miserable humiliation out of Eden. The tree of the knowledge of "good" was not enough. There hung, in ruddy beauty, the more luscious fruit of the knowledge of "evil" as well. Why not eat of that? Knowledge can do no harm. Seeing things as they are! Nature is a safe study. "Thou shalt *not* surely die." Six thousand years the story has been told over and over. You need not go for it to the beginning of Genesis. It was acted last night close to where you live,— happy for you if not by some soul that you love. Indiscriminate knowledge, unhallowed curiosity, the lust of the mind looking through eager eyes, is the unceasing temptation of man. So he falls first into sin, then into shame. "Seeing life" turns out to be tasting of death.

Make one or two all-important discriminations.

There is a difference between kinds of sin. Some sins, far more than others, are sins first of the imagination. They are such that to think of them is to be tempted by them. To harbor their images, to gaze on their portraits, is to open wide the way for the guilty realities themselves. With other offences it is not so, or is so only in slighter degrees. The most vivid and picturesque stories of theft, for instance, most of us here could probably read, to any extent, without much danger of becoming kleptomaniacs or robbers. Such crimes as come of cool calculation, not stimulated by feeling, invested by no halo of voluptuous fancy, we are not much more drawn to by becoming familiar with their history. Yet it is observed even of these, like suicide and murder, that they have their run at periods, like diseases, showing that the constant contemplation of any evil thing, by some secret fascination or sympathy, weakens the securities that save us from its power. Especially true is this of those which are secret in their very nature, loving darkness rather than light, born and nursed in hidden chambers where no eye of man can reach, till they gain the satanic strength, finally, to break openly over the bounds of law; but at any rate corroding, corrupting, and spoiling the chaste heart, till it is pure no longer. So certainly teaches Christ, He who knows this human heart so well in all its weakness,—when He insists that sin is in the glance of the eye and the desire of the mind. Hence the supreme importance He assigns in His teaching to the government of the thoughts, the imagination, the "hidden man." Hence His terrific calling of the *unuttered* and *unacted* desire by the name of the most unfaithful of all committed crimes. There are sins that you can no more paint on the airy walls of your contemplation, and keep there, without being made sinful by them, than you can stamp inky types on paper and leave no mark, or handle pitch without its cleaving to your fingers. You may say, "Unto the pure all things are pure," and so you will go and look, and listen, as you please; you will let meretricious art and ambiguous literature and bold company tempt you to the full bent of their unbridled will. Yes—"Unto the pure all things are pure"; that declares a principle. But who are the "pure"? Will any one of us here in God's house, right-minded as he may be, looking up honestly toward the great white Throne, dare say, "I am pure"? and if you are, how does it happen that you willingly suffer impurity to be the tolerated guest of your heart's hospitality?

Granted that some insight into evil is necessary, how is that knowledge to be gained?

A good deal of it is given to every mind by divinely planted instincts,—about as much, if they are kept alive, as is needful for the practical management of life. In some sense we know evil by knowing good. If a soul loves God, then it finds intuitively that there is a something opposite and hateful to God, which it must hate. Right suggests its eternal enemy, wrong. Charity conveys some quick intimation of its dark shadow, malice. The dove trembles at the sound of the wings of the hawk it never saw before. Cynics sneer at the weakness of innocence. But there are saints who are also heroes, known and read of all men, who never went to school to license, but have grown up clean-hearted and clean-handed from their cradles, "unspotted from the world"; and yet they are shrewd, strong, keen-sighted men, and masters of men,—hard to beguile, and hard to circumvent. St. Anthony in the picture shuts his eyes; but the rock in his desert is not more unyielding, or the moonlight on his forehead while he prays more chaste. You have read the melodious sermon on purity in Milton's "Comus,"—and what *stronger* woman do you expect to meet anywhere than the guileless heroine there? Sin is pollution: the very name is like the wild and warning cry heard by travellers in the East at night from the camp of the lepers—"Unclean, unclean!" Solomon understood it. "Go not near it, pass not by it, turn from it":—touch it not, taste it not, handle it not. These are the counsels of Almighty Virtue, tempted as men are tempted, yet without sin. You may be "simple concerning evil," and yet, by being "wise unto that which is good," armed *against* evil, and triumphing over it.

A brilliant biography was published not long ago, presenting the career of one of the most conspicuous men of letters of the generation just past, in which the theory is advocated that genius is an apology for vice, and that he who would portray society and life skilfully must mix in their muddiest currents and try the whole circle of indulgence: as if those who are to enlighten or entertain mankind must first taste of filthy cups, and descend to vulgarity on their way to refinement: as if any lawless nature had only to set up a claim to originality, in order to take a license for sensuality: as if the Almighty now and then suspended the everlasting laws of righteousness in favor of anybody's mental gifts! It is a denial of fact, and an impiety to God. Put the case respecting any heart near your own. Would you not recoil from the practical application of any such romantic paganism there? Of any *friend* we have, would we not rather be assured he has borne always an untainted breast, than that he has dragged it through a slough? Or do we ever imagine him less "wise unto that which is good," for his being "simple concerning evil"?

So thought some of the old Germans, in their wholesome forest life, who, according to their Roman historian, buried the details of private vices in oblivion, farbade their publication, and were blest with the chaster manners.

A pure character is a growth, and follows the analogy of growing things. Make the tree good, and the fruit will be good—the Saviour says. Out of the pure heart the pure life will come. But how do you make the tree good? You provide the natural conditions of a strong, healthy vegetation. You take care for a good soil, a genial climate, a free play of the sunshine, moisture in its season, a shelter from frost. And if there are any influences destructive of the tree's health, or unfavorable to its fruitage, you keep them out of the way. You do not bring the noxious things into your orchard, or your nursery, to try how near you can place them to the tree without their taking effect on it, or how much injury it will bear, and live through after all. None but a fool does that. You do not import canker-worms and caterpillars and scatter them in the next field, to see whether they will make their way into your horticulture; or whether, if they do, the trial will not strengthen the tree's constitution; or whether the tree may possibly have robustness enough to put out a second supply of leaves, after the first have been riddled and blasted. You know that if you plant your tree where the gases and smoke of a smelting establishment pour a corroding breath upon it, it will perish. "The end of these things is death." You know that if you place a peach-tree near others already tainted with the yellows, the contagion will spread, the blossoms will curl and drop, and no fruit will grow on the blighted branches. "What fruit had you then in those things whereof now you are ashamed?" God, my friends, has not entrusted these sensitive souls to us to be experimented upon by a vain curiosity or a headstrong self-confidence. They are to be guarded at every point from all that blights, and all that defiles. They are to be surrounded with blameless associations,—with companions that act and speak no guile. Every hour while contamination is postponed, and corruption kept away, is so much saved for virtue. The powers of right in the soul are strengthening. Good habits are getting formed and confirmed. The currents of desire, of thought, and of emotion, are learning to run in fixed and lawful channels. The man is growing daily wiser and wiser into that which is good, in a blessed ignorance of evil.

It is said, on the other hand, that Providence, in the actual operation of human life, exposes us to a great deal of evil, and therefore that we are at liberty to expose ourselves to it. So, in some sense, Providence exposes us to physical disease. We do not, therefore, approximate as much as we can to the resorts of miasma and fever. We do not seek to inhale the air breathed through consumptive lungs. We never cultivate the acquaintance of the plague. The maxim, "The greater the sinner the greater the saint," was never true, except to a shallow judgment which takes intensity of zeal for the balanced and solid power of Christian character, to say nothing of the small chances that out of a hundred "great sinners" you will get a single "saint."

No! we pray, if we pray at all, "Lead us not into temptation." There is meaning in that prayer. Our Lord knew us better than we know ourselves, when He included it in the seven brief petitions of that universal liturgy He gave to mankind. The man must have learnt little of the infirmities of his own conscience and will who fancies himself strong enough to dispense with it. "Lead us not into temptation." Who can repeat it, without insult and hypocrisy, if, having said it to the Most High, he goes to *seek* temptation, or lets his children seek it in unprincipled books, in dissolute companionships, or among any of the residences of guilt?

For one, I can never hear parents speak of sending their offspring purposely into perilous company, in order that they may see the world's worst side early, without painful memories of horrors unutterable which that shallow maxim has sown, hopes it has broken to pieces, spiritual beauty it has disfigured, and the gray hairs it has brought down with sorrow to the grave. Let virtue have the vantage-ground of youth; let holy shapes of purity and love and truth preoccupy the soul, before the rabble of hateful tormentors rush in. The longer these blameless guests pitch their white tents on the unsullied field of the child's heart, the more will we rejoice and thank the protecting God. Give the first delicate years to goodness; let right principles grow by exercise; let the habits of life learn to run in the even channels of piety and obedience, and it shall be harder by and by to break the blessed barriers down.

But we want, it is said, a robust, an exposed, tried virtue, not a virtue feebly grown in solitude, and too sickly to bear the sun. Beyond all question we do. But they who think to find here an apology for commerce with sin, forget that there is just as much discipline and a far greater blessing in resisting the inclination to look at sin, as in resisting the increase of it after looking and listening have rooted it in the soul. The point where the first offenders were to learn how to strengthen their principles was in refusing to *taste* the forbidden fruit, not in seeing how they could escape it when its virus was once in their blood It was enough that it *was forbidden.* The trial of obedience and of faith was there.

There is another light, still, under which we may look at this whole matter. We throw ourselves forward a few years, when, by the silent laws of God working out surely and silently their deep and awful issues, the consequences of our indulgence will become plain to our experience. If reason, Scripture, the Spirit's testimony, companions, history, the holy dead, did not teach us, time shall. For then, as habit grows obstinate, as the abused spirit begins to turn and prey upon itself, as a perverted imagination wreaks its revengeful retribution, as age or an opening eternity shall displace fleeting fancies with everlasting realities,—then will not all these illusions pass away, and the sternest self-denial appear our happiest wisdom? Then we shall look back on every familiar tampering with vice with infinite disgust and unavailing remorse. Then, to have turned away our eyes and our ears from every dubious or tempting thing will be an unspeakable joy, and to have been "simple concerning evil," will have proved the noblest way of being "wise unto" all that is "good."

If we look back even over the little way we have gone in our life, our memories will instruct us. Whether we fancy we have conquered or fallen, there are few of us, I suspect, that cannot recall some foolish toleration of ourselves in an unhallowed curiosity which we would now gladly blot out with tears or drops of blood,—some evil companionship in childhood which threw a shadow across our lives, or fixed a stain on our hearts, that has hindered, or saddened, or somehow cursed us ever since. Let us be frank and confess. Whenever we have lingered in the presence of low conceits, or have let some lower inclination prevail, has not a secret feeling of having been degraded come, as sure and self-evidencing testimony to our guilt? "What fruit had ye then of those things?"

The best protection against inward impurity is to preoccupy the inward world with better guests, and hold it for them with ceaseless vigilance. As with the body so with the spirit; if we would have health we must honor the laws of health. Fill your life with spiritual service and there will be no room for the thoughts, imaginations or desires which assault and hurt the soul. Instead of fighting them after they enter, keep them out; tell them at the gate you have better company. Tell them so in the name of Him who, when He had peremptorily put the seducing spirit behind Him, because He had His Father's will to do, found angels ministering to Him. "Overcome evil with good." There is many a secret sin that is best contended against not by first thinking about it and then resisting it,—for, while you think about it, it takes the form of a temptation,—but by crowding our days so full of duty that the tempter will find no treacherous door open. Work is chaste. Work hallowed by prayer is chaster still. Have no fears that God will not help. "Every branch that beareth fruit, He purgeth it." From this, as from every other danger, Christ formed within is safety, is salvation.

We must end, as we began, on the mount of the Beatitudes. "Blessed are the pure in heart, for they shall see God." It is only another announcement of that wonderful and glorious principle which runs all through the inspiring Gospel. The motive power lies far beyond all selfish hopes or fears. At every step the disciple takes his rewards as he goes on; and they are rewards in the kind of his toil. For the charity that suffereth long and thinketh no evil there will be given a mightier power of love, till tongues shall cease and that which is perfect is come. For the struggles of uncomplaining patience there will be the grand endurance which smiles on pain. For faith, the sunlit country where no doubt ever casts a shadow. And for that Christlike purity of heart which is the transparent air in which all spiritual graces live and move, the vision Beatific and Divine, which eye hath not yet seen, which no heart hath yet conceived. Nevertheless, it is a vision not to be wholly postponed and waited for till death changes us. Death to sin is always changing us; victory over evil is always transfiguring us. The knowledge of the Son of God will begin where the purity begins. It will be an immediate and ever-growing "blessedness" even here. The vision will be ever-brightening, till we see not in the least " as through a glass darkly," but " face to face."

# STRENGTH OUT OF WEAKNESS.

*Fourth Sunday in Lent.*

"My strength is made perfect in weakness."—*II. Corinthians* xii. 9.

Along with other new forces brought in by the Gospel, spiritualizing society and regenerating humanity, there came an original doctrine of what makes weakness and strength. Up to that time, man was accounted strong in proportion as he was able to overmaster the persons and things about him. Matching his own resources against the elements, or against the capacities of other men, his power was measured by his ability to maintain his superiority in these quarrels or rivalries. Till the death of Christ, the strong man was the man strong with his sinews and his hands, or, at best, with the cunning and calculation of his brain. He was first who could strike down most enemies, gather most wealth, march longest at the head of his army, pile the most perfect pyramid, or most fascinate an Athenian assembly by the subtle charm of eloquent speech.

Corresponding to this heathenish estimate of what makes up "strength" was the view taken of bodily "weakness." It was either to be simply deplored as a calamity, or despised as a shame. No spiritual illumination, shining through, transfigured the sick face; no submission of faith dignified the poor frame prostrate with pain. The men, and even the women, looked on disease with a kind of dry disgust. Some of the best of them proposed to kill off the old people as unserviceable to the State. Virtue consisted in keeping up the animal vigor as long as possible, and when it failed, all that the most faithful friendship could do was to draw back in helpless embarrassment, just where Christian sympathy is most eager to press forward and reach out its merciful hands. It was imbecility gazing at infirmity in despair. Instead of hospitals for disorder and retreats for the disabled, you have only the Greek tragedies chanting in superb poetry their melancholly wail at human suffering, or Latin comedies laughing at it. We see the apostle of Christ standing in the presence of such a proud civilization as that, and quietly saying to it, "When I am weak, then am I strong." And we cannot wonder that to the mere children of nature then, as to men and women of the mere natural reason still, such a saying was a riddle, with hardly a clue to its meaning.

The meaning is that in order to get very near to God, or to let the glorious attractions of almighty love and light lay hold of us, and lift us up,—we must be somehow impoverished first, belittled, disappointed, baffled, weakened. Whereas we had imagined we were strong in proportion as we could *make our own way*, it turns out, quite to the contrary, that we are really strong in proportion as we are conscious of needing and receiving help from above us, as we feel dependent on the Divine Man, and keep our hearts open to His inward-working power. Whereas we thought, with those old pagans, that we should be strong by pride, it proves that pride is just the feeblest thing in us, and that we must be emptied clean of it before we can be sure of any real honor,— because pride separates us effectually from the fountain of inward life. Whereas a growing fortune, or a lucrative business, seemed to be a means of safety, it turns out that this depends altogether on the man who holds it, and the spirit in which he uses it; and that unless he can do without it, or give it away, when God calls him, he is as weak as that very promising young man,—promising, but only promising,—who came to Jesus complacent, but went away mortified;—a moral failure. Whereas a robust body and sharp senses looked like strength, the true powers of a glorious manhood are quite as apt to be manifest in men of broken health or slender constitutions. At any rate, by the Christian plan of life, we must begin with penitence, or sorrow for the past; and what is that but a confession of weakness? We must become as little children, in feeling, the Saviour says; and what is childhood but dependence? We must take up a cross; and that is a taking down of the selfish part. We must believe; and faith is an acknowledgment that we are not sufficient to ourselves. So this new kingdom begins in this wonderful way. "When I am weak, then am I strong." Obstacles, sicknesses, losses, defeats of our plans, the breakings up of our securities, are God's opportunities; and He knows how to use them. We watch the course of our lives, and we see that what is best has generally come by self-subjection. And at last our experience answers to this mystical account given of the heroes of the Bible,—"Out of weakness they were made strong."

St. Paul finds it necessary for once to vindicate his apostleship, and in order to that, a rare thing with him, to vindicate himself. After alluding to certain extraordinary revelations which had lifted him into the third heaven, and would naturally tempt him to religious vanity, he emphatically discards any such presumption, and goes on to say that he counts it a signal blessing that he has always been kept down and saved from self-confidence by bodily disadvantages. What this "thorn in the flesh" was he does not mention; the Corinthians he was writing to knew:—a weak voice, possibly,—weak eyes, more likely,—for he several times alludes to his eyes pathetically; and if they were permanently hurt by the intense light at Damascus, he might very well say of them, "I bear in my body the marks of the Lord Jesus:—let no man trouble me." (Jewish traditions refer it to convulsions.) At any rate it prevented his presence being admired, limited his powers as an orator, and quenched the hopes of public ambition. He felt it the more because by temperament he evidently relished great natural vigor. He knew, too, with his "like passions," that the men he preached to had a habit of sneering at physical disfigurements. Of course they would take occasion from his infirmity to disparage his ministry and discredit his message. And so he reached this triumph of self-humiliation,—our special Lenten grace,—only by a tremendous struggle. He carried it, as his devout spirit took everything, into his prayers. Probably he put his petition on the ground that his deformity abridged his usefulness as a preacher. So we all pray when we are not quite clear whether we are thinking more of God's glory or of our own comfort: in other words, whether it is simple faith or a disgusted self-will that prompts the supplication. As with Peter, and with Christ, the tempter came three times. Three times Paul besought the Lord that the vexation might depart from him. For some mysterious purpose it was God's plan that it should remain. But then there rang in his ears an answer to that supplication which thrilled his soul more profoundly, and awoke in him a far more comforting assurance that he was answered, than if a miracle had instantly healed every disordered fibre in his frame. The Lord said, "My grace is sufficient for thee." This trial must continue and try thee still; to take it away would be to imperil the purity of that human vessel which I am refining to carry the treasure of eternal life to the gentile world, but My imparted grace shall continue too, and never fail. Be that sufficient for thee. Let the thorn still sting the flesh. It will not weaken, nay, it will stimulate and redouble the real power.

Now if this had been a sentence spoken for effect, it would be a paradox in rhetoric, and nothing more. Coming from the lips of our Lord, it declares a principle of all Christian life and growth. On the one side we see feebleness, trembling, ignorance, perplexity, a dying body, earthen vessels :—on the other side, strength, courage, the demonstration of the Spirit, the excellency of the power, the immortal life of Christ. In that contrast, made a personal experience in our Christian discipline, lie the trial of character, the ministry of temptation, the shame and splendor of the cross, and the victory of faith which overcometh the world.

Something like this we are continually seeing, as the common working of God's Spirit, in the characters of men. Not one in fifty of those who have their hearts made alive and earnest for Christian service are led that way by increased prosperity; by high health; by having their own way; by any personal advantages whatever. Most of us must have seen man after man, yes, score of men after score of men, and it is a sad sight enough, who have once taken up a Christian's work, and vowed themselves to Christ at His altar, grow negligent of religious duty, and gradually relax all the exercises of a good soldier of the Cross, just in proportion as they flourished in business, rose in office, took what might be called an easy place in the world, or became "strong" in the world's sense. Accordingly we are just in the best way of being made secure when we are cast on rough conditions. Poor boys from the country, with their whole wordly estate swinging in a small satchel at their side, are the strong-handed builders of institutions, roads, cities, ships, and become masters of all the grand enterprises of the world. David was a great deal stronger when he was a stripling with a ruddy face, coming up from the brook with a few stones for his sling, or when he was a hunted exile, flying from one rocky hiding-place to another, or when he was on his knees pouring out of a broken heart the fifty-first psalm, than when he sat in purple on his throne, and in the fulness of his table forgot his Maker, and had to tremble before the prophet. How many there are who first take firmly hold of the everlasting Hand, when they have felt all around them in the dark and could find no other hand! A man of business on the full current of success, a fortune at his command, and a multitude dependent on him, *looks* strong no doubt to himself, and to other men. But some day he goes home from his office with a strange weakness in his frame; he creeps up to his chamber with it; he lies on his bed and is faint under it; his business goes on well enough without him; and weeks after, when his flesh and his will and his pride are all worn down, he tells you, with an accent that has such a sound of reality in it as you have heard in nothing he ever said before, that all his past career has been a superficial and miserable mistake, because obedience to Christ, and self-surrender to His holy will, were not in him. In his weakness he is for the first time strong. A woman moves in brilliant circles, admired, accomplished, obeyed: for there is a certain sway that seems like power. But changes of fortune shut her up in a narrow estate; they unclasp her jewels; set her to tending fretful invalids, teaching dull children, or dragging a feeble frame through the drudgeries of some hard lot; all the radiant visions vanished. But there has risen, meantime, another vision: the open way of life, and the light that is on the Face of the crucified. A voice has been heard saying, "Thou art mine; forgiven; redeemed; My daughter; I am with thee in thy poverty, made poor Myself for thy sake; My grace is sufficient for thee; no man shall pluck thee out of My hand." And now her day of power has come, and with power, perfect peace.

Familiar instances,—you say. Yes, very familiar. Look where we will, the proofs will multiply upon us that here is a great law of the Divine discipline with men,— not wholly confined indeed to spiritual things, but most brightly manifest there and yielding its most blessed fruits there. By some means or other passion, pride, self-will,—the "strong men armed" that keep this world's house,—must be turned out before the King of Glory can come in. We might, no doubt, if we would, let God's goodness lead us to repentance; we might, if we would, grow straight up and go straight on in the path of the justified. But, humiliating as it is, most of us have to be scourged into our rest. The sunshine of the Lord's love is not let in on many eyes till the walls of the house we trusted are shaken apart. As an old English poet wrote,

"The soul's dark cottage, battered and decayed,
  Lets in new light through chinks that time has made."

You see St. Paul before his conversion, with his commanding intellect and iron will swinging his sword from city to city to strike down Christian disciples, everything else in him powerful but charity: and yet it is only when he is sitting in darkness, or led about by another's hand, sightless, helpless, that his passions grow cool, his heart's flesh comes like the flesh of a little child, and the power of Christ rises in his soul. Blindness, solitude, humility, these stern hands fashion him into that brave and irresistible leader of the Church whom all the swords and dungeons between Syria and Spain cannot terrify or silence. Elijah must hunger; John the Baptist must eat locusts and wild honey in the desert; the twelve must leave their homes and their property; St. Peter must weep bitterly—before they can be mighty witnesses, standing before kings. Nay more: the King himself, in the beautiful language of the Visitation Office, "went not up to joy, but first He suffered pain." Our infirmities are the springs of our victories,—and hence, that we might be made conquerors *through* Him, He took our infirmities upon Him.

Perhaps something in us prompts us to answer, "This is a very strange order of things. Why should it be so? Why should not the full health and vigor of all parts of our nature go on and ripen harmoniously together? Health is certainly the normal state of man. Property is useful. Why should we have to be spoilt in one part of us to strengthen another part? Something must be the matter."

Exactly so; something is the matter, and that something is the bitter cause of all the misery, the pain, the disappointment, the emptiness and aching of heart in the children of men. It is the sin that doth so easily beset us. God's loving order was disturbed because a hateful human disorder came in, and has never gone out. Therefore the way to life must be just what it is:— through suffering to peace; through a wilderness to the land of olive gardens; through forty Lenten days to a resurrection jubilee day; through loneliness, self-disgust, and emptiness into the city of the living God, and fulness of joy.

Remember, strength will be poured into our breasts from God, provided only the bar that keeps it out is taken down. God is always love. If ye, human parents, know how to give good gifts unto your children, how much more the Heavenly Father! Only one thing is wanting, that the two bolts,—self-will and self-indulgence, —be weakened till they give way. Weaken them, my friends; weaken them in every way,—by self-reproach, by discipline, by taking up a cross, by fasting, by doing duties that you dislike to do, by disinterested work for other men, and the blessed energy of the Spirit will flow in. In your weakness God's strength will be made perfect. And then you will know, with St. Paul, what it is to glory in tribulations. Then you will learn to entertain sickness and sorrow in your houses as the royal ambassadors of the King of Peace. At first Paul called his thorn a messenger of Satan buffeting him. After he found out why it came, he called it a gift, a love token, a sign of heavenly favor from his Master. If Satan's angels are sometimes clothed as angels of light, why not God's angels in shadows? If it keeps you humble, the thorn is finally woven into the crown of rejoicing. O blessed infirmities, blemishes, ugliness, pain, poor success, mortified ambition, ye are prophets and heralds of salvation; ye are our securities from deeper and more lasting shame! We ought to learn some anthems to sing your honors as pledges of our heavenly deliverance. To accept bodily pain, or an insignificant reputation, or a ruined plan, even after having prayed against it, as the veiled minister of mercy, and heartily to give thanks for the scourge,—this is *to have*

*Christ formed by faith within.* It opens the interpretation of that wonderful saying:—" Always bearing about in the body the dying of the Lord Jesus, that the life of Jesus might be made manifest in our mortal flesh."

In a prayer repeated since last Sunday, all through this week, the Church makes us bold enough to ask for "abstinence," that "the flesh may be subdued to the spirit." The ground we have gone over brings us to the basis of all this penitence and self-denial. It lies in our nature and constitution as well as in the Scriptures.

Finally, you may turn to society at large. Look at a whole city, in the full tide of commercial prosperity and social indulgence. Abundance shall run down all the streets like rivers of water. Every scene of entertainment, from the glittering play-house to the lowest haunt of dissipation, shall be nightly thronged and illuminated. The men shall build palaces as playthings, and the women string diamonds as beads. The talk of the town shall be of the last night's brilliancy and jewelry, raiment and banquet. Night itself shall be turned into day, not for vigils of prayer or praises of the Great Benefactor,—if *that* were done the whole population would laugh aloud at the fanaticism,—but it shall be done night after night for frivolity, for dancing and eating and drinking, for this world's god, and no lip shall sneer at it. There shall be wealth enough for all this; and every new form of ostentation, and every new avenue of traffic, and every addition to the trappings of a material estate that wealth could provide, shall heighten the pomp. Now, would this be the strong city? What are the attributes of strength? Self-command, courage, faith, endurance, moderation: these are the signs of *human* strength. Has it these? God alone, the Almighty, is the source of strength; and that city alone is strong of which it can be said that "God is in the midst of her." Can it be said of that city? Character is strength, and there is no character there. It is weakness at the foundation, weakness in the superstructure, weakness at the gates; weakness in the chambers; weakness at the heart. You have read history; and you know whether Tyre and Babylon and Rome just before they fell were strong.

Turn from that spectacle to another. By some Providence, the city is humbled. Its face is sober and thoughtful. Manners are simple; dress is plain; industry is more plentiful than entertainment; luxuries are not seen, but charities are abundant; its sanctuaries are thronged; its nights are still; its people are walking with God; its children's indulgence is restrained. Wisdom is the ornament of grace about its neck. There are household prayers in all the houses. Righteousness is its law; and God is its king. Here is strength: "Clean hands and a pure heart." Strong as well as happy is that people whose God is the Lord.

Man is not strongest when his head is full of dreams and calculations of gain, his heart full of promotion and admiration, his hand full of this world's gifts, and his mouth full of meat and wine. He is strong when he rules his spirit; strong when he works, and consecrates his work to God; strong when he is on his knees; strong when he forgets himself, and lives in the spirit of the apostle's declaration: "It is no more I that live, but Christ liveth in me."

# A HEAVENLY MIND HERE.

*Fifth Sunday in Lent.*

"For our conversation is in heaven."—*Philippians* iii. 20.

WHATEVER apparent incompatibility there may be between having a residence in one world and a conversation in another, the religion of Christ boldly meets that difficulty and puts it out of the way. A life which reconciles these contradictory things is not only possible but is the practical object and the triumph of every Christian man. Not only apostles but the whole congregation, not only ministers but men of business and young people, can have their conversation in heaven every day and be none the weaker for it, but greatly stronger, for all the work of this world.

A case easily supposed will illustrate St. Paul's meaning; and it is suggested by the word translated in the text "conversation." The actual sense of that word, as he wrote it, is *citizenship*. In the old English of the Bible and Prayer Book, a man's "conversation" meant not the mere act of his tongue, but the entire expression of his life in conduct, and so it revealed to what kingdom his heart belonged. An American agent or ambassador has a temporary dwelling in Athens. Living on that foreign soil, occupied daily, for the time, with its local affairs, respectful to its institutions, a good neighbor, he never forgets his allegiance to a distant republic.

The landscape about him may show a beauty that wins his admiration; the Greek faces and manners and hospitalities may gain his good-will; yet they are not those of his native land. He remembers that his stay is short; sometimes he is homesick; he expects to be called back, not long hence, where his treasure is laid up and his untravelled heart abides; he is a stranger and sojourner, away from home.

This simple comparison answers the better, because it shows that when our faith commands us to have our conversation in heaven it does not require us to be bad citizens of the world where we now are. We are not bidden to be absent minded; if we were we should do poor work here, and lead ineffectual lives. The man may form hearty attachments where he tarries; he may pay willing tribute to the city that temporarily befriends him; he may live cheerfully and helpfully, neither a complaining guest nor a fastidious and sullen recluse. And yet, none the less, as the Epistle to the Hebrews so grandly says of the patriarch who is the type of the Christian believer, he desires always a better country, which he knows,—a "city" first in his honor, dearer to his love, and always in his hopes. So Christ, by His doctrine and spirit, reconciles a regular and happy labor among the fields and streets and markets of this world with a constant recollection that we have an eternal citizenship above it. He teaches here, as He taught at Nazareth and Jerusalem, in the fishing-boats and on the mount, and as it had never been taught before, that we can be religiously faithful to every present-relationship, and yet never forget that celestial patriotism which keeps us obedient to "the powers of the world to come." We can be busy, neighborly, charitable, enterprising, getting our livelihood, making some earthly spot more beautiful as well as more righteous, and all the time "looking for and hastening unto" an immortality infinitely better,—wearing on our whole manhood or womanhood the stamp of a consecrated purpose and an unworldly secret in the soul. No man living to himself, no man dying to himself, life and death are both transfigured by an indestructible communion with an invisible Friend and Lord. We *can*, by the Spirit's help, be *in* the world without "minding" earthly things selfishly, greedily, ambitiously, or irreligiously. This is the original glory of our Christian estate, and nothing less than this is our personal calling, as learners in Christ's school and worshippers in His Church.

I say, the glory is original. Till Christ came, this majestic fact in our condition, that our little human tent here is overarched by an infinite heaven of light and love which really opens and pours down a living influence upon us, scarcely anywhere broke through the pagan shadows. It neither lightened the dull monotony of mortal labor nor consoled the bitterness and blindness of mortal sorrow. Here and there, in some half-awakened soul, there was a religious dream or guess,—some glimmer of the light that was to rise on rich and poor alike,— some Athenian thinker, such as Paul found "feeling after God, if haply he might find Him,"—some solitary flash like the stoic maxim, "Deny thyself and aspire," *almost* worthy of the Son of Man,—some morning-star like the reason of Plato. But these harbingers of the day only cast slender streaks on a few hill-tops, showing how broad and deep the darkness lay on all the lands below. Men looked downward at matter, or else across the surface of the earth on their own level, and their "conversation" was of its wars and lusts. It was a civilization born of appetite and self-will, suckled by a wolf, bred in battles, glorified in statues and epics splendid in form but barbarian in subject and spirit. In all the Asiatic pomp there was not one house of charity for sickness, insanity, orphanage, or old age; in the Alexandrian science not one school of virtue or lesson of pure self-renunciation; in the Greek beauty no beauty of holiness; in the discipline of Roman armies not one crucifixion of the flesh to the heavenly law of righteousness. "The law of the members," as the Epistle to those very Romans so graphically calls it, ruled the race:—the "law of the spirit of life in Christ Jesus" had not come. The city they called "eternal" was rotting into ruins, and the "citizenship," or "conversation," was far this side of heaven. How the errors of the mind, when let loose from the obedience of Faith, run round in circles and return! One of the audacities of modern sceptical speculation, reported from France, is a proposition that science may so dispense with the Almighty as, among the achievements of the future, to take command of the forces of nature, stop the process of decay, and insure the globe itself against the waste of time and the judgment for its sins. You call it the babbling blasphemy of fools. But it is the logical termination of human thought, cut off by itself from God, living an utterly earthly life. In the midst of such a society as that we see Christ's great convert to the cross standing and saying, "Our conversation is in heaven."

*The earthly and the heavenly mind*, then. The choice between these two is what our Gospel, with its anxious earnestness, is pressing on our conscience.

What hinders? First it is said, with an accent of complacent cleverness, "We must take the world as it is: there is no use of flying in the face of an immense majority: no scattered picket-guard of saints, however pure, can make head against this tremendous mass of worldliness, especially in crowded and eager centres of population. Your ideal is lovely: it is well enough to hold it up in church, a seventh-day picture of impossible sanctity. But while we live in an earthly commonwealth, if we expect to *get on with it*, we must keep on pleasant terms with it, sit at its feasts, drink its health, and not be over-critical as to its principles."

If this answer were valid, it would settle the whole question at once, on the anti-Christian side. The Church would be an organized failure. Instead of a fearless witnessing for Christ, and fighting against wrong, we should have a supple and cowardly system of mutual compromises and flatteries. Men and women would go into society to learn how to live down to each other's weaknesses and prejudices. Christian salvation would be an amiable dream, and moral courage a romantic fiction. But then, even the common, careless mind has a deeper-toned conviction than this. There rise up before us all images of heavenly-minded persons whom we have known. Most people know enough of the story of the past to know that its principal grandeurs and glories have gathered about the heads of a few brave and suffering and rather solitary men, who have earned their immortal names by standing out against the fashionable corruptions and falsehoods of their times. Inward voices respond in almost every breast to the righteousness of this order of souls, whether many or few. Before they give away their manhood for the sake of getting on with the world, *some* citizens will inquire *to what end* the world is getting on. And then, whatever *we* do or say, the Word of God refuses to be altered, and that from first to last tells us not only that we *can*, but that we *must*, unless we mean to die eternally, live above the world while we live in it.

Besides, falsehood and sensuality were never yet prevalent enough or popular enough, anywhere, in Babylon, or Corinth, or Vienna, or Paris, or here, to incapacitate any soul for a clean and godly life, if that soul chose and willed, religiously, to live it. However low the reigning tone of morals about you, in club, or brokers' board, or ball-room, or political cabal, yet in your clearer moments you feel that your freedom is not crippled, your independence not crushed, your power to strike out and keep up a line of consistent Christian action not abrogated or subdued. Though nineteen out of twenty fall disgraced, you are able to be the twentieth and stand upright. If offences must come, you can refuse to be the offender, and refuse successfully to the end, because the Almighty is on that side, giving both secret inspirations and a shield that no temptation can pierce through and no bankruptcy can break. "Faithful found among the faithless" is the record of many a noble and modest citizen here, true to his secular trusts, as well as of the steadfast seraph Abdiel wearing his crown in heaven. All the crimes and scandals which debase high places, till it seems as if no places would be high very long, ought not to tempt us to forget the ten righteous in a city that save it in spite of the ten thousand that are willing it should be lost, and to be lost with it.

And further, nothing in society or custom takes off the wrong-doer's sin, or its retribution; numbers, situation, opportunity, example, rulers and chief-priests, being utterly incompetent to alter an iota the eternal contradiction between wrong and right. They may color or drape or baptize wrong-doing, but they never change its essence. The citizen in a bad community who does nothing, says nothing, gives nothing, to purify its iniquities, cannot say, " This is a very wicked place, but that is nothing to me; it allows horrible abuses and facilities for profligacy, but that is not my concern; *I* have no son or daughter to lose temperance or modesty; extravagance and dissipation are shockingly conspicuous, but that is no reason why I should not indulge myself privately if I please." He cannot say that, because in that heaven where his heart ought to turn every day, there lives a God with whom multitudes of people, and established usages, and municipal officers, and polite concealments, are not of the least account; to whom there is no privacy, and from whom no secrets, of chamber or alley or intrigue or fraud, are hid. No more can a dishonest merchant excuse himself by quoting unscrupulous or accommodating maxims of trade, and saying, " My business is adjusted to the moral scale of my class; as long as I am up to the average mark I am safe; if I do bring up my sons or my clerks to take advantages which will not bear daylight,—that is the fault of commerce, and not mine." He cannot say that, because neither buyer nor seller, or the board of trade, makes the moral law or modifies it; and God has set you down there, an individual soul, on purpose to bear testimony, by straight accounts and fair bargains, against the vast and evil thing, and not to hide behind it. The partisan, in Church or State, cannot say, " Reckon with my party, not with me." He has, if not a citizenship, a judge in a country where he must reckon, without his party, for what he helped make his party to be. We who take our shameful part so easily in petty apologies and artifices and winkings at social laxity, cannot say, at the Divine tribunal, " Blame society;—I only went with the rest, and was no worse than they." For God's practical Truth will answer us, How then is Christ's kingdom ever to come? How is the load of the world's iniquity ever to be thrown off? You may presume that these sins will continue, do what you will,—and that may be true. Offences will come, but " woe to that man by whom they come."

Before it has done, Christianity means undoubtedly to reach *society*, on the broad scale; but it must reach it through persons, gathered one by one into its own heavenly "citizenship." It has to do with conviction, affection, faith; and these are always properties of persons before they can be of nations or communities. The Saviour did not publish a plan of political reform, or a schedule of social science. Meeting His countrymen in little groups, or one by one, as they came, He showed them what was in His heart, and showed them the ineffable beauty of a holy and blessed "conversation" with His Father, while they were yet fishermen and publicans, and reapers and water-carriers, about their houses and fields. So began the everlasting empire and the everlasting age of righteousness through love, which was in time to lift itself over the palaces at Constantinople and Rome. Before men knew it, He had planted a kingdom to fill and possess the earth,—planted it just where alone it could be planted, in the living heart and will of certain individuals who had ceased minding earthly things, or minded heavenly things far more. And so, precisely, He meets us to-day. With all His spirit of sacrifice and mighty power of redemption, with the cross on His shoulders and the scar in His side, He comes to each one of us, and speaks. We all desire to have America a Christian country. Then we must be Christian men in America. We would all, I am sure, have ours a Church practically Christian, in the power of the Spirit and in all holy and charitable action, arising and shining on the tops of the mountains, like an army with peaceable banners. Then we must be Christian members of it, in conviction, in principle, in what we do and what we refuse to do, in the company we keep and the company we let alone, sustaining as consistently as we can, and without ostentation, a heavenly conversation. Precisely the strength of our practical endeavor to do this will be the measure of our Christian sincerity and progress.

My friends, there is a particular reason for these thoughts. There are, doubtless, persons in this House who have not consciously made up their minds to keep God's commandments out and out, through and through, asking God for help,—and yet they would be shocked at the idea of our social life returning to barbarism. There are others farther on, nominally Christian, publicly complimenting general religion and applauding Christian institutions, without pretending to conform their personal practice to Christ's law of spiritual life. This notion that we are any safer or any better for living in a land of a professed Christianity, whose principles we daily ignore and whose most sacred duties we shuffle aside, is one of those delusions that show their absurdity the moment they are noted in language. What our most intelligent Christians need to realize far more clearly than they do is that every scheme attempting to cure the bad morals of the people comes short and must fail, unless it goes down to the root and heart of the matter by beginning with faith in God, and putting the soul into a direct and earnest conversation with Him.

In these times the Faith is put back and kept down not so much by persecution as by corruption. We live in days of indulgence, and days of education, and so temptation comes in under physical and literary luxury. Ever since Eve's parley with Satan in Eden it has been the strategy of evil to gain admission without having its character suspected. If the moral sense is obstinate and will not yield, teach it to call evil good. If conscience defies a sword, drug it with narcotics. This is the generalship that captures a besieged city by poisoning the fountains at which the people drink, when the walls are too thick to be battered down by assault. Once radically unsettle a man's mind as to the obligations of duty, and you work a far more comprehensive depravity in him than by only enticing him now and then into single bad actions, against which his conscience continues to cry out. You make him the servant of all unclean work in the household of the senses. If, by listening to the sophistry of the appetites, I can really come to believe that things are tolerable which God has declared sinful, I see no breakwater after that to keep the whole muddy sea of sensuality from pouring its foul flood over me. For as the whole quality of a Christian lies in the *choice of the heart,* so the lowest and last perdition is where the very faculty of choice is perverted. As this deterioration goes on, so gradual is it that we have to look over a long interval to mark the steps of the decline. It is vain to deny, for instance, that respectable families allow their sons and daughters the forms of social liberty which fifty years ago their wiser fathers would have been ashamed of, and which now yield no particle of addition to their joy or honor. There are encroaching irreverences that take down, little by little, the strict and holy standard which keeps the soul near to Christ, and which, like the flying fiery cross among the faithful Highlanders, should recall brave hearts to the front-places in the Christian fight. These are the perils to be watched if our Christian stability, our civil order, our public virtue, our Church of Christ are to stand fast, or our own souls are to live.

And so the true confessors of this age are the men and women who exercise their consciences day by day to discern between evil and good; men and women who replenish their spiritual strength by prayers in their families, and prayers in their closets; souls that keep so far back within the entrenchments of a heavenly citizenship as to be out of all risk of slipping over into dishonor; men of business that will not take a second look at the tempter for an additional thousand in their year's income; young men who will sooner resign profitable places and turn to less tasteful work than let an initiation into meanness and lying be a part of their training to "success"; women who choose that good part with Mary's Friend, rather than wade through ambiguities neck-deep to conquests of social ambition; children that would rather be laughed at than disobey, and rather master their passions than each other:—all souls that have made the glorious choice between Christ and this world, while in this world, these are they that live heavenly lives, and make this world heavenlike.

There are certainly two worlds within us, as well as earth and heaven without us; and one of them is apt to get the mastery and press the other down. Take as the divine image of the one of these, the Saviour's sacramental prayers in the seventeenth chapter of St. John, or St. Paul's description, at the close of the eighth to the Romans, of the love of God, from which neither life nor death will separate him. For the other take any unbelieving sensualist's frank testimony:—take Lord Chesterfield's, who was a type of his class. "I have run," he says, "the rounds of business and pleasure, and have done with them all. Shall I tell you that I bear this melancholy situation with resignation? No; I bear it because I *must*. I think of nothing but killing time, now it has become my enemy, and my resolution is to sleep in the carriage to the end of the journey." Now to say nothing of what happens when the journey ends, and of the waking out of sleep, and of the new question that will rise before a man who has so poorly succeeded in killing time, that time killed him,—viz., how to kill eternity,—leaving all that, we see the contradiction between the two worlds complete. The warfare between the principles that lie at the roots of them is a deadly warfare, and still it goes on.

It has gone on another season. All around you the lower life has had more than its share. This is not a professional judgment. It comes from those who live in the midst of it. The tide runs over-fast, and over-full. This world has had enough, too much, for a nation needing regeneration as much as ours; too much for a Church which is yet a Church in the wilderness; too much for earnest followers of a Master who hungered and sorrowed for them, owing all they have to Him. Look up, above it. Set your hurried ways and self-delighting houses into a holier order. Keep under the body, and bring it into subjection. Standing in these Lenten days under the shadow of the cross, gather clear-sightedness, and inward power, and by dying to sin live unto God.

# SPIRITUAL WASTE AND WEALTH.

*Palm Sunday, or Sunday before Easter.*

"He that gathereth not with Me scattereth."—*St. Luke* xi. 23.

In the material economy no such rule is laid down; no such necessity exists. We can fold our hands and stand still, neither scattering nor gathering. We can direct our energies or withhold them. In all that sphere of life which man holds in common with the inferior animal orders he can expend his force here or there without being said to rob merely because he does not give.

But when we rise into the range of relations that are spiritual we pass under a new and peculiar law. Freedom remains. It is enlarged. But irrespective of our own arrangement, we find we are subject to this condition, in respect to one Supreme Spirit,—that if we are not serving Him we are wronging Him; if we are not working in the line of His loving and bountiful plans, we are striving against Him; if we are not gathering with Him,—gathering wisdom and strength and purity and greater capacity for good and other "fruit unto everlasting life,"—then we are wasting what belongs to Him. We are in a necessary stewardship, and this is one of its laws. The law may look exacting in the statement, but it is glorious in its operation. Neutrality, not only in the posture of our affections, but in the use of our active powers, is impossible.

Not far from each of the great scenes of our Saviour's ministry there was a third party, taking no apparent share in the transaction. Those that sided openly with Him and publicly confessed their loyalty, on the one hand, and those that expressly opposed Him, on the other, became of course conspicuous in the conflicts that sprang up about Him. By their direct opposition to each other, Apostles and Pharisees, the family at Bethany and the Council at Jerusalem, John and Judas, Zaccheus and Herod, Joseph of Arimathea and Pilate, immediately suggest to us two distinct classes of people,—the friends and the enemies of the Son of God. Decided convictions always throw men into definite positions.

Near by, however, you might always find another class, more numerous, probably, than either of them. They are not brought forward into notice, because no real interest or choice brought them visibly into the struggle that was going on. Other things absorbed their attention. This Divine, disinterested Redeemer, who had come from heaven to speak to what was deepest and best in their hearts, to take all their burdens and sicknesses upon Himself that He might call them more effectually to honor and immortality, was walking their streets and waiting at their doors. It was told along the highways, in villages and cities, "Jesus of Nazareth is passing by." They neither hindered nor followed Him. The routine of the day's business, family festivities, social pleasure, bargains to be begun or closed in the market, each one's little busy world of care or display or profit, was enough. What if the Lord of all life, the Healer of all miseries, and final Judge of all souls, is passing by? Let Him pass. Give us a little more of this world; give us the meat that perisheth; give us popular envy and ascendency; give us to-day's abundance. What is Nazareth or its Prophet to us? Answer Him as He stands at the door and knocks, and tell Him there is no room for Him in our houses; we are engaged and cannot see Him; in this great tavern of a world, as in the inn at Bethlehem, there is no room for Him. The world ignores its King.

It was so on that strange, excited morning, at the beginning of Passion-week, which this Palm Sunday commemorates. For some unexplained reason, there must be the outward spectacle of a royal reception of the Messiah into His own city. He comes unto His own nation, and His own received Him not, because He came as a sacrifice and a servant. Yet they must *appear* to receive him. Hosannas, branches of the palm, the olive and the cedar, torn from the trees, garments spread in the road, must make up the wild and melancholy demonstration of a hollow or at best a half-instinctive enthusiasm. Christ's journey towards the cross begins with this sacrificial anguish at the acclamations of a populace who knew not what they did:—hosannas on their lips to-day, but maledictions and "Crucify Him," five days hence! Palm-branches waving on the heights of Olivet one day, slumbers of heavy eyes or careless vigils in the garden of agony four days after! In the midst of this jubilant concourse, He wept. Here were the two parties then:— a frenzied and mistaken multitude in the streets; a plotting and hating cabal of jealous rulers and scribes at the court-room in the city. But, remember, between these, and all around them both, was a greater company, that we hear nothing about: indifferent, undecided; not planning murder for the Nazarene, with the Pharisees;

not following in admiration with his friends; but caring for none of these things. These were travellers making their way, that day, engrossed with their own affairs, from Jerusalem out to Bethany, or on to Jericho, or over to the Jordan, who only uttered an exclamation of impatience or contempt that their way was blocked up, and their business delayed, by this intruding stranger,— just as men complain now when the Church interrupts their traffic with her worship, or when Providence shuts them into a sick-chamber that they may repent and lay hold of life. Very likely there were men and even women there that He had healed once, or whose children He had healed, who had gone back to their houses to enjoy an ungrateful comfort, and to make a selfish waste of the lives His mercy had lengthened out; blind men whose eyes He had opened, that looked upon everything else than His blessed countenance; withered hands that He had made whole, which gathered not for His garner, nor even reached out for a palm-branch to honor Him; tongues there, whose strings He had loosened, that would not speak His name or join in the hosannas. They probably imagined they took no part against Him. They certainly took no part for Him, or against His enemies.

It was so with the still more august and solemn events that followed. It was so on the night of the Supper, when the little band went out in silence, under the Paschal moon, from the upper chamber to Gethsemane, and when the soldiers, led by the traitor, crept into the shaded garden with their torches, and fell to the ground before the face of the Son of Man. It was so the day after, when a few persons collected about the Judgment Hall. It was so, later, from the sixth to the ninth hour, when the sudden darkness and the earthquake startled the people with the exclamation that the Lamb of God, "slain from the foundation of the world," was dying. It was so in the wonderful reports that filled the air, Easter morning. It has been so ever since, in all the Palm Sundays, all the Good Fridays and Easter Sundays, all the fasts and feasts, all the days of death and burial, all the years, all the ages. It will be so this coming week. The greater number are those that take no open part for the Master or against Him. Doing nothing,—by honest confession, by a brave enrolment, by the obedience of faith,—to gather treasure for Christ, they imagine they are doing nothing to scatter and waste it.

He speaks to that large third class among you to-day. If there is any question about that position,—as to its rightfulness, or its safety, or where those that are trying to hold it really belong,—does He not settle that question by the text? "He that gathereth not *with Me* scattereth."

Just before, the evangelist says, Christ had been speaking, with fearful emphasis, of the two hostile kingdoms, which forever confront each other in this world. The strong one armed keepeth his own palace. He will never surrender it, or one particle of it, in any human soul, till a stronger than he,—and there is only one stronger,—binds him. He will seem to surrender it; he will call it by some innocent name; he will cover it with a Christian title; he will deceive, flatter, promise, and manage; he will transform himself into an angel of light; but he will do it all to keep his own. Equally exclusive, over against that dark kingdom, is the kingdom of light: open, candid, without concealment or evasion, rejoicing in the truth, all its deeds done in the day, but admitting no admixture, no compromise, no neutrality. Everywhere, what fellowship hath light with darkness? Anywhere, what part hath the true subject with the traitor? In every soul, these two kingdoms and their laws are contrary the one to the other. It is remarkable, in all the Gospel, how invariable and how clear Christ makes this doctrine of absolute and necessary separation. There is *no* third party after all. There is no place for one. Non-profession does not make non-allegiance, or neutrality. It makes allegiance to the enemy. It makes disloyalty. "He that is not with Me is against Me."

The universality of this twofold law, therefore, and the impossibility that any human being in Christendom should so escape from it as to stand neither with God nor with His enemies, is the first great truth of the subject. Into that sharp conflict that is going on between the two kingdoms everything is drawn. Nobody lives; nothing by any moral agent, any man, is done; nothing is thought, written, spoken, built, bought or sold, begun or finished, outside the field of that warfare and the necessity of that choice.

The next truth to be remembered is our dangerous liability to be deceived just at that point, *i. e.*, to reckon as harmless or safe courses of life that are really anti-Christian. Between the Church and the dens of gamblers, drunkards, thieves, and profligates, between the communion-table and the jail, there runs a broad strip of moral territory, wearing a respectable look; it seems to belong neither to the one nor to the other. Why not set up over that territory, including so much of business, society, study, and so many people, the name of Christianity? Why not let it pass as Christian ground, with all its mixed companies, selfish passions, and worldly practices? "Heathenism" has a bad sound.

All this might very well be if Christ had not come and revealed another law and another judgment. The moment He appears,—and wherever the Gospel is preached He does appear,—then separation begins. Reveal to any community a new truth or propose a new reform, and it acts at once as a touchstone of their quality. According as they receive or reject it they are driven apart. But when Christ comes, He comes as the Lord of every soul that lives; the truth He reveals is universal truth. He is not concerned for a majority; He wants purity: "first pure, then peaceable." The more He can gain, the more will the infinite compassion of His loving heart rejoice; but be the penitents and the believers many or few, the repentance must be true, the faith hearty, the *allegiance* above suspicion. So He says, "He that gathereth not with Me scattereth." If there are any, here or elsewhere, who think they do enough because they are not positive opponents, mockers or infidels; who think that, because they never persecute, or revile, or take a traitor's silver, or meet to plot with Scribes and Pharisees for Herod, therefore they are not secretly fighting against their eternal King, Christ here assigns them their place with terrible distinctness. Unlike the politic leaders of earthly kingdoms, He fearlessly casts this middle-party from Him,—that it may thereby become truly His. All are scatterers that are not gatherers *with Him*. There is a striking record, in the Book of Numbers, of a prophet who tried, in perilous days, to be on neither side, and paltered with a double tongue between the true God and His enemies; but at last the issue between the two armies could be no longer evaded, and, after the battle, the body of this compromising neutral, Balaam, was found on the enemy's side, where it fell fighting *against* the Lord.

It is in this sense that Christ comes to put men and families of men "at variance" with one another,—a strange thing to be written of Him. It is not for division's sake, but only that truth may not be confounded with a lie, darkness be called light, and the very foundations of all honor guilt. There can be no lasting harmony, no healthy peace, but in Him in whom all things in their unity consist.

"First pure, then peaceable." Man cannot be really reconciled to man, save as he is first reconciled to his God; and there is only one Reconciler. In Him alone is humanity restored, and man made one with his brother. Not to gather with Him and for Him, is to divide and scatter. It is He that "maketh men to be of one mind in a house," in a nation, in a Church, in heaven.

This eternal doctrine needed never to be more plainly repeated than now, when the contest is not with Baal and Ashtaroth, Jupiter or Minerva, or any god of the old mythologies, or with avowed infidelity, so much as with a habit of dropping out, one by one, all the divine and glorious elements of Christ's own peculiar kingdom, and thinking to gather for human comfort or wealth, for social or sanitary or literary "progress," without gathering for Him. A few years ago a charitable sisterhood for the benefit of the poor was established in London. A writer in one of the public periodicals described a visit he had made to their establishment, and after giving a most interesting account of the self-denying labors of these refined and delicately bred women, he says, "he was curious to learn the motives that prompted them to take up sacrifices so irksome and repulsive. He supposed it was human pity, or a natural benevolence toward the beneficiaries; on inquiry he was surprised to find this was not the case at all, but the strong principle which actuated them was a religious self-renunciation for Christ's sake." They loved the wretched and the poor because they saw in them the objects of the Saviour's tenderness, souls for which He died, immortal spirits they were to meet hereafter in His kingdom wearing His image. They gathered for Him. That is the deepest, strongest, and only lasting power of good works. We may fancy we can substitute other things: amiability, philanthropy, political economy, a material civilization: —they are all excellent *as parts of Christ's kingdom*, but all weak, illusory, a mere scattering under the appearance of gathering, if they are taken apart from Him and set up for a religion. The Gospel never admits for a moment the possibility of such a thing as a Christianity without Christ. It is not enough to keep the old name; we must cling to the Eternal Person, if we would live His everlasting life.

O Divine Teacher and Prophet, persuade us of this! Good Shepherd, who wouldst gather us all together when we were scattered abroad; Blessed Friend, who wast for us when all else were against us, suffer us not to be found indifferent, undecided; for so we shall be found against Thee!

All is wasted then that is not done with a heart of love, and that toward God; all time that is not spent for Him,—these days of busy labor, in trades and professions; these unsatisfying contortions of effort to be a little richer, or a little more noticed, or to climb one round more on the ladder that you will slip from the instant death touches your fingers; these plans, schemes, travels, bargains, buildings;—they look like gathering, but they are only scattering, unless in the midst of them all your character is daily built up, a spiritual house, Jesus Christ himself being the chief corner-stone.

Gather with Him and all the parts of your life which are yet alien or infirm He will steadily draw into the unity of His own Body, making it strong and pure and immortal, knit together and making increase by the edifying of His love.

This morning, not with palms but with praises, we welcome Christ as our King. He is our King; we are His subjects;—but what kind of subjects? decided or wavering? hiding the badge and colors of His calling, or bravely confessing Him before the world? Behold, thy King cometh! Open to him the heart, the true Zion where he loves to dwell; otherwise He will look upon it only to weep over it. Bring Him into the city of your souls with the acclamations of a full faith, and follow Him to His Passion with a sincere repentance, that you may rise with Him, at his Resurrection, into newness of life.

# THE WATER AND THE BLOOD.

## *Good Friday.*

"This is He that came by water and blood, even Jesus Christ; not by water only, but by water and blood.—*I. St. John* v. 6.

By the form of the expression, "not by water only,"—it is implied that there are two beliefs as to the object of Jesus Christ's coming into the world,—one of them going beyond the other, and taking in something that the other leaves out. St. John lived and wrote close to the very heart of his Master. He rarely touches anything that is not essential to the substance of the Gospel, and he dwells most on what most distinguishes it from other systems of religion.

In a few simple sentences this marvellously illuminated mind has just thrown out some most profound and comprehensive statements. "Whosoever believeth that Jesus is the Christ, is born of God." "Whosoever is born of God overcometh the world." "By this we know that we are the children of God, when we love God and keep His commandments." "This is the victory that overcometh the world, even our faith." Then he goes on from this general doctrine to a more particular definition of it. It is evidently in his mind that some readers of what he is writing will say:—"But *what is this* 'faith'? Faith in what? If it is a force so mighty that it overcomes the world, it must have in it the divine energy of Him who gives it. Who is He, and what is the mysterious power of His coming which makes Him the Giver of eternal life to those that believe, in all lands and ages of the world?"

He answers thus:—"It is He that came by water and blood; not by water only, but by water and blood." There were probably those then, there are certainly those now, who would have no difficulty in accepting the main facts of Christ's birth and biography, would admit Him to be a memorable teacher, a reformer of society, a leader among moralists and philanthropists; but they would allow nothing further in His claims, as the Head of the Church or the Saviour of mankind. They would probably declare that nothing further was needed to make men all that they ought to be.

So, even among those who are disposed to call themselves Christians, we meet these two classes; and what they differ about is just that august event at Calvary which on this day millions of men are remembering.

As to the transaction itself, so much as this is almost universally allowed,—that at a certain date in history, Tiberias being emperor at Rome, a man called Jesus, of Nazareth, of pure life, having the appearance of a prophet, arraigning and rebuking fervently the prevailing life of society around Him, and claiming a mysterious connection with the One God, after a public career was crucified in the obscure province of Judea, near the city of Jerusalem, by the combined action of the imperial and ecclesiastical authorities, assisted by a traitor among His own followers. Along with this fact, so far away from us in time and place, is commonly admitted another, which rises at once into solitary majesty, and becomes a matter of unspeakable personal concern. It is that, *in some way,* following upon the crucifixion, and springing from that spot, a steadily advancing wave of spiritual, moral, and intellectual light went out, and has been ever since spreading over the globe. The feelings and convictions, the institutions, the principles of personal action and the spirit of society,—what we call the character of mankind,—have been changed and formed anew from that hour. Mark this, too, especially,—this change has been brought in the name of that Person. It has not been a revolution of abstruse opinions or impersonal ideas, like the progress of philosophy among the Greeks, or the breaking up of mediaeval stagnation at the crusades, or the transformation of European religion in the sixteenth century, or the political theories of the eighteenth and nineteenth;—it has always and everywhere gone on by a personal appeal, a personal loyalty, a personal enthusiasm,—there is a better word yet,—a personal faith towards that crucified Man, Christ Jesus. There is no such name among men. It has made the nations that have rceived it strong. The governing forces of the world have not been superior to it; almost the whole line of commanding men, since the Caesars, have acknowledged Him to be greater than themselves,—having a Lordship different in kind, and loftier in rank.

So much is almost universally granted. But, around the cross where this Personage died, there stood four groups or classes of men, representing very various opinions of His actual title to honor. There were first the people whom the Prayer Book, in the service of this Good Friday, teaches us so tenderly to pray for; as the Saviour himself while on the cross, murdered by their malignity, taught His whole Church Catholic to pray for them,—the Jews. *They* treated His suffering as a proper penalty for a disturber of the peace who had promised to emancipate them from foreign masters, but had provoked the aristocracy, and failed. A second class, Romans and other strangers, looked on with indifference, sneering, with Pilate's sarcasm, at a fickle rabble so excitable as to pour out in a procession with palms and hosannas after a fanatic, who five days after takes His turn as a victim of their caprice. Thirdly, friends in perplexity, amazed women, their hearts torn with many kinds of pain, watched from a distance the dear form where their gratitude and affection were sacredly enshrined.

But, scattered among all these, few in number, and yet the vanguard of a mighty army, unrecognized builders of a kingdom that was to rise from that spot and conquer and outlive every empire under the sun, there were certain men on whose souls the truth *had* taken hold. They knew very soon why their Master died, and what it is to believe in the cross. Afterwards, instructed by a risen Redeemer for forty days, they laid the foundations, they drew the outlines, they set in order the worship, and they spoke the creed of the Church,— the Eternal House which should gather and shelter the family of Christ. When *they* are inquired of, what this dying on the cross signifies, they answer, " This death was not only the last crowning act of that most merciful and life-giving life which began at Bethlehem; it was more than that; it was the opening of the door into life eternal for men who had broken from their Father and were spiritually dead; it was a perfect offering of Love, obedient to Law, for the sins of all mankind; it was a sacrifice of atonement, of such ineffable and Divine power that it melts away the wall of separation which the transgressions of the race had built up, and opens the kingdom of heaven to all believers. There was disobedience everywhere. Four thousand years of Jewish and

Gentile self-righteousness had proved that there is no self-recovering power in humanity alone. That power must be lodged in a Person who has in Him both of the estranged natures that are to be reconciled to each other;—it must be a mediation between an everlasting law of purity and right, which every man is concerned in having kept honorable and inviolate, and the weak but repenting soul, which has violated its commandment;— it must be a suffering so free and so glorious in its charity that it shall be a bond of union between believers, mightier than the wall of partition which it broke down. Beyond all the blessings of the Saviour's life among men was the mediatorial mercy and reconciliation of His death. So runs the teaching and testimony of the Gospel, from first to last.

Each of the New Testament writers clothes this truth in his own characteristic dress. St. John presents it, with peculiar beauty, under the original image of the text. Taking two of the most familiar substances of the material world,—water and blood,—he turns them into a figure of the great central doctrine of the Gospel and the Church.

First the "water." Water is the emblem of spiritual purification, because it is the common instrument of outward washing. Our Lord himself, who was able to set all symbols and all forms aside if He chose, went down into the water, at the beginning of His life's work, in order, we are told, that He might fulfil all righteousness. He "came by water." There must have been weighty reasons for this water-ceremony, so solemnly observed, or He never could have made place for it among His crowded days of teaching, healing, and comforting His countrymen. He takes peculiar pains to say that every Christian life must begin in the same way. "Except a man be born of water and of the Spirit,"—an outward and an inward washing,—" he cannot enter into the kingdom of God." Nothing plainer is written. " Go teach the nations of the earth and baptize them," with *water*, was His last commission, when His work was done. "Repent, believe, and be baptized," with water, " every one of you," was the preaching that converted the world and planted the Church. So it is that each individual Christian life, as well as the whole body of Christ, after Him, came " by water."

Why is this? Because one great part of our Saviour's work is to purify men's lives. Do they not need purifying? The stains are everywhere. In this congregation there is not one clean conscience. We can all *see* the stains when we look sharply into ourselves, or into society. Manners are not clean ; business is not clean ; politics are not clean ; our literature and our tongues are not clean. In their business dealings few men dare to say that they are perfectly clean-handed ; and in their solitude, fewer still will claim that there is nothing unclean in their imaginations. The Church herself has not yet been presented to the Bridegroom a Bride without spot. And therefore, in taking upon Him all the plagues and sorrows of His human brethren, Christ came into such close and vital sympathy with them that He desired to go through all the outer as well as inner forms of their experience. Human nature was in Him, too; it was tempted in Him ; evil came all round it and beset it ;—and therefore He treated Himself as all these human transgressors are treated. He was baptized with their baptism, and they with His. The world was to smite and sneer at Him, and spit upon Him, in spite of His purity: in being holy for them He will also be washed with them. He " came by water."

Accordingly, one great part of the power of Christ among men, through the Gospel and the Church, is the cleansing away of moral corruptions. Whenever a professed Christianity, or nominal Church, has not gone steadily and effectually to reforming men's conduct and institutions, by righteous education and a higher spirit, there has been some falsehood at the heart, some hypocrisy under the ecclesiastical cloak. "He that hath this hope in him purifieth himself." Stains on the lips, the hands, the habits; stains on social courtesies, domestic dispositions, every room of the house, and even on Church observances; worst of all, stains on the sacred temple walls of the soul itself;—these all have to be washed away, first by one true repentance and regeneration, having water for their sacramental sign, and then, afterwards, by the repeated washings of Christ's truth and spirit, applied faithfully to all the departments of our action. Christ came to cleanse His followers from all unrighteousness. He "came by water."

But now shall we not only say, "*This* is true," but shall we go on to say, "This is all that our Saviour gives us, and this is the whole of His Gospel:—Christianity is a system of moral education and religious improvement; nothing more"?

Is obedience to a perfect Law, and such obedience as we at best can give, the only salvation? If it is, I, for one, must wonder how it is going with me; and I shall have to doubt whether your message to me can be called a gospel of glad tidings at all. I confess to you, preacher of this Law, that while I honor it as a law, "holy, just," beneficent, and know that it comes from God, I fail in keeping it: it is not only exceeding broad, as David found it, but exceeding deep and exceeding difficult. I fail in keeping it, have failed all along from the first, and shall fail to the end; for the more I keep it the more I see its breadth and depth, the farther up its splendid standard flies, and the more shameful seem my sins. You answer, "Yes, you fail, no doubt, very often; but you must keep trying: try again, and then try again. You are defiled, but wash yourself. Here are Christian truths and Christian precepts and the Christian spirit: take them and cleanse yourself with them. What you want is more of the water. Christ came by water. It is all He brings. More water,— more water to make you clean!"

Systems of religion have made that answer. But, my friends, there comes a time in the experience of earnest people's minds when they feel that this is no answer for them. They know, by a secret conviction, and no rationalizing and no philosophizing can drive it out of them, that they need more than this; that for them to be saved into the everlasting life, and into the presence and communion of God, by a perfect mortal righteousness and a blameless obedience is a fantasy so utterly out of all fact and reason both, that to offer it to them as a ground of salvation is a mockery. They believe that somewhere there must be *another half* to match this fragmentary piece of a mutilated revelation, and they are not mistaken. "This is He that came by water and blood; *not by water only*, but by water and blood." The daily sacrifice of four thousand preparatory years had presignified it to a waiting world. As the passion-flower sprang out of the common earth, and held up its bright blossom and natural image of the tree at Calvary, ages before the real cross was planted in its soil, so the passion-promise of prophecy bloomed in the expectant faith of the race at the very gates of Eden. The serpent had polluted Paradise; but after all, the woman's seed should bruise the serpent's head. Man knew from the beginning that he must have a Saviour to look to, or he was gone; humanity itself would die. He knows it now just as well. Something tells you that though you had an ever springing font at your side, a well of water, a river, a Jordan, an ocean, in which you should be baptized every day of your life, it would not wash out one of these deep-struck spots in your conscience and your heart. Somewhere among the sons of men there must be One Perfect Obedience, One Sufficient Sacrifice, needing not, like those shadowy sacrifices which prepared the way, to be often offered, but " once offered."

Then a living and loving faith in Him will work out the true and healing life in every believing heart. "There is a fountain opened for sin, and for uncleanness"; but it is not a water fountain. This day we approach it. The more earnest our soul's life grows within us, the more the conscience, while struggling bravely with all its might for the keeping of the commandments, cries out for this peace. The past, the bad, mean, selfish, sinful, guilty life of days gone by, with all its accumulated corruption, we cannot remember it without remorse; we cannot look back into it without anguish. Only he who *doeth* the deeds of the Law—so it reads—will live by them. Who of us has done them? *Where* are we then, my brethren, if there is "water only," example and precept only, commandments only, sorrow upon sorrow when they are broken, and the breaking repeated still? It certainly looks very much like sorrow without end.

From our Lord's first coming in the flesh He knew that He came not by water only, but by water and blood. Among the most remarkable of Overbeck's striking series of pictures illustrating the life of Jesus, there is one that represents Him as a Child in the carpenter's shop. Like other children, He has been playing with the tools, and has taken up the saw. A look of solemnity passes over His radiant face; and by the shadow that falls on the floor underneath you see that the block of wood He is sawing out is taking the shape of a cross. Joseph looks on in a kind of perplexed reverence, and the Virgin-mother by his side with a sad admiration, as if Simeon's prediction were already beginning to have its acccomplishment, and the sword were piercing her own soul also. This is not imagination; it is rather interpretation. The artist is only an expositor of the evangelist. "This is He that came by water and blood." From the outset of His personal ministry,—as it had been from the foundation of the world,—the Saviour was pointing to the sacrifice,—journeying always towards Calvary. Other prophets and reformers had come "by water," preaching purification for the future. He alone came "by blood," giving, in Himself, atonement for past and future both. The august sorrowfulness of the end rested evidently on His spirit. As fast as they were able to bear it He unfolded to His disciples this real object of His being born. He spoke to them of His flesh and blood, to be given for the life of the world. He explained, very early, to a Jewish rabbi, the symbol in Jewish history, the serpent lifted up in the wilderness, an emblem of the cross to which men have to look in faith to be healed. He accepted, at His baptism in the Jordan, the Baptist's ascription to Him as the sacrificial Lamb of God, taking away the sins of the world. On the mount of Transfiguration He announced more openly "the decease that He should accomplish at Jerusalem."

To quote the testimony of each of the apostles would be to copy a principal part of their several sermons and epistles. A very few concise phrases will call up more pages to your memory, and show how the whole strain of their doctrine proceeds: "Having made peace by the blood of His cross, by Him to reconcile all things to Himself"; "Ye were redeemed by the precious blood of Christ"; "While we were yet sinners, Christ died for us"; "We which were far off, are made nigh by the blood of Christ"; "Justified freely by His grace, through the redemption that is in Christ Jesus, whom God hath set forth to be a propitiation, through faith in His blood for the remission of sins that are past." We read what is written to the Hebrews: "Without the shedding of blood there is no remission of sins. Having therefore boldness to enter by the blood of Jesus,—let us draw near,—with full assurance of faith." We hear the voices of the Apocalypse: "Unto Him that loved us and washed us from our sins in His own blood,—to Him be glory and dominion." We hear the mighty song of heaven, like the sound of many waters, but singing of a purification that no oceans of water could ever accomplish: "Thou art worthy, for Thou wast slain, and hast redeemed us to God by Thy blood out of every kindred and tongue." Even if all other tongues were still, in heaven or in earth, we have the truth from Him who speaks alone as men never speak: "This cup is the New Testament in My blood, which is shed for you. He that eateth My flesh and drinketh My blood, dwelleth in Me, and I in him; and I give unto him everlasting life."

Can anybody think it strange, after we have repeated affirmations of Holy Scripture like these, that we repeat, also, every year, with reverent adoration, the commemoration of this day? The day of the sacrifice on the cross? I can imagine, I think, the total disbelief, of pride or delusion, that shuts the Bible up, with a sweeping denial, or drops it in despair. It is more difficult to conceive how any clear mind can hold on upon it, to call it a message of moral education, with no atonement :—the water without the blood.

We stand once more to-day at the foot of the cross. I am half-ashamed to be handling cavils and objections, before this mystic miracle of love, which fills a universe with comfort and light. You can read, if you please, the long line of argument, from Justin Martyr and Augustine to the last modern speculation, on this vast wonder of time, into which, we are told, angels look with humility. But how plain the whole truth that we need is found to be! We are but children. Your soul, mine, every soul in the world, under its temptation, its infirmity, its bad desires, was sinking into death. We had our unsuccessful projects of relief, failing one by one. Infinite love reaches out the cross to save us. God says to us in His Son, " Take hold of this: believe on this, and live forever,—in thankful service to your Lord." O thou of little faith, wherefore didst thou doubt?" " The blood of Jesus Christ cleanseth us from all sin":—not " water only, but the water and the blood."

The whole Gospel of our salvation gathers itself into a personal blessing.

Whatever my personal fortunes, for the present, may happen to be, I know that I am in the midst of a world full of suffering and failure;—things most valued are passing away, and the best-beloved friends are dying and carried out to be buried. Here is the body;—not a fibre of the flesh but is liable and sensitive to pain. One little nerve pierced by a needle fills days and years with distress. A careless shot alters the whole course of a young man just furnished for a successful career, blinds him, cripples him; or a crash on a railway crushes out fifty lives at once, and leaves five hundred precious interests, or attachments hanging upon them, broken up and mourning. There is not a faculty of the mind but has its frightful capacity of torture. Disorder, shortcoming, wrong-doing, desertion, hatred, loneliness, orphanage, shame, despair: what names these are! And what realities are under them! The great world's history is tragical,—a history of war and crime. Now, in the midst of this sorrow-struck humanity, stands a soul, seeing it all and feeling it. Perhaps it is yours. It is told that above it all there is a God, and partly believes it. But is He *only* above, looking down upon it? Does that God *feel* for this wretchedness? Is there a *heart* in heaven? Does the Everlasting King love *us*, and come close to us? You read the epistle for this day. You look on the face of HIM despised and rejected, His countenance marred more than any of the sons of men. Behold the Man! You know that He is more than man,—God's only Son. He prays, "Father, forgive them." He dies. You know, now, whether there is a heart in heaven; whether your God has entered into your humanity. "Herein is love!" We have a suffering and a sympathizing Lord.

Sorrow is always venerable; but the degree of it is proportioned to the sensibility. Only a nature infinitely refined, infinitely delicate, and infinitely pure, with an *infinite capacity* for sorrow, could suffer as the Saviour suffered. No other atonement could be complete. And herein was the love.

But there is a power and a glory of love beyond even this. Taking one more look around this great world's chamber of sickness and groaning, you discover faint occasional gleams of a brighter law breaking in. There is not only fellow-suffering, and not only suffering freely borne for others' *help*, but here and there some nobler spirits, the noblest of all, are gloriously taking up and bearing crosses in one another's stead, that the guilty may be spared, that the lost may not perish, that the worst may be saved. There is such a thing as voluntary suffering to save the hateful and the hating, the spiteful, the evil, the foul. *Whence*, in all the universe, from what one spot of singular and central glory, do these beams of heavenly charity arise? From that hill of sacrifice,—and only there,—where we gather our remembrances and assemble our affections and offer our praises this day. The revilers spoke a deeper truth than they knew: "He saved others: Himself He could not save." He whom the faithful Abraham, of the morning lesson, dimly prefigured, sadly building his altar and saying, "God will provide Himself a lamb," spared not His Son. Herein is the love that is Divine,—the love of the Son of God, on the cross!

We come, then, finally, to the great confession,—beginning in humiliation and ending in triumph,—the confession of the sinful, redeemed soul. I am sure it is mine. May it not be made, must it not be,—by every soul here? I am weak; I am unclean; I am broken in my will; I am evil, proud, selfish, passionate at my heart; I am stained all over with sin;—and I am fighting against adversaries mightier than I, where all that trust themselves go down. Give me the water to cleanse. But, O Son of God, keep not from me the precious blood, to sprinkle, to pardon, to redeem. I was far off; make me nigh by that! I was dying; let me live by that!

"I saw again. Behold heaven's open door.
　　Behold a throne! The seraphim stood o'er it.
　The white-robed elders fell upon the floor,
　　And flung their crowns before it.

"I saw a wondrous book. An angel strong
　　To heaven and earth proclaimed his loud appeals.
　But a hush passd across the seraph's song,
　　For none might loose the seals.

"And straightway up above,
　　Stood in the midst a wondrous Lamb, snow-white,
　As it were slain with the deep wounds of love,
　　Eternal, infinite.

"Then rose the song no ear had heard before;
　　Then from the white-robed host an anthem woke;
　And fast as spring-tide on the sounding shore
　　The hallelujahs broke!"

# THE POWER OF THE RESURRECTION.

*Easter Day.*

"To this end Christ both died, and rose, and revived (or lived again), that He might be Lord both of the dead and living."—*Romans* xiv. 9.

In the facts of our Lord's personal history there is a special satisfaction provided by each great event for some special want that is common to men. From the need of reconciliation with a broken law of right and with Him whose perfect will that law is, met by the Sacrifice, we pass this morning to our need of reconciliation with our own future. Even the firmest believer, as he looks along the uncertain years before him, and beyond them all, sees that much must be lost. Is he to receive anything in its place? Three kinds of separation look particularly forbidding:—the separation from human companionship, family and friends; the separation from the present outward scene, as a familiar sphere of activity; and the separation of the soul from the body. It is around these three portentous mysteries that the sorrow and anxiety gather, which Christ's rising from the dead scatters. He meets them, as on this day, by the demonstration of His living and eternal Headship over the spiritual creation. All souls alive in Him not only live forever, but they are in Him forever one. "To this end He both died, and rose, that He might be Lord both of the dead and living." By virtue of His inextinguishable Divinity we shall know our Christian friends again. Dying, the decays of disease, the dust of dissolution, will not permanently overmaster the vitality which has its springs in Him. The earth swings, half in light and half in shadow, around the central sun. But to the Household of Faith, such alternations are transient:—the part now shaded and the part shining in joy will be contrasted hemispheres no more, but will move into a boundless noon, one bright and perfect globe, with no need of sun or stars. This is the assurance, the consolation, of Easter Day.

There are, however, two senses in which man is said to be immortal. Natural immortality is simply the lengthening out of bare existence, irrespective of those loftier and nobler qualities which belong to what the Christian calls *life*. If we take the idea of the best of the old Greek thinkers, making humanity threefold,—body, soul, and spirit,—we should say that beyond the body, which alone dies, there is a second element, an "animal soul," which escapes destruction and survives. What kind of existence that would be, with nothing added to it, animal immortality, we have not the faintest conception. Nature casts not a beam of illumination there; and Revelation itself is dumb.

It is striking,—a fact in which it is impossible for men who follow at all the courses of modern thought, and who watch the bearing of science on the great problems of the soul and the dogmas of the Faith, not to be interested,—that the most prominent scientific assailant of the Bible distinctly declares his belief in a future life. While holding that the human race has been gradually *formed upward*, or developed from the lowest animal type, instead of having been originally set by the

Maker at the head of creation, he yet admits that somewhere on that line of transmutations, this marvellous and majestic attribute of immortality, or imperishableness, has been acquired. How far this sort of "life to come" differs from the ancient heathen idea, has not yet been made to appear.

What we have to notice is that,—being sublimely indifferent to all the speculative or naturalistic theories,—the New Testament starts from an entirely different point, leaves the conjectures of philosophy wholly aside, but offers to our faith what harmonizes indeed with all true philosophy, and what no measure of knowledge can ever possibly deny or ever touch,—the doctrine of eternal life in Jesus Christ our Lord.

The matter stands there in a sublime simplicity. They that live the spiritual life have it from the Son of God, and by believing in Him:—He rises from the dead and lives forever;—therefore they also live immortally. These are the short, clear steps in that evangelic argument. But no line of reasoning establishes the conclusion. No dialectical demonstration ever attempted,—not even the famous one of Bishop Butler,—is without its weak spot. We are dealing not with the parts or conditions of a problem, but with a living fact and a personal reality. "*I am* the Resurrection and the Life: —whosoever liveth and believeth in Me shall never die": —this carries us beyond the region of premise and inference. We believe, or not; and are blessed, or wretched, accordingly; but we are not argued into the conviction, or out of it. The faith, however, in its certainty, amounts to sight or knowledge; and hence it is no exaggeration when all Christendom, moving ever towards the grave in the procession of its generations, declares in the burial sentence, "*I know* that my Redeemer liveth."

It is remarkable, too, that in the New Testament the common term for this Christian immortality is the eternal or everlasting "*Life*,"—or sometimes simply *the Life:*—as if it meant to say that there is really no other life worth living but this one of purity and honor, love and prayer, beginning in a Christian here, becoming afterwards the life of heaven: so surpassing, whether in this world or the next, is its richness, its joy, its satisfaction, its glory. When we examine and weigh them carefully, Scripture statements that we had not perhaps before looked at in the same light come to confirm this view. Christ himself says, in His last prayer before the Supper, that it is *now*, not merely that it *will be* in the future,—it is now eternal life to know the Father and the Son with this affectionate knowledge. When He speaks of going to prepare a place for His followers, it is that this personal intercourse may continue,—" that ye may be with Me, where I am." He says, "He that eateth My flesh and drinketh My blood," —which is the mystical description of a deep and inward union,—"hath eternal life." Everywhere He teaches that immortality is not a gift conferred upon us from without, as from hand to hand, but that it grows up in the soul, as the sure consequence or fruitage of obedience and trust toward God. St. John is full of this idea,— that you may know whether you will live forever by knowing whether you are following that Master, from the love of Him. St. Paul speaks of being "absent from the body and present with the Lord," and of his desire to depart and be with Christ,—evidently regarding a Christian death as a merely physical incident, an emancipation from the flesh,—leaving the spirit more at liberty to be in direct and active communion with its unseen Friend. This is his magnificent message to the

Corinthians:—" Not for that we would be unclothed, but clothed upon, that mortality might be swallowed up of life."

So we come to the text. It is the culminating of a rapid and rising stream of devout thought, where the one object that stands supreme is the risen Redeemer. The real import of the Easter event is that Jesus, risen from the dead, becomes thereby the personal centre and giver of all spiritual life to His Church, and is a Lord of the living and the dead. Observe some inferences.

In the first place, this Lordship of the risen Christ over the living and the dead provides the only solid and satisfactory assurance of the future reunion and recognition of His followers. The question that rises oftener than any other to the lips of the bereaved touches this point of reunion. "Shall I see him again,—my brother, my child, my friend? Will the hand that lies there white upon the breast be reached out to me when we meet? Will the eyes of my mother, whose light opened on me with my life, welcome my coming? Each dear and trusted face,—by some celestial sense will its mysterious meanings and attractions be felt as they were here,

"'Lovelier in heaven's sweet climate, yet the same'"?

There is no need to put these intense longings into words. Without saying that they are universal, it can certainly be said that they are common; and they are generally eager in proportion to the affectionateness of the survivor's nature. You may try to construct a heaven cut clean off in all its sympathies and attachments and recognitions from this world we are in now. But you will almost certainly then have before the mind a heaven practically destitute of any sympathies and attachments whatever; too vague to awaken expectation, too unreal to inspire enthusiasm; bleak, cheerless, and quite too feeble in its attraction to meet the meaning of that grand apostolic expression,—" the *powers* of the world to come."

He who rose and lives again is the Lord of the living and the dead. They are not two families, but one, because they are all in Him, in spite of the transient curtain that hangs between the departed and ourselves,— a curtain that probably has its only *substance* in the eyes of our flesh. The resurrection of the body of Jesus, as the Church has always taught by the stress she has laid upon it in the Creed, signifies the literal reality of all that is promised the Christian in his future home,—the actual identity of the person here and the person there,— the actual renewal of affections and their interchange,— for what is the identity, or the blessing of it, if the heart has got to begin its whole history afresh? It signifies the actual restoration, too, of the society, the acquaintanceships, in other words, the common life and common worship, only in purer and more exalted forms, of those who have believed together, and worshipped the same Saviour, here.

There will be no confusion of persons, no obliteration of the lines that mark off one soul from another. The individuality of the disciple is not *absorbed* even in that of his Lord,—which would make a Pantheist's heaven,— or in an undistinguished mass of strange life,—which would make a heaven of pagan "shades." We shall be just as distinct persons, with all personal faculties, affections, sympathies, substances, yes, and appearances, as we are now. In those celestial congregations there will, no doubt, be something to be recognized by, in feature or form, inbred on earth, and indestructible by dissolution.

Hence the need of a glorified, resurrection body, to be set free, at the last change,—following the *analogy* still of His body who died and rose the same. Character is getting fashioned under an inward sculpture of moral experience, so that the second life will be the orderly outbirth and continuation of the first,—only the gross, material elements giving place to those that are refined and ethereal, wearing a dignity and beauty of their own, and with every trace of earthliness and defilement purged away forever.

As the preparatory process of the natural life goes on in secret awhile,—as the seed must lie some time hidden and decaying, till suddenly the end of that patient waiting is found in the budding beauty of the leaf and flower,—so a Christian man's entire mortal education is but an obscure making ready for that moment when this mortal shall put on immortality.

So, precisely, teaches St. Paul. "There is a natural body, and there is a spiritual body. Howbeit, that is not first which is spiritual; but that which is natural, and afterward that which is spiritual." "To every seed his own body." That is the identity. This is all we know about it; but it is enough. Everything beyond is speculation, and not revealed on authority. In due time the resurrection-body will be made complete in all its substantial parts, and will become the perfect organ of the spirit of life in Christ Jesus. "Them also that sleep in Jesus, God will bring unto Him." The power of their rising,—the secret spring of their new-born life, in the regeneration that brings new heavens and the new earth, will be the eternal Life-Giver himself, the Head of the whole Family of Faith, the Lord of the dead and the living,—having been first received here by faith, and indwelling in the believer's heart.

Again,—through Christ our resurrection-life will be social, as well as individual. As everything in the kingdom of heaven has its type and model in the Person of our Lord, so in the rising of His form, and the subsequent interviews with His disciples, we see a promise that, literally and forever, those to whom He imparts His spirit will move together, in a family order and freedom about Him,—whatever their employments and spheres of action may be. Nothing less than this can be taught us by the parable of Lazarus with the patriarch, by the inspired images of St. John in the Apocalypse, by the *company* of saints made perfect, by the hymns and amens of the redeemed, by the assembled spirits of just men made perfect, by the whole family in heaven and earth,—but, more than all these, by the reappearing, in the body, of the Lord of the dead and the living. Reason, to be sure, might conjecture or dream out an individual immortality,—as four or five of the ancients did. But the universe is very large. Whither would the forth-going soul take its strange journey, if there were no *centre* of spiritual attraction, no living Head around whom the society must circle, making a heaven by His light and love, no Christ receiving the believer to Himself, where He is?

Another assurance, given by the fact of the Saviour's bodily resurrection, is that of the *independence* of the spiritual life on the material conditions and their changes, which accompany dissolution. One of the sources of materialism is the disturbance or utter eclipse of the mental faculties by physical disease, or by old age. You stand by a bed and watch this distressing process, perhaps the utter wreck and dislocation of a superbly balanced intellect by a fever, or you observe the breaking up of memory and all coherent thought, between eighty and ninety years of age. You see sometimes the finest judgment inverted, the sweetest temper irritated, the holiest piety become petulant, the strength of manhood sunk to a melancholy childishness. If you were observing this dismal spectacle for the first time, you might say, as many a medical student has said in the haste of his half-way science: "It looks here as if man were nothing after all but a piece of anatomical or automatic mechanism. A few drops of blood too many on his brain, a jar of the delicate machinery by friction, will unsettle the soul from her seat, and, before the lamp finally goes out, the flame burns so low in the socket that it seems that body and spirit will be buried in one grave. The soul must be but an accidental appendage to the corporeal organization, and must perish with it." Such thoughts pass through minds that take no pleasure in them; and faith reaches out her hand, trembling, for some support.

You pass then to the death scene at Calvary, between the sixth to the ninth hour. There is no mental eclipse in the august Sufferer; but there is one sign set there to show us how completely the experience of the Redeemer includes the infirmities and agonies of our humanity, in its inward as well as its outward trial,—the cry, "My God, My God, why hast Thou forsaken Me?" We know that the death was *real*, till the giving up of the ghost. Yet through all this sinking and final going out of life, we see the indestructible soul asserting her immortality; unhurt she takes back all the energy and capacity of which destruction appeared to deprive her. It is a visible triumph. The bonds of death are loosed, because it is not possible He should be holden of them. The third morning brings every slumbering faculty and every lifeless fibre up, living, to its place. The Jesus that speaks to Mary at the tomb, and to the disciples for forty days, is the same Jesus that prays, "Let this cup pass from Me." And because He is ours, and we are His, in the exact language of our prayer at the eucharist, in the bonds of an inward and spiritual possession, therefore all signs of decay and weakness pass away with their transient causes. Beyond the tottering frame, the faltering reason, the failing memory, beyond delirium and dotage, beyond lethargy and all the lapses of the mind, the soul resumes its power, its health, its vigor of immortal love, because its risen life is in the risen Mediator, hid with Christ in God.

Once more, we want this bond of unity between the dead and the living to throw a purifying and ennobling influence into our present daily life, to save it from sinking, as our life is so terribly tempted to, into a besotted mammonism, an insane frivolity, or a miserable selfishness; —to make it a noble and ever more perfect preparation for what is to come. How is it with us here? We want this constant "power" of a practical connection between the two worlds, to keep the present from being a mere scramble and carnival of the senses, a place to eat and dress and sleep in—as well as to keep the future from being a sentimental fantasy, or a dead blank. The apostles join the most inspiring prospects of the glory to be revealed with their sharpest protests against common sins. We are immersed in falsehoods and wrongs, in lusts and ambitions. There is no resurrection for them. We are tempted hourly,—nobody denies it,—to unclean transactions, to covetousness and bad temper, to envying and evil-speaking, to indolence, impatience, and unbelief. Now, one of the great powers by which we are to struggle against these successfully, and finally overcome, is the certainty of a day when Christ,—who is life to those that love Him, and whose eyes are like a flame of fire to those that are untrue to Him and unrighteous to each other,—shall appear. The new man in Him is to be put on immediately. Even in these self-seeking earthly streets the Christian is to walk unselfishly and unblamably, his pride humbled, his temper controlled, his motives godly. Whatever is done in word or deed is to be done in the name and spirit of the Lord Jesus, risen from the dead, by those that are on the way to meet Him. The true Christian's way through the world is somewhat like the walk of the disciples with Christ through the corn-field on the Sabbath. He does not object to their rubbing the ears of corn for food,—*i. e.*, to their hands doing the ordinary and necessary business,—because they are bound on His service, and need strength to do it with for His kingdom's sake. But they must work with Him. Try to make a little heaven where you are,—in the house where you live, in the scene of your daily toil,—and there will be little doubt of the heaven hereafter. Do your daily work and do it cheerfully:—this is God's world, good enough for you and me,—bad as some things in it are. Christ thought it not too bad for His holy feet to press for three and thirty sad, hard-working years. We are the workmen of a Master who is as much here as there;—the Lord of the living as of the dead, and of the dead as of the living.

When we are asked, therefore, how we know that we shall live forever, we reply, Not because some book of arguments, or pledge in paper and ink, or some pretty parable of spring-blossoms and butterflies tells us we may; but because every Christian can say for himself, "I know in whom I have believed. My Redeemer liveth, and no member abiding in Him can perish. He that believeth hath the witness in himself."

We lift up our hearts to the True Tabernacle in the

heavens, which the Lord hath pitched and not man,—which will abide when all these houses of our earthly tabernacle are dissolved, and with gates ever open to all the separated dwelling-places of the one catholic and pilgrim flock,—gates through which "they go no more out." Blessed be He who died for us and rose again, that the entrance is not shut at all, day or night, and that those angels which keep it are not partial or prejudiced angels, not mercenary or fastidious angels. The poorest Lazarus will not have to wait for room to be made for him by prouder people. The woman whose sins are many and the man whose demons are legion, penitent and healed,—the Publican if he believes and the Pharisee if he is humbled, the Samaritan if he is "good" and the Priest and Levite if they are converted, the Prodigal if he has gone home and the rich Zaccheus if he has made himself poor for Christ's sake,—they all not only enter in, but they are willing to be equal there. They count themselves to be all unworthy, and therefore are made kings and priests together, in a spiritual royalty and a priesthood of likeness to the High Priest who is touched with the feeling of our infirmities. He suffers little children to come in, remembering that He was once a little child in Bethlehem for them;—He welcomes aged saints, like Simeon in whose arms He was laid.

Last night some veteran believer turned his face away from the world and went to look for the place prepared for him,—a good soldier and servant to his life's end. Close by his side will be found the spirit of an infant, lying down to sleep amidst his playthings, never conscious what the sign of the baptismal cross on his forehead meant. The flesh of the old man's heart will have become as the flesh of a little child. The soul in the baby's breast will spring forward into a seraph's strength, keeping its childish innocence. And both will bear a part with the same thanksgiving in the Hymn like the voice of many waters, saying, "Amen; blessing and thanksgiving be unto God and to the Lamb that was slain." To this end Christ died and rose. And still, to each one of us, as these seasons of the resurrection come and go, the Spirit and the Bride say "Come"; and "Whosoever will, let him come."

# HOW THE RISEN CHRIST IS SEEN.

### *First Sunday after Easter.*

"AND as they went to tell His disciples, behold, Jesus met them, saying, All hail! And they came and held Him by the feet, and worshipped Him."—*St. Matthew* xxviii. 9.

A FEW souls that had been most intimate with Jesus up to the terrible night at Gethsemane, to whom He had become more than all of life or love besides, pass in one moment of surprise from the dismay of His crucifixion to the complete comfort of having Him with them again alive, His form invested with the mystery of this new miracle of His resurrection. On the part of the women it seems to have been an act of *silent* adoration, not a syllable being spoken; and we can well understand why it should have been so. The Lord himself at first, and for some time, says but a single word. That word which would be as literally rendered "Rejoice," our text translates into the statelier salutation, "All hail." The verse before tells us that the disciples had received the angel's announcement of His rising from the dead with a mixture of contradictory emotions:—"They departed from the sepulchre with fear and great joy";—and this, too, we can all comprehend, if we know much of what the heart contains, and how it fluctuates when it scarcely dares to believe that it has actually grasped the one blessedness it has most longed for. But what is of fear is not of faith. The Saviour joins Himself, therefore, to the believing side of their hearts, sends away the last remaining traces of their doubts, and makes their joy full.

There are six separate occasions, at least, recorded by the four Evangelists, when our Lord, after His resurrection, appeared to human eyes. That every particular of these is brought into the narrative is more than we are at liberty to affirm. St. Luke's statement, at the opening of the Book of the Acts, that during the forty days, until the ascension, Christ was occupied in giving instructions to the apostles respecting the constitution and administration of His Church, now perfectly established and set up in the world, only waiting for the descent of the Spirit from the ascended Head, at Pentecost, to set its wheels of life into their wonderful operation for all time, would rather seem to imply that much is left unrelated, to be brought out, from time to time, into practical shape, in the planting and training of the Church, after the heavenly pattern. Nor do we get an entire description of even these successive appearances in their order from either one of the four biographies, but only by placing them all side by side, examining carefully to see where each incident falls in, and so obtaining a consistent and perfect record. What gives a new meaning, however, to the whole account, when it is thus arranged, and what has been singularly left almost entirely out of view in the ordinary expositions of it, is that there is evidently from first to last, running through all these manifestations, an order of another sort; that is, an intentional and remarkable progress in the kind and manner of Christ's showing Himself, according to the spiritual condition of the persons to whom He appeared. Each individual sees just so much of Christ as his state of mind and heart, his religious quality and habits, prepare him and enable him to see. In all religious matters we receive and are blessed according to our own willingness, that is, our faith. With this clew in hand you will find there is something here of much greater signification and beauty and power than will be gathered from a fragmentary reading of the several passages, or from treating the manifestations as so many disconnected occurrences without any secret law of internal connection relating them to each other, or to the religious frame and capacity of those who beheld them.

Of the several believing women that had agreed, the night before, to meet each other at the sepulchre in the morning, after their Jewish Sabbath was over, Mary Magdalene was found to be first in keeping the appointment. That eager promptness was a remarkable and very beautiful illustration of the saying of Christ, when He had melted this woman's perverted heart and changed her bad life, that they to whom most is forgiven love most. She came very early, before the daylight had fairly divided the shadows of the olive-garden; she came alone; her love casting out the fear of the solitude, of the darkness, and of the soldiers keeping guard. As she comes close to the mouth of the tomb, a single glance shows that it has been opened. It seems to be the popular notion,—and many hymns as well as sermons have perpetuated the mistake,—that the stone was rolled away from the door by the angel *before* the resurrection, as if to open the way for the Lord's arising. But if you look accurately you see that the Lord's resurrection was self-accomplished and independent; and herein was the special proof of His divinity. In all other returns of life to the dead some visible outward agency wrought the miracle; but, unlike Lazarus and Jairus's daughter, Christ raises *Himself*: the omnipotence that first voluntarily yields, lets death have its way, and sleeps under that face of death, puts forth now its own mysterious energy, and the sepulchre is broken, not from without but from within. It is afterwards that the angel moves the stone, revealing the emptiness of the place, and the *fact* of the resurrection accomplished,—first seating himself upon it, as if to say, "You, hostile Roman sentinels, are now dismissed from your post; a celestial watch relieves you; the earthquake bids you be gone";—then passing in to sit where the vanished body had lain. Mary does not look into the chamber itself; but full of one thought only,—that the rulers in their spite have robbed the grave,—she turns back in her alarm and grief into the city to tell the disciples. Two of them,—Peter and John, run to the spot,—John outrunning Peter, Peter leaping down into the sepulchre to make the search more sure, and Mary Magdalene, having followed them out, coming up less rapidly, but arriving while they are there. What is especially to be observed, thus far, is this,—that although Christ had actually arisen and was there, these two men, Peter and John, did not see Him. They went back into the city not knowing what had taken place. And it is only then, when they have gone, that to other eyes than theirs, to another kind of nature, of finer mould and quicker sight, a woman,—a penitent, a soul in which the mighty wonder of another resurrection had been first achieved, weeping because they seemed to have taken away her Lord, and she knows not where they have laid Him,—it is to her that the Lord first appears. He speaks only her name, in that tone which, after she had heard it once say, "Thy faith hath saved thee, go in peace," she never could mistake; she knows Him; she cries "Master," with reverent gladness; and she throws her arms about those feet which she had once washed with her tears and wiped with her hair.

The second manifestation,—that mentioned in the text,—follows immediately after. Other women come up, with their spices and ointments. At the sepulchre itself they see only angels,—some of them one, others two,—giving rise to the differing statements of the different evangelists,—each one seeing according to her spiritual vision, her measure of faith, or her susceptibility to the message to be communicated. That message was that they should go and inform the apostles that Christ was alive from the dead. On their way the Divine Form meets them, speaks to them, gives them joy, and they, letting their clogging fears fly, fall on their knees before Him, cling to Him, and worship Him. Is it possible that a part of the motive for this holding Him by the feet, in a kind of convulsive clinging, was an apprehension that He was somehow to be again torn from them,—caused perhaps by Mary's repeating to them His strange language, "I am not yet ascended to My Father"?

It is not to be supposed that the impartial Christ, or the Christianity of His Gospel, literally prefers the one sex to the other. But He respects the nature of each, and does not abrogate the laws of that nature. Had this great principle never been forgotten, how much miserable babble the modern world would have been spared, and with what dignity woman might rise to her real superiority, in spite of the wrongs of men! To that one, therefore, which has the cleaner and clearer spiritual eyesight, Christ will disclose the first radiancy of His glory,—the lustre of His resurrection-face. In that sex which loves most, and therefore suffers most, and is perhaps capable of sinning most, He finds the faith-faculty most ready to recognize Him, and on that therefore,—as if in a kind of compensation for the first sin, the greater weakness, and the tenderer sensitiveness to all injury,—He bestows the blessing of the earliest benediction of His resurrection-voice. He makes women the private messengers, not the public preachers, of His Eternal Life; they are to tell it to His disciples, the disciples are to set it into a system and to proclaim it openly to the world. It is not till after many hours of thinking and wondering, of anxiety, scepticism, incredulity, weighing of evidence, and conquest of the reluctances of pride, that the slow masculine understanding comes up to faith at all, and finally concludes that it *must* believe. Even these apostolic men treated the testimony of the women, that day, as idle tales and believed them not.

But this is not all. The general spiritual distinction thus drawn between the sexes reappears, in its measure, between individuals of each of the two. And thus there is a similar advance of clearness in the other succeeding manifestations. The circle continually enlarges, from the solitary Mary to a great company of men, as they are gradually prepared to see and believe. Toward the evening of that same first day, Jesus joined Himself to two of the disciples,—evidently the more spiritually-minded of them,—on their walk to Emmaus;—but though He converses long and wonderfully with them and makes their hearts burn as He opens the Scriptures, yet their eyes are holden; and it is not till they are brought under the solemnity of the supper at the end of the day, as He blesses the bread, that they know Him at all. In the course of the same day, St. Peter, creeping slowly out of his doubts, is suffered to catch somewhere a momentary glimpse of the blessed countenance that had always such a mysterious power over him;—notice that he also is a forgiven penitent, and has a heart of such tenderness as is rare among men. That evening, at a small assembled company of them in Jerusalem, the doors being shut for fear, Jesus is suddenly seen in the midst. But they are still slow of heart, fail to recognize Him, take Him for a phantom, and are only convinced by the condescending demonstration to their very senses: "Handle Me and see; a spectre has not flesh and bones. Behold My hands and feet, touch them and know that it is I Myself"; and then, to make their faltering belief more sure, He eats with them. A week later, the same scene is repeated, only that Thomas's doubts are still more obstinate and are subdued only by the same patient proofs presented to His fingers and hands. Later still, there is a promised meeting on the shores of the Lake of Galilee; but there is something of the same slowness of recognition on the part of the fishermen, the same mingling of apprehension with belief. Still the circle of witnesses widens. On the Galilean mount, probably the same mount where He had been transfigured, he is seen of "above five hundred at once." Returned to Jerusalem, He gathers the twelve about Him to give them their great commission, and makes the appointment of the perpetual ministry with its inward grace and outward seal. The ascension is drawing near, to be followed by Pentecost. So He assures them, "Ye shall receive power after that the Holy Ghost is come upon you." With each new meeting, as you see, these interviews grow more and more natural. The disciples are less troubled and more at ease. At last, when all is accomplished, when they have become so familiar with His risen form as to be certain and trustworthy witnesses, and when from the outward evidence of the bodily senses they have been patiently lifted up to receive the finer credentials of the Spirit, the communion having become very close and very like that which they look for, through all their sufferings and testimonies for Him till His coming again, then He leads them out toward Bethany; the final words spoken, His form rises into the heavens; they cannot hold Him longer, with all their love, to the earth; henceforth they can only worship Him in that heaven of glorious life to which He is ascended, and from which they look for Him to appear once more.

Let us return now to that point in this series of marvels where the words of the text come in, and take out of them three or four great truths to carry with us into our life.

First is the certification afforded by our Saviour's resurrection to the fact of His divinity. "They came, and held Him by the feet, and worshipped Him." They worshipped Him; and He neither forbade nor checked that worship. Was not He the one true Teacher of what true worship is? Who so quick and sure as He to detect the slightest traces of sacrilege? Who was ever so prompt and so thorough in putting away everything that was not His own? He had said, at the temptation, "Thou shalt worship the Lord thy God, and Him only shalt thou serve." He had repeated to a scribe the fundamental dogma of the monotheism of the Old Testament. "Hear, O Israel, the Lord our God is one Lord." Yet He permits Himself to be worshipped. Either the very root and essence of His transcendent nature is so included within the essence and unity of God that He is God in man, or else He is a created being. If He is the latter, then worship paid to Him is profanation. If He is the former, then this accepted adoration of His followers is only a consistent offering of the faith He had Himself warranted when he said, "I and My Father are one,"—"that all men should honor the Son even as they honor the Father."

It is noticeable that two of the most unqualified declarations of Christ's essential deity were made to Him, and sanctioned by Him, after His resurrection:—this one of the actual paying of divine honors to Him, which was repeated by the disciples just before the ascension, and St. Thomas's hearty confession, "My Lord and my God!" We see in this just that steady development of Gospel truth which is most natural. Up to the time of His death on the cross, marvellous as the tokens of the Lord's superhuman character were, both in His words and in His acts, it was the human side of His nature that was kept constantly in view. A being having all the visible attributes of a man, subject in the body to mortal limitations,—to weakness, pain, fatigue, sleep, hunger, tears,—moving and feeling as other men move and feel, must leave on all about him the impression of a human nature; nor would it be very strange if the daily sight of these external qualities should partly obscure, for the time, the marks of a loftier origin and make a belief in His divinity difficult. But the sepulchre had now put a different aspect on all these mortal signs; the resurrection had transfigured them and, as it were, *divinized* them. It had never been heard before that a man lifted himself, by his own will, out of the grave and asserted his superiority to all the forces of destruction. Surely here must be nothing less than the Creator's majesty. The divinity broke through the mortal investiture. In the glorified form the "Son of God" stood revealed not less than the "Son of Man." They worshipped Him, and He received their worship.

Unless it belonged to Him, He must fall instantly in our esteem to a lower place than any modest, clear-headed reformer, or teacher, of tolerable self-knowledge, in all history; for no such human creature could endure for an instant to accept these honors. Henceforth to all the Church and to eternity Christ should be owned in the Christian creed and adored in the Christian heart, as " very God of very God." The resurrection sealed that doctrine. And so when we find it everywhere said in the New Testament afterward that the apostles preached " Jesus and the Resurrection," the meaning clearly is, they preached Christ in both His humanity and His divinity, and thus a perfect, almighty, all-suffering Saviour, —Jesus, the man, our brother, Mary's child, and *the Risen One*,—our eternal Lord and Judge. Begotten of the Father before all worlds! Begotten, not made, who for our sake became man!

Place beside this truth another. These faithful believers were not believers in a one-sided or ultra spiritualism. They "*held Him by the feet*, and worshipped Him." It is contained in the original sense of the latter clause, that they knelt down to Him. Here were two outward signs of a living faith, and the faith was evidently the more living for them both:—the touch and clasping of the hands, and bended knees. Both were welcome to Him who knows every secret spring of the soul's strength, and who replaces the dead formalism of the Jew with the vital forms of a spiritual kingdom. So two principles pervade the whole system of redemption, from end to end. The Redeemer conforms to both when, from being unseen in the heavens, He puts on our material flesh and blood, to reach us men. He conforms to them again, when, in that glorified body, after His resurrection,—which He has the power to render visible or invisible at His pleasure,—He yet lets the women fold their arms about His feet, bids the incredulous apostles touch and handle Him, and convinces Thomas by putting his hand into His side. He conforms to them both when He solemnly establishes the two sacraments and the visible ordinances of worship in His Church;—He gives grace, and its sign.

Again, a supreme value is set here, for the Christian life, on the Saviour's personal presence. To us, and to the Church for eighteen hundred years, that presence has not been corporeal; yet it has been literal and real. What would life immediately become, to any Christian who has really learned or even tasted what it is to live in Christ and to have Christ live in him, if that reality of *Jesus Christ present with him* were stricken out of his soul! What would his days of loneliness be, his times of depression and discouragement, when all that he has done seems vain and all that he tries to do unattainable, his hours of extreme suffering, his bereavements, his seasons of repentance or remorse? How could they be borne at all if we could not do as the women did, go to Him, hold Him by the feet, look into His face, be sure of His sympathy and His abiding love?

Men of action, men of thought, if any of you do not answer to this, or feel any reality in it, I do not know how to reason with you about it. We can only tell what we have seen or felt,—and that always very inadequately and feebly to those that have seen nothing and felt nothing of the kind. This much some of us cannot help seeing. Those institutions and movements in the world, however moral or religious their object, and however brisk their activity, seem to have no deep or strong or permanent life in them which are without this living and conscious connection with the presence and person of Christ, so as to draw their constant supplies of power from Him. Those, on the other hand, however few their numbers, or scanty their treasuries, or apparently insignificant their results, which are rooted and grounded in Him, animated by the daily breath of prayers to Him, in their members and leaders consecrated to Him personally, holding Him by the feet and worshipping Him, —these seem to have in them a certain tranquil and immortal power for good, and to be the salt of the earth. So too with the souls of men. With whatever good intentions, honorable aims, charitable feelings, and abundant energy, they that are without this conscious connection with the living and personal Head seem like streams, however full, which run from a cistern and not from the fountain in the hills. They have all that human goodness and zeal can have without that one secret and ineffable element of Christian love, eternal and inexhaustible; and therefore, while they are never to be judged uncharitably, they are not to be trusted as we trust what Christ holds in His almighty hand and stamps with His cross. He does not say to them, "All hail," and they do not hold Him by the feet and worship Him. More than that, some of us, I am sure, have seen this. A pure and aspiring heart, praying and struggling for a deeper peace than it has ever found, generous, disinterested, devout, yet always restless and always dissatisfied because not conscious of an embraced and worshipped Christ, at last begins, perhaps without argument or theological process, to open its spiritual eyes on the form of the Son of God,—to say, timidly and yet confidently, "I know not yet how to frame this trust in me into phrases and formularies, and yet I know that Jesus Christ is with me, is my Saviour, and has for me all the power and love I need; I am sure He lives greatly in me and for me, and that I live a little in Him; I know that my God comes to me in Him; I know that all I am capable of receiving of God I find in Christ; I meet Him in the furnace of fire; I have found Him at Gethsemane; I have felt Him when I was tempted in some wilderness; I have rejoiced to behold Him *risen* when I have walked among the graves of those whose lives have sunk away as water sinks into the sand;—yes, Him whom having not seen I love, and in whom though now I see Him not, yet believing I rejoice. I have known Him in the breaking of bread, I have heard His voice forgiving me when I confessed to Him, and His 'Be of good cheer, I have overcome the world,' when the world seemed to be overcoming me. All this is real to me." Whenever this has so been said, we must have felt, I am sure, that there was a new birth into an altogether different and higher life; and that this life in a man is precisely what the Gospel means for him, comes to give him, and what nothing else is. Blessed, oh blessed are they who whereas they have been blind, now so see! Define or explain their faith as they will, they have found out what it is to hold Jesus by the feet and to worship Him.

Finally, what we saw to be true of the several disciples in their witnessings of Christ's manifestations after He arose is equally true, only in a slightly different way, of His followers here. They that were spiritually best prepared, by affection, by earnestness, by sympathy with the spirit of His life and cross, and by love for Him, had the clearest and earliest disclosures of His glorified presence. It is just so now. They that are least occupied with themselves, least engrossed with a business that is all of this world, or with a social life and its fashions that are all afar off from the simplicity of His beatitudes, they that are trying to do and bear His will in their houses, they that are busy looking after His lost sheep, they that are ready to believe more because they use the faith they have, they that repent most sorrowfully and put not their boast in anything that they do,— these are the souls to which He will unveil the glory of His face, whose eyes He will touch and open that they may see more and more of His truth, and in whose hearts He will dwell as He dwells in no temple that is made with hands.

# WHAT IS HEAVEN?

*Second Sunday after Easter.*

"FATHER, I will that they also, whom Thou hast given Me, be with Me where I am."—*St. John* xvii. 24.

FROM the accounts we have of the teaching of both Christ and His apostles, they seem to have given less space than we might have expected to the particulars of the soul's condition after death. A few great, simple, commanding, comprehensive assurances are made to stand out before us, with outlines that are very sharp and foundations that are very broad and firm, like the mountain peaks of a country towards which we sail. The region around them lies indistinct, till we come to it; it is enough that the summits, with their heads lifted to the sun, tell us that the continent is there, with only some general intimations of its extent, and the mark of the shore. The fact of the Christian's immortality, the fact of the judgment at the entrance, the fact of the separation of the righteous from the wicked, the fact that this judgment proceeds on one principle, and that this separation is determined by one affection or the absence of it, the fact that afterward there are two parted families, each of them a social state, the perfect blessedness of the one consisting supremely in the fully recognized presence and love of the Lord, and the complete wretchedness of the other in absence from Him,—these are all. However much besides a Christian intelligence may reasonably infer or Christian hope habitually expect, gathering it up from scriptural allusions or natural analogies, these only are the established verities. They are taken out of the realm of doubt, or conjecture, and are settled, as the hills are settled. On these the Scriptures lay all the stress. Around and under them they spread out all that immortal land. To the faithful who seek by patient well-doing there shall be glory, honor, and immortality;—but tribulation and anguish to every soul that loveth and doeth evil. And yet to every Christian mind there must always be an intense interest in the questions that arise about that future life. It is not the intellect only, but the heart, that asks them. What kind of a life will it be? What is heaven? In what part of the universe will it be found? What will be its appearance or scenery? What can those occupations be that,—when this world and all its business and all its resources, its lights and shadows, its cares and comforts, have swept away into the common darkness,—will come in to fill up and satisfy the desires of the soul, forever and ever? Who will our companions be? How much of what we know and feel, and call "ours," in this present life, will in any form be restored or renewed to us there? Other kindred inquiries will occur to many of you as having visited and revisited your minds, dwelling there perhaps unanswered, till the silence became oppressive. Meantime, modern science pushes forward nearly all its investigations on the plane of physical phenomena and terrestrial life. Enterprise, labor, discovery, commerce, art, civilization,—these passionate and vigorous interests tell us nothing of the spiritual world, —which nevertheless girds and besets us all about, and hangs close above us;—they sometimes rather blind us to it, though they need not. And so, unless Faith lifts her hand and opens the veil, our life, whether intellectual or industrial, is all only a one-sided movement, and our souls are bereft of their grandest strength and peace.

Now, the New Testament has its own way of meeting all these questions. Instead of taking them up one by one, and attempting to give us particular information, —which we should, of necessity, from the difference between that other world and this, be unable to understand, and which would do little for us but excite an unhealthy curiosity and disqualify us for what we have to do here,—it takes us by the hand and draws us directly to Jesus Christ. It puts us into immediate communication with Him. It points us to His person. It persuades us that all the good we can hope for or receive will come from Him. It assures us, by the cross He bears, that all our sins, under which we were dying an endless death, have remission and cleansing through His sacrifice. It shows us in Him a *Love* that is infinite in its tenderness and patience,—but at the same time a Power to take care of us, a Wisdom to enlighten and guide us, and a Holiness to sanctify us, in equal measure with that Love. *Then*, when it has drawn and fastened to Him our supreme faith, so that we feel there is no really good thing that we can have or desire but it will come to us through Him, it begins to speak to us of the other world to come. It lets us hear Him say, "Father, I will that they also, whom Thou hast given Me, be with Me where I am." Heaven will be *to be with Him*, forever,—with Him in a deeper and larger and more perfect sense than we ever can be here; having a deeper knowledge of Him than is possible here, a clearer sight, a closer and more actual communion, larger receptions of His spirit. Heaven will be to see more, and more constantly, the wonderful richness of His character, its tenderness and grandeur, its purity and holiness, its glory and beauty. Heaven will be to comprehend more entirely what it was that He did for us when He so loved us as to give Himself for us, and what the suffering and the sin were from which His sinless suffering saved us. Heaven will be to be made like Him, fashioned into that mysterious and most excellent living image. "We know not what we shall be, but we know that we shall be like Him, for we shall see Him as He is."

Mark how the doctrine opens by this method. Heaven is not, then, as it is often represented, a mere appendage or supplement to this life, affixed to its end. Nor is it a foreign territory with which we become acquainted by an outside description, and then enter by a second existence. It is rather the perfecting and widening out of that *life of Christ within the disciple*, or of the disciple's life with Him,—whichever way we express it, for it is really both,—only in conditions of greater freedom and power. This life was "new" whenever we chose to take up our Christian privileges, and to treat them as realities. But whenever it began, once begun it is everlasting. Heaven is the great part of it yet to come, and we know it is by far the best part, because it will be more Christ-like. His spirit and His will must act with unhindered and unlimited power, through all hearts. The obstacles and drawbacks of sin and sorrow, remorse and suffering, of bad passions and misunderstandings, of weakness and guilt, of parsimony, pride and conceit, of disease and death, will have come to an end. You have held between your fingers in April a little black powder rubbed from the pods of a lily; and you have seen, at midsummer, the superb blossom that seems as if it might have been transplanted from Eden. That heavenly life so grows out of this Christian life here, as the perfect, splendid flower grows out of the small, plain seed in the dirt,—yet not by any law of material nature, but by the law of the Spirit of life in Christ Jesus. Heaven is not a place to which Christ goes as a foreigner, finding it heaven already. He makes it heaven. It will be heaven to any one of us only as we have Him *first* in our hearts. Heaven to us is included in Christ, as the less is included in the greater. It is the unfolding or flowering out of the energy of His Light and Love. We are not to speak of "going to heaven," as if that were the first thing; but of becoming one with Christ,—and then going to heaven will come in, in its time, as a part, the perfect part of that. Once united in living sympathies and affections with Him, so that we live for the same holy and blessed things for which He lives, heaven comes of course.

Christ himself says in His prayer that it *is now*,—not merely that it will be,—eternal life to know the Father and the Son. He tells His followers that He goes to prepare a place for them, that they may be with Him where He is. He says, "He that eateth My flesh and drinketh My blood hath eternal life." Everywhere He teaches that immortality is not a gift conferred from without, as when we are transported from one country to another, but that it grows up in the soul as the necessary fruit of faith and holiness. St. John says you may *know* whether you have eternal life by knowing whether you believe in the Son of God. None of the apostles has any conception of heaven and its happiness, except in direct connection with the presence of the Redeemer. The glimpses we have in the Apocalypse of heavenly employments always disclose Him to us as the Life of the place.

It may be inquired, whether this would not somehow confine or narrow down the range of the heavenly enjoyments. Would there not be a wearisome monotony in the unvaried celebration, through eternity, of *any*, the most glorious King, the most enthusiastically loved and admired Leader, or even of a Divine Deliverer? But it needs to read Scripture with only a moderate intelligence to correct any such impression. The sacred writers never meant to say that the total and uninterrupted occupation of the future state will be a literal offering of vocal praise, in song, to the Saviour. They freely picture that life under strong imagery. Worship will be there, as here, the highest and most satisfying act of the spirit. Think of the immortal sublimity of those celestial liturgies; of the great harmonies that will lift up the multitude of souls that no man can number, and of the real "marriage supper"! It will be the highest sense of satisfaction and rapture that we ever have in these services and sanctuaries on earth, multiplied and intensified ten thousand fold; and then it would not be strange if it were more frequent or longer continued. But we must remember that we shall remain social beings there, and carry all our individuality along with us, and have all the powers and faculties there that we have here. Of course they must be used. There is not the least reason to doubt that our actual employments in heaven will not only be loftier but far more diversified and wide-spread than they are here or than we can even conceive of their being made here. When any soul becomes inspired and enlarged with a personal devotion to the Saviour in this world, that certainly does not restrict its energies, or make its movements monotonous. On the contrary, every capacity is quickened by this grand affection. And so in heaven. Christian love being the motive of every act, the acts themselves may be infinitely various; and, thankful service to the Saviour being the delight of that Eternal Day, the service may show itself in such differing ministries as the busiest and most useful Christians here are not able to imagine; and there shall be among them things that God hath prepared for those that love Him which eye hath not seen, or ear heard, or heart conceived.

And yet, my friends, if we take any one of those great changes in our condition which we should all alike agree in considering the most desirable as we pass from the earthly to the heavenly state, and dwell upon it, we shall see how it must proceed directly from the influence and the power of the presence of Christ, judging only by what He revealed Himself as being and doing in this world. We should all desire, for example, an increase of the powers of life and love and motion. See, then, how when He was on earth He wrought just that invigorating and quickening effect on every soul that gave itself to Him, illuminating ordinary intellects in such a way that they became the teachers of all ages, turning mechanics into masters of the minds of scholars and thinkers, making a few fishermen the famous men of the world, and establishing among jealous nations and races a brotherhood that outlasts all their revolutions. We should desire exemption from what hurts and afflicts us here, especially from disease and death. Consider how much of the Saviour's time on earth was given to the removal of these evils, and especially that there is no trace of any such thing on earth as the restoration of life to the dead, since the world began, except through His interposition. We should long for a society where mutual charity would take the place of selfishness, strife, and over-reaching, as the principle of social commerce and advancement. And how plain it is, from Christ's teachings and sacrifices here, that just that blessed change must come in a society where His spirit would be the unresisted law. We should hope to be freed from sin. And who could doubt that He who left heaven and came into the world on purpose to cleanse and deliver it from sin would banish it forever from that heaven which is fashioned after His own likeness, and is the fruit of His own spirit? No night, no tears, no suffering, no sin,—what better marks than these could there be of a world where the compassion of the Son of God reigns without limit and without restraint?

Observe, in the next place, how this doctrine harmonizes with the fact that the Scripture representations of the heavenly world differ so much from each other. They differ because they are not literal but figurative; they are figurative because their object is not to inform the understanding but to animate the affections and inspire a glorious hope; and, for the same reason, these images are not made to be consistent with one another. God designs that we shall expect and desire the heaven He has prepared, not because we know in detail what is there, but because we trust Him, and believe that it is a world where the law of Christ has unobstructed and perfect sway. To kindle and sustain in us that faith, His Word represents heaven under images which, in their natural sense, are quite incompatible with each other. It is a city of gems and gold, it is an open country with trees and running water, it is a world with no more sea and it is a sea of glass, it is a house and it is an innumerable multitude of worshippers on a mountain top, before the throne. These are the helps applied to our feeble spiritual sense, through the imagination, which is the faculty most easily reached and moved, according to the whole practice of Revelation, from end to end. But we are not *left* to these uncertainties of the imagination. Underneath these there is a fixed and solid substance of revealed truth. To this truth every separate image points, exhibiting some one or another of its attractive faces. The truth itself is, that of that society of redeemed souls, glad in their infinite joy, Jesus Christ is the centre, the light, and the life. There is no discord or division there, because He is love,—and there,—as it is not here,—every spirit and the whole place take their law and temper from Him. Nothing that is defiled or that maketh a lie enters there, because He is pure and true. If the memory of the miseries of this life remains at all, such recollections will not be painful; the knotted problems will all be loosened and dissolved in the celestial chemistry of some strange, new light; for He has pledged Himself that there shall be no pain there. No sick-beds; no watching all night for the last breath of your child; no anxious question what that secret symptom means which looks like the beginning of the end; no broken friendships; no lost love; no aching heart; no bitterness of a rebellious and profligate child; they shall hunger no more. There will be no wretchedness of unfulfilled desire, of failure to do right, of unanswered affection, of baffled aspiration and poor performance,—because, having chosen Him before all, and got clear of all the earthly competitions and shortcomings, we shall have enough in having Him, and shall be satisfied with His likeness.

It is another and very practical blessing of the same doctrine that it makes large room for the differing notions and differing degrees of sensibility that Christian men may have, according to their constitutions and circumstances, about that next world. If you find your mind less disposed to dwell upon the pleasures there than the duties here, that need not trouble the conscience, provided only your devotion to your Lord is undivided, and your life is consecrated to the doing of His will. That, rest assured, is the main thing. Some of the most godly, self-sacrificing, and Christlike Christians I have ever known have never said very much about what is to come after death. Heart and hands and mind were all too busy doing the Master's work here, where it needs to be done so much, day by day. Other Christians dwell largely on that future, and gather a needed refreshment from the labor or the endurance of the present by anticipating the glory that is to be revealed. Of these, again, some fasten on one and some on another of the scriptural aspects of that coming world, for their consolation and encouragement, just as the Spirit of inspiration, suiting the supply to every necessity, intended they should. You meet these diversities constantly in the biographies of saintly men. Robert Hall said once to Wilberforce, "My chief conception of heaven is rest." "Mine," replied Wilberforce, "is love,—love to God, and love to every bright and holy inhabitant of that glorious place." Now Robert Hall spent a great part of his time under acute bodily anguish, and no wonder he longed for rest. Wilberforce, a man whose whole energies, in parliament and private life, were given to efforts for the realization of the law of love in legislation and society, naturally thought of the better country as a social state founded on the same principle. Intellectual Christians may long for the wider knowledge, when they shall see no more as through a glass, but face to face. Gentle natures, reading all secrets and learning all truth through their hearts, long and thirst for such measures of affection as they have waited for and never found among men. The evening before he died, the devout and profound German student, Spener, a reformer of his time, court preacher of Dresden, and one of the founders of the University at Halle, asked for the reading of the seventeenth chapter of St. John, saying that it never could be comprehended in this world, but that he was now glad to be going where all would be explained. Poor people may very well think of the abundance so often promised them in the resurrection,—like a woman in consumption I knew of, lying under a few rags on a heap of straw, who answered to the visitor's question, "Is this all you have?" "It is all, except Christ. It will do well enough; I shall exchange it very soon for His unspeakable riches." Strong-handed and enterprising people may wonder whether there will be enough to do there, and turn right eagerly only to the prospect of running on the active errands of their King. The parents of dead children cannot help looking day and night, to see the sweet faces and kiss the bright foreheads that are missing.

In all these varieties of expectation we find only the permitted, harmless workings of a law of our nature. They remind us of one of the serious sayings of Charles Lamb, that "the shapings of our heavens are the modifications of our constitution." They run into danger, and encourage irreligion, and undermine faith, only when they tempt us to put anything else in heaven before Him who alone opens it to us, or makes it what it is; when they dispose us to insist on anything whatever as *essential* to our future peace save what He may see fit to give us, or when they hide the one real and certain glory there behind mortal forms. It is a false and not a true Christianity which tells us first to be sure and get to heaven, sending us to Christ only as a means to get there and be happy. True Christianity calls us first to Christ, for what He is, and then tells us in its gracious promises that if we follow Him faithfully we shall be with Him where He is forever, satisfied to awake in His likeness.

No doubt, sad thoughts may pass through some of your minds about some of the dead, and anxious thoughts about some of the living, as to where this truth of the Gospel may leave them,—and with what a gulf of separation between. For the first, we had better dismiss them, committing all the departed,—and the more so, the more we loved them,—in faith, in hope, in charity, to Him who mercifully has all judgment assigned to Him, because He is Son of man, and has borne our infirmities. For the others, our anxious thoughts of the living that we love best, lest there should be some dreary separation hereafter from them,—only let these beget in us more faithful intercessions for them, more consistent and blameless lives to convince them, more of Christ reflected in our daily dispositions and conduct to draw them after Him. There is something excellent in the quaint saying of one of the most heavenly-minded of men:—"If I ever come to heaven, I may very likely see three wonders there: the first, that I shall miss many persons whom I expected to meet; the second, that I shall meet there many I never expected to see; the third, and the greatest wonder of all, that I shall be there myself." But, after all, this doctrine is not one that we can use to the best advantage for other men. It searches, it warns, it ought to purify and quicken ourselves. For, construct whatever other theory of immortality we may, so far as we look to revelation for our guide, and to Him who alone brings life and immortality to light, we have no glimpse or ray of light on any other heaven than that which is created for us by the Living and Risen Redeemer of our souls, opened by His cross, and entered through repentance and faith toward Him.

A few more holy Easter-times at most; a few more offerings of this struggling and broken worship, mingled with mourning,—"missing some one at a sacrament"; a few more strains of that

> "———sad mysterious music,
> Wailing through the woods and on the shore,
> Burdened with a grand majestic secret
> That keeps sweeping from us evermore";

a few more bright or clouded sunsets fading along the western walls of our earthly sanctuary, and then the curtains will be lifted up. Then no longer as through a glass darkly, but face to face; then the vision of the Countenance which no eye hath seen,—and the new song before the throne, that no ear hath heard! We know not what we shall be, but we shall be with Him, and we shall see Him as He is!

> " Oh the rest forever, and the rapture!
> Oh the hand that wipes the tears away!
> Oh the golden homes beyond the sunset,
> And the hope that watches o'er the clay!"

# WHY THERE WILL BE NO MORE SEA.

*Third Sunday after Easter.*

"AND I saw a new heaven and a new earth; . . . and there was no more sea."—*Revelation* xxi. 1.

THERE is this remarkable respecting the New Testament disclosures of the future life:—for everything that approaches definite details of description, we have to depend on the language not of our Lord himself but of His apostles. In the communications of both there is a conspicuous reserve; but it is most striking in Him who *is Himself* the resurrection and the life. There is no fulness of explanation. The picture of the Revelation is drawn large; there is no filling up of the severe, sparing outline. However much there is for faith, there is nothing for curiosity; and a great part of the message to faith is that we must wait.

This silence is the more significant when we connect it with two facts: First, the whole history of human thought shows that there is an almost irresistible fascination in that invisible country, lying as it does directly on the path before us, and closely related to the life we are living now; and this interest has always been found to be lively, in proportion as men's minds were active; second, we are urged up to these inquiries not only by the intellectual problems that meet us but by the homely troubles of the common heart; we have to deal all the while with a world where the graves of the dead occupy a large space in our scenery; where the alarm-bells of disease are ringing in some of our chambers every night; where memorials of the departed, who are felt to be *only* departed, not annihilated, color the atmosphere and change the look of almost every house, and where, around the death of more than half of those who die, there hangs a sad sense of incompleteness, capacities not yet developed, powers not yet used, aspirations not realized, and a work not done. Nevertheless, Revelation does lay a solemn stress on the fact itself of immortality. It creates a conviction in every Christian that he ought to pass through his whole course here with the eyes of his faith and hope turned forward,—a purifying influence from his future home perpetually breathing upon him:—what St. Paul calls "the powers of the world to come."

The farther we go on, however, in the examination of the matter, as it lies in the Scriptures, the better satisfied we shall be that the reserve spoken of has good reasons. The scantiness of information is itself a kind of instruction. We find that whatever is essential to *the beginnings* of a heavenly state is sufficiently disclosed: and as we have nothing to do here with anything else *but* the beginnings, it becomes plainer and plainer that we are under the safe leading of a strong Hand,—which is a master of all the mystery, and will be able to lift the veil as soon as we can bear the light that springs and flames behind it. In other words, in the New Testament, from Matthew to Revelation, just as in the steps of our own growing experience, the increase of information is gradual.

Look, for example, at the distinction, just alluded to, between the teachings of the Saviour himself on this subject and the comparatively enlarged expressions of His apostles. Observe that there is an order, a very striking and beautiful order, in the opening of the Truth. In the words of Christ, as they are written down by the four evangelists, only the fewest features of the great resurrection doctrine are unfolded. They can be mentioned in a moment. One of these is that the faithful will form groups of a single family, and yet be distributed into companies; because, Christ says, it is all our "Father's house," and yet there are many "mansions" in it; this introduces the animating idea of variety in unity, with personal characteristics, yet a single society;—that same grand result of diversity of operation within one all-including bond of law which science has been groping after so long, and which the ablest scientific men now begin to think they can catch glimpses of, as a single Force, in the kingdoms of nature. That recognitions will take place among those who have been spiritually and truly united here follows from every scriptural principle and intimation. But the one great fact on which all these others are made to depend,—that around which they are all ranged, and out of which they all grow, is that of our Easter-tide doctrine, that every Christian has his eternal and blessed life directly from his having been spiritually united with Christ before. This is the intense personality of His power, as the Head and Fountain of the whole spiritual creation. It will not be a pantheistic absorption of finite spirits in the Infinite:—the personality of every soul will be as sacredly kept and guarded as that of the Redeemer himself; for every one is precious in His sight. If I, the Good Shepherd, He says, "know my sheep," "I am known of Mine." It is a reciprocal intercouse, a seeing and being seen, a giving and receiving, a rejoicing of each with each. And yet such is the fulness and perfection of that divine life in Him, that all the immeasurable sphere, and all the countless differences of heavenly occupation, will take their quality of blessedness, and their peculiar light, from the glorious presence of Him by whose love each soul has been counted worthy to be saved, and is permitted to be there.

To draw out the more particular consequences comprehended in that truth, and to unfold its subordinate aspects, must be left to the twelve apostles, after the actual rising of Christ should have secured the doctrine in their minds.

We pass on to their testimony, and we see the same gradual order, only opening a little further. First these apostolic witnesses, as in the Acts, content themselves with preaching, wherever they can get a hearing, THREE GREAT REALITIES that are to convert the world and regenerate the race, *i. e.*, Christ the Living Man; Christ the One Sacrifice for sin, and Christ the Divine Head of a spiritual and everlasting kingdom, in which all live from Him. In their busy life of incessant activity and travel, proclaiming this Gospel and planting the Church from Jerusalem to Spain, there was room only for this, with practical exhortations to repentance and faith,—illustrated as it all was with those tranquil martyrdoms where they went cheerfully to death, not careful themselves about the lesser features of the glory beyond, but counting it enough to look up and see their Master, as He had foretold, waiting to receive them to Himself.

The next stage we reach in their epistles. As they sat in prison cells and thought out the sublime system of this "Faith" which they were delivering once for all to the saints, or as they saw the need of applying its fundamental principles to the agitated minds and practical necessities of the churches they gathered, they were able, through the Spirit's illumination, to offer some additional light on the questions that were sure to arise respecting the Christian immortality. So we find St. Paul writing to the Corinthians—who had thinkers among them—as in last Sunday's evening lesson, more especially of the nature of the spiritual body, and its analogies to the terrestrial or fleshly body, telling them how we are to be not unclothed but clothed upon, indicating somewhat the succession of events in the second coming and the general resurrection, and giving also to the Church, to kindle its *hope* through all ages, some magnificent glimpses of the heavenly *worship*, where there will be "no temple," only because the whole new heaven and new earth are one open temple, where the liturgies of the unnumbered multitude are as the voice of many waters, and the praise is unceasing.

Later still, however, just as the high strain of inspiration is about concluding, St. John, standing last of the twelve in this life, is suffered to raise the curtain of that which is to come a little further. What he reports, to be sure, is not all perfectly plain, at least to any eyes that have searched it hitherto; how could we, short-sighted scholars, and reading at best through a hazy and clouded air, be foolish enough to expect it would be? It is enough that mysteries are set partly open there which have stimulated the adoring wonder, and have fed the faith, too, of all the generations since the beloved disciple fell asleep. In this last Book of the Bible, the sketches of the celestial country are made more clear; we see a likeness there to what is brightest and best in our familiar landscapes here, which makes it seem more like a home that we should be glad to move into and take comfort in; the ranks of the innumerable congregation become more distinct; the anthems seem to grow louder as we listen at the door set open; and the very words of the "Thrice holy" of the great Supper are sent down to us, so that we might begin to use them around our earthly altars, in anticipation. It is a great deal, for example,—considering how often our bodies ache, and how often we have to watch over disease, and are tired out with our work and with seeing how little our work comes to,—to be assured expressly, and again and again, that there shall be there none of the torments that distress us in this flesh; that we shall hunger no more, thirst no more, burn with no fever-heats, never be weary, ache with no more pain; and that all these immortal liberties and enjoyments shall be given us, in Him, freely, as fruits of faith.

Now, it is among these most exhilarating and consoling prospects that we come to the singular expression of the text. St. John is faithfully reporting his vision; he tells, in the historic tense, what he had seen and heard; there could be no illusion about it. "*I, John, saw.*" Εγω Ιωαννης ειδον ταυτα. The first heaven and the first earth had passed away. A new heaven and a new earth,—not a new "heaven" merely, but a new earth as well,—have taken their place;—this must be to prove to us how close and real the connection is between this life we are living now with that which is to come after. But there is one unexplained change. *One* of the features of these earthly landscapes,—one of the most majestic and mysterious of them,—has vanished. "There was no more sea."

Where all the declarations of the Bible are so brief and yet so significant, we cannot afford to let one of them slip by, as if it were a mere superfluous metaphor. There must have been, to this inspired and eagle-eyed evangelist, some special and some religious meaning in this absence of the sea.

I recall, as one clew to that meaning, the situation where St. John saw the vision and wrote this Apocalypse. As he grew old in his episcopate at Ephesus, surviving all his fellow-witnesses and companions,—now sixty years after the resurrection,—the fury of persecution under the Emperor Domitian banished him from his ministry, along with many noble men and one consul of the empire, and drove him into exile. The *prison-house* that was found for him was a sterile, rocky, island in the Aegean, or Greek Archipelago, and his prison-wall was the "sea." There is an old Latin hymn that says:

> "Through Rome, infuriate city,
> From Caesar's judgment chair,
> They drag Christ's loved disciple,
> The saint with silver hair.
> To *desert islands* banished,
> With God the exile dwells,
> And sees the future glory
> His mystic writing tells."

Travellers point out a wild cave or grotto, on the southern side, midway up the desolate promontory, looking out over the waters of the Mediterranean, near enough to catch the roar and beat of their waves against the cliffs at the foot. It is not strange that tradition afterwards associated John's figure with the eagles. Here he received the "Revelation." He saw and heard such things as were never given to man, before or since, to see, or to hear, or to utter. He was in the Spirit on the Lord's-day. The Master whom he had seen standing by the Lake of Galilee in the day-dawn after the resurrection, His countenance now as the sun shining in His strength, with the same voice that had comfortingly said,

"Fear not," stands once more before Him. He is in the midst of the seven golden lamps, and in His hand, an emblem of the Churches, the cluster of those seven stars of the "Pleiades," to which the Almighty pointed the patriarch as the symbol of His everlasting strength, among which astronomy has since found the one central star around which the same Hand swings all the stars and suns in the universe. "I, John, who also am your brother, and companion in tribulation, and in the kingdom and patience of Jesus Christ, was in the isle that is called Patmos, for the word of God, and for the testimony of Jesus Christ. And I heard behind me a great voice, as of a trumpet, saying, I am Alpha and Omega, the First and the Last, and what thou seest, write in a book."

Now in that mingling of divine and human together which runs through the Bible, nearly every separate writing in it is stamped with the geography where it was produced. And so the imagery of St. John, which portrays the realities of the unseen world, is not less true to those realities because its features are taken from around that mountain of stone, sea-girt and solitary.

St. John writes of the blessed life of the new creation, where holy souls are at rest, that there is "no more sea." What *was* the sea, then, to him,—what is it everywhere, —that he should choose it to symbolize something that is *un*-heavenly;—something that is to be done away with when that which is perfect is come? The sea is that which sunders man from man. To St. John himself, as I said, it was a prison-wall. He looked out across it, homesick, towards the eastern line of coast where the friends he loved, the dwellings of Ephesus, the Churches he had planted, waited and mourned for him. There is no such wall of separation on earth as the sea. It divides nation from nation, as well as land from land. Whatever the original unity of the race, it breaks that unity apart. That is the very epithet that a Latin poet (Horace), who lived just before St. John's time, applied to it,—the "dissociable" ocean. It rolls in its immense barrier between kindred, between friends, and no longing of love can bridge it. Every voyager across it is practically an exile. The two forbidding, repellent shores cannot be drawn together by any clamps. If you stand on a bluff and let your eyes rest on any water where you can see no coast-line, one of the first things in your mind will be of something beyond; something you cannot reach. So long as the seas intervene, this is a divided world. The family of souls cannot be *literally* one;—the universal neighborhood and brotherhood at which the Gospel aims cannot be actually represented, till the first earth is passed away, and there is no more sea.

But if there is one thought that lies nearer the heart of the Gospel than any other, it is that of the perfect oneness, or flowing together, and living together, of the nations and souls of men. Prophets and evangelists promise, in the new Christian age, a reconciliation of what was estranged,—the absolute extinguishment of all the causes of division. The blessed bond of that harmony began, in fact, to be woven when Christ was born, and the angels predicted peace at His coming, at Bethlehem.

The old political constitutions were framed on the idea of exclusive rights. In Babylon and Persia and the heathen empires of the West, no matter whether Nimrod, or Tamerlane, or Xerxes, or Alexander, or Caesar was on the throne, selfish power was always king, and hate always prime minister. This very Domitian hunted the Christians through his empire, from jealousy of their rising commonwealth. He charged the two sons of St. Jude with plotting to restore the old line of David. They told him they were poor, hard-working men, and held up their hands, rough and black with the spade and soil. "What, then, is this kingdom?" asked the emperor. They answered, according to the annals, in the words of our text:—"It is a kingdom far away. We look not for it till the world is at an end, and our King cometh to make a new heaven and a new earth." With Christ every human government was to come under a new law,—disinterested charity. Instead of military aggressions there were to be missions of the Cross; for hostilities, hands of help reached out; for battles, sacraments. One was a civilization of conquest; the other of sacrifice.

We know well enough how slowly the consummation has advanced against wars, crusades, caste, slavery, the complicated injustices and wrongs of a selfish society! Hereafter it will not be so. Hatreds, suspicions, oppressions, cruelties, quarrels, are all to be swept away. *Men* will not crowd each other back from the places of privilege. *Women* will not envy each other beauty or love. Scholars will not rob each other's reputations. The tongue will stop its poisonous, garrulous business of detraction. There will be no "classes" in the celestial society, except such as move on agreeing and merciful errands about a common centre, obeying one impulse of love. The spirit of Christ's mediation shall be the reigning force. There shall be one fold under one Shepherd. All shall be like Christ, for they shall behold Him as He is; and sympathy will beget resemblance. There shall be no more separating sea. Another heaven; another earth; but "no more sea"!

So much for the society at large. Think, too, of the heavenly comfort it must bring to *private* hearts to have all the sorrows of personal separations ended. We know how much of the *pain* of affection, whose first instinct is to bring hearts that are alike *together*, proceeds from parting. In the perfect life to come, the pure and good, being always with Christ, will always be consciously and truly together. They "go no more out." To those of us that travel a great deal, or take leave very often of those we love, there is a special meaning in that phrase. We know nothing, to be sure, of the modes of movement or the means of intercourse there; but we know there can be none of those partings that have sorrow in them, no sad farewells, no constrained, untimely, and unwilling absence. A sick mother will not wait in agony on one side of an ocean for news from the bed of her dying child on the other. There will be no empty rooms that *feel* empty, or deserted hearts. There will be no melancholy embarkations, no looking out after receding sails, no watching for the last breath. Communion, fellowship, love, the *presence of the loved*, will be perpetual. There will be no more dividing sea.

There is a second character of the sea which probably likewise suggested it to St. John, for Christian comfort, as an image of what is of the earth earthy, and must therefore pass away before the coming in of an everlasting satisfaction. The ocean is all a field of nothing but barrenness. Those wide spaces of water, interposed between the lands, two thirds of the earth's acres, are bitter and fruitless. Nothing green or sweet or nourishing grows on them. They are literally what poetry calls them,—a "waste." Nobody makes a home on that restless, fluctuating floor. The sailor is a ceaseless fugitive. Nothing settles or abides on that restless breast. All the life it ever sees or supports is a transitional, passing life,—moving from one tarrying-place or coast to another. What an image it is of the fickle and transient elements of this world that now is, compared with the fixedness and stability and blooming life of that which Christ has opened!

More than this; there is a key to this second part of the meaning of the text in the closing passage of the chapter that goes just before. St. John has there been representing the last judgment: "I saw the dead," he writes, "small and great, stand before God; and the books were opened, and another book was opened, which is the book of life, and the dead were judged out of those things which were written in the books, according to their works. And *the sea* gave up the dead which were in it." The sea is a great graveyard. It is the home of the drowned and buried that it has swallowed up by thousands. One of its bravest vessels grinds against a rock in the night, and instantly it becomes a coffin, sinking six hundred bodies,—and two nations are full of fright and mourning. And it never allows affection to set up a sign where the dead go down. There is no harvest from it, except the harvest of the resurrection. But then, following this scene of the judgment is the new creation, and when the evangelist comes just after to speak of that, his mind goes back to the sepulchral sea. And lo! it is gone forever. There is no place in that universe of trustful joy for the hungry, insatiable, treacherous waters. "Old Ocean's gray and melancholy waste" will not be found around the "continent of living green." In other words, dropping the figure, that new world—the *Christian* home—is all a dwelling-place of life —life everywhere; life without sleep; life forever. Desolations and destructions are come to a perpetual end. If there is any appearance of the sea at all in that Apocalyptic imagery, it is the "sea of glass," on which the redeemed stand with their harps. Everything there must be as useful as it is beautiful, and as fruitful as it is fair. You may say there is a wild and wondrous beauty about the ocean; and no doubt in this material world it has its uses; but neither the Gospel in this world nor the evangelic descriptions of the next recognize any beauty that is not the source of peace, or life, or benefaction. Heathen beauty, Greek beauty, cold, restless, faithless intellectual beauty, must be baptized into the warm "spirit of life" in Christ Jesus, or there is no room for it in the heaven Christ opens.

> "Here below, imaginations quivering
>   Through our human spirits like the wind,
> Thoughts that toss like waves about the woodland,
>   Hopes like sea-birds flashed across the mind.
> Up above, the host no man can number
>   In white robes, a palm in every hand,
> Each some work sublime forever working
>   In the spacious traits of that great land.
> Down below, the Church, to whose poor window
>   Glory by autumnal leaves is lent,
> And a knot of worshippers, in mourning,
>   Missing some one at the sacrament.
> Up above, the shout of hallelujah,
>   And without the sacramental mist,
> Wrapt all round us like a sunlit halo
>   The great vision of the face of Christ."

Brethren, we must endeavor not to let the poetic dress of the doctrine blind us to its practical solemnity and spiritual power. But we do discover, under the image which the Spirit of God suggested to the seer at Patmos, two of the principal characteristics of that spiritual world where all of us, who are joined by faith to Christ, will very soon be going. It will be a world of undivided spiritual fellowship, and it will be a world of living and fruitful action. In still simpler and more comprehensive words, it will be a world of love, and a world of life. Both are intimated in the prophecy that there will be no more sea,—no cruel sea or barren sea, no sea to divide or sea to destroy.

I spoke of this prediction as having a practical effect. The best thoughts we can have about the future life are thoughts that make us better men now,—more fit to live under the eye of God, and in daily intercourse with our neighbors, just where we are,—kinder and purer at home, more just and honorable in business, more reverent and humble in prayer, more charitable in our judgments of each other. The metaphors and poetry even of an evangelist will amount to nothing, if we do not come to this. Unless we are very thoughtless indeed, there cannot fail to be a strong and salutary influence breathing on us continually by remembering this :—that we are so near, one day's march nearer every night, to a world that is *all love* and *all life*,—without selfishness and without death ;—and that world eternal. The prospect itself, if we realized it, would shed some new sanctity, it seems to me, over the life we are living. It would be more quickening and more sanctifying than any sermon.

But something more than this is also true. Everything that will belong to our Christian state hereafter has its root and its beginning in our convictions and our conscience, our affections and our habits, here. Your individual interest in this subject, and in all that can be said about it, depends on how much of the germ and sentiment of the heavenly service is in you already. Heaven will be only the outgrowth and completing of a heavenly character formed on earth. No one of us can plant the tree of life after he dies.

Property, business, houses, dress, and furniture,—the banks, and the warehouses, and the dividends,—they all seem strong enough, and half satisfying,—so long as there is nothing to take our minds below the surface. But there comes to us, one by one, a breaking up. God sends it, because He loves us. A sickness, a death, a failure, a broken heart or broken hope, shakes them all to pieces; and all at once the world feels hollow. Have you any hold, then, on another inheritance? What is that hold? Is there One stronger than the sea? The Son of God has walked in victory upon it. By Him we can conquer the bitterness:—for love is of God, and he that loveth is born of God, and knoweth God, and overcometh the world. By Him we can get the better of the unfruitfulness:—"Herein is My Father glorified, that ye bear much fruit." "The branch cannot bear fruit of itself, except it abide in the vine; no more can ye, except ye abide in Me." "And even now, being made free from sin, ye have your fruit unto holiness, and the end everlasting life."

# ALONE AT ATHENS.

*Fourth Sunday after Easter.*

"WHEREFORE . . . we thought it good to be left at Athens alone."
—*I Thessalonians* iii. 1.

ST. PAUL is speaking of himself personally. What he says here, in the evening lesson for this day, is that he puts upon himself the sacrifice of solitude in a strange city, simply because it comes in the line of his duty to do so, as a preacher and a missionary of Christ to men. To his tastes other appointments would be more agreeable. Some familiar place would suit better his passionate longing for sympathy. He is a scholar, and would prefer retirement. He is the scarred and worn hero of many hard battles, and would like to rest in the fellowship of some peaceful household of Faith. That he cannot do and be faithful; and this, with any honest soul, settles the question. Having formerly planted a Church at Thessalonica, a post of importance as lying on the great Roman road to the East, and a Macedonian seaport, he had afterwards journeyed westward, plunging, with the cross in his hand, into pagan Europe. Arriving at Athens, busy as he is, he remembers the affectionate little band he had left behind. So cordial is his feeling for them, that he determines to part with his only companion, Timothy, who is like a son to him, and send him back to "establish" them; and with him goes this touching despatch: "Now we live if ye stand fast in the Lord." To that warm fireside-circle of spiritual life this strong man's heart looks back across the separating sea, homesick, no doubt, but not a whit the weaker or less brave in God's work for that.

Turn a moment from that bright picture of primitive Church-fellowship in Asia to St. Paul's loneliness at Athens. Launching on his missionary expedition from the East, and sailing up among the islands of the Thessalian Archipelago, he had brought the new truth, to proclaim it in this capital of men's intellectual life. In his person, on his landing at the Piraeus, the morning light of the new age rose on a second continent. Yet everything about him was appallingly bleak, every face was unfriendly. Any courage less valiant than that of the Son of God in his heart must have quailed before the overpowering splendor and despotism of the old heathenism, in the very stronghold of its dominion. Athens was the brain of the world. The apostle had come to it, as fearless of its sophistries and arrogance as he had been of the swords and dungeons of Syria. He had come to say: "You classic Greeks, artists, poets, philosophers, are seeking after wisdom; but the foolishness of God is wiser than the wisest of you. One God made you; one Saviour died for you. Your Olympus is a fiction. I preach unto you Christ, and Him crucified, the wisdom of God and the power of God; your Saviour, if you will be saved."

Without some common interests, cities are wildernesses, and society is the saddest of solitudes. From the moment St. Paul's feet touched the pier at the lower end of the town, the monuments of the dominant mythology began to lift themselves forbiddingly before him, to make him feel himself "alone." His own heart burning with loyal love for the Shepherd of Galilee and Lamb of Calvary, the first objects that greet him, as he passes, a stranger, up the principal street, are the statue of Neptune with his trident, a sensual temple of the god of wine, and sculptured images of Mercury and Minerva, Apollo and Jupiter, with all the flaunting signals of an idolatry rooted in the prejudices and habits of centuries. Reaching the market-place, his sense of separation only deepens at every step. The buildings are memorials of a foreign history. Their walls are covered with paintings that celebrate barbarous exploits, and illustrate alien manners. Processions of disgusting ceremonies meet him on the way. If he looks up, figures of religious falsehood are hung out along the carved ledges and balconies. From the water-side, all the way up to the Acropolis, the city is one vast museum of unhallowed art, of an unclean civilization, of a Christless worship. If he turns from the world of sight to the world of thought, he finds the schools of unbelieving speculation, Porch and Academy, Stoa and Gardens, strong in great names to be sure, but distracted with debate between doubt and delusion, and full of eloquent error. The most that he could hope from any of them was that, after the glorious testimony to his Master at Mars Hill, they would set him down as a fanatical adventurer, advertising an unheard of sect,—a " setter-forth of strange gods." What was all this to the sorrowful, earnest, straitened spirit which was there in the form of a worn and sunburnt traveller from Tarsus, secretly so absorbed in the power of a holy affection for a Personage executed long ago as a disturber of the public peace in the distant province of Judaea, that he could say, "It is no more I that live; I have no life of my own; Christ liveth in me"? The round of festal novelties, the decorations of

Attic taste, the splendid learning, the subtle wit, the riches and refinements of a proud prosperity,—what would they all be to one whose heart was in the unseen court of the King of Kings, and who was willing to give his body to be burnt, or his blood to bubble for the One True God? Deeper and darker his solitude grew. And yet even there he could send away from his side the single sympathizing friend that had followed him; he could banish himself into a completer exile, and be utterly "alone at Athens," for the confirmation and comforting's sake of the little band of Christians far off at Thessalonica.

There opens out of this casual circumstance a matter of general concern in personal religion.

In God's appointments for us there are two kinds of loneliness:—one outward and physical, the other a loneliness of feeling, conviction, and character. Both of them have important connections with our Christian education and moral strength; and both have their dangers.

1. First, the providential conditions of life are so settled for very many persons that they have much less than the average share of social communication. Sometimes by a shrinking turn of the constitution, or by shyness or natural reserve, or by the lack of that magnetic quality which draws up sympathy and confidence from others, or by a fatal propensity to say the wrong thing and repel instead of conciliating, or else by necessities of residence or occupation, they are cut off from society. There is also a solitude of temperament, the inmost heart all the while yearning and crying for companionship, and yet strangely fettered, held back, and sealed up in a dumb secrecy, which the will cannot find out how to break through. There is a solitude of pride,

where social pleasures and advantages are voluntarily but bitterly given up, to escape making an appearance inferior to that of one's class, in the style of hospitality, dress, or equipage, or of literary culture and accomplishment. There is a solitude of obligation, created by the sheer necessity of unceasing toil, by filial or conjugal or sisterly devotion,—by poverty or pity imprisoning both body and mind alike. And there is a solitude of bodily infirmity or sickness

Among the perils of such a situation to Christian character we must set down a tendency to too much self-consideration. A continual confinement of attention to ourselves, or to those who by belonging to us become only a slight extension of self, belittles us. The soul takes petty proportions, sees with a narrow vision, and is warped to one-sided judgments. Finding nothing beyond self to fasten upon, affection settles back and stagnates or sours in the breast, till mere self-preservation becomes the end of living. Religion, though her hand is on the invisible world, will have hard work to save such a life from contempt. It has been the snare of all anchorites and monks and nuns. It is a spirit directly opposite to the charity and cross of Christ.

In other cases, from the same cause, we see censoriousness. Rigid standards are applied to other people's motives and conduct. Allowances are not made for unavoidable differences, and so, again, the first commandment, of love, is broken.

Along with these bigoted and intolerant ways of thinking comes envy, a morbid estimate of your neighbor's fortunes, and a cynical discouragement. *You* have never had, you think, your fair chance in the world. Companions that started with you at school have gained brilliant successes. Past the invalid's still chamber, out in the street, the children of health and wealth are rolling away to luxurious gayety. It needs a singularly steady faith in God's impartiality to keep down your discontent. So Martha felt her solitude when she complained to Christ,—"Carest Thou not that my sister hath left me to serve alone?" And so felt Peter when he asked, "Lord, and what shall this man do?"—contrasting John's brighter lot with his own predicted desolate martyrdom.

Add to these temptations that of a certain unwholesome daintiness or fastidiousness, which is apt to arise from constant preoccupation with private tastes, and is quite unlike the rugged readiness for Christian service to all the ugliest forms of humanity, in the good soldier of Jesus Christ. Grievances, in the long and gloomy hours of retirement, are nursed and exaggerated. Suspicions grow rank and poisonous. The hand is withheld from many a useful office, and the tongue from many a cordial utterance. Opportunities for Christian benefaction are despairingly thrown away, and life is miserably bereft of its true spiritual glory.

2. If now we look at the involuntary and moral loneliness, we shall see that while this too has its dangers, it may be made the occasion, as it was with St. Paul, of great spiritual gains and victories. It is indeed almost indispensable that, at some period of their lives, souls which follow Christ should be stripped of the support and separated from the countenance of company, and stand morally apart, without leaning on human arms or opinions about them; without popular honor; without much encouragement or sympathy, this side of heaven. It is one of the crosses which brave men, determined to be true at any cost, sooner or later have to take up. It is a school where strong principles

are planted, strong convictions are nourished, and strong energies are trained. Rules of action taken up merely out of deference to prevailing notions fluctuate with change of place and time. Those wrought into the conscience in solitude are more apt to come at first hand from God. Here is the test of courage, and of all *real* characters. Can you live, work, suffer, stand out, move forward, alone? Can you go where everybody refuses to go with you, and only the clear command of the Holy Spirit calls? Can you stay at your post, and hold your own, when the whole multitude, the class whose favor you prize most, the set that claims you, some of them perhaps as conscientious as yourself, decline, or retreat? This settles it whether you are merely a piece of movable furniture in the halls of a worldly society, a manufacture moulded by the hands of fashion, or a living and independent soul, satisfied to walk with that Man of men who had not where to lay His head while He was showing the world the truth and love of God; satisfied to live with the apostle who thought it good to be left alone at Athens, for duty's sake, and who tarried another time at Ephesus because, around the door that was opened to him to testify for Christ, there were " many adversaries."

In all the biographies of human greatness we find this proved by examples. I try in vain to think of one victorious and memorable saint who has not had, some time or other, the discipline of the desert, some seasons of awful retirement to a mountain, in a night,—away from where men are coming and going. It was there that these leaders of the world's life have gathered gifts from on high, have broken the bondage of ambition and vanity, and have come so close to Christ that His own sacrificial power entered into them. Men that have been much in solitude have generally been the heroic figures of history,—men coming out of the wilderness, back from deserts, down from the mount,—Abraham and Moses, Samuel and Elijah, David and John the Baptist. Out of the Bible no less than in it, it is remarkable how the master-men have been at some period lonely men. They had to break friendship with the average social morality, too honest for compromise, too loyal for the buying and selling of conscience, too pure for popularity, and therefore, after they had walked apart in the world with the Man of sorrows and solitude, we see them walking out of it at last with the triumphant step of believers who had kept the faith,—conquerors who finished their course with joy.

Hence, too, the defect you are sure to find in people that have never accepted or created for themselves these intervals of seclusion. They may be stirring characters but thin, loud but shallow, wanting in reverence and steady power, over-anxious about results and appearances, over-deferential to the popular cry, leaning upon social judgments, appealing to social maxims, never quite easy "alone,"—at home only in the "multitude" but afraid of the "mount," shrill men, easy to find, and serviceable in some ways, but with no deep, subtonic notes in their manhood, and no heavenly signification in their faces. Dr. Johnson, in his imaginary world of Oriental luxury, describes a merry feast, inaccessible to care or pain, "at which, nevertheless," he says, "there was not one guest who did not dread the moment when solitude should deliver him to the tyranny of reflection." A "tyranny" perhaps to the cowards who dare not face their own consciences; but, if society makes them afraid of self-knowledge and uneasy before God, society itself is the tyrant. Most gay companies have more or less of this covered foreboding and unrest in them: no music drowns it, and no smiles can make it beautiful. It is the earnest, hearty workmen, with God and for God, who know how to use society and how to welcome solitude,— how to take with equal joy active service for Christ in the world, or retirement with Him when He says, "Come ye apart"; how to be refreshed with fellowships at Thessalonica, and to be left at Athens alone.

If it is true, as seems to be generally agreed, that the evangelist's expression, "Many were coming and going, and there was no leisure," pictures in one vivid phrase the manners of our own times,—if it is an outward-living and fast-living and self-indulgent generation,—a noisy and showy age, then the Church never needed more than now to repeat her Lord's great doctrine of religious retirement and private prayer. The more engrossing our tendencies to secular arrogance and a mere surface morality, varnishing vice instead of uprooting it, the more watchfully you who are Christians ought to guard the sacred retreats of meditation and worship. This nation could hardly have been what it is, or done what it has, if our ancestors had brought up their sons and daughters in the glaring public parlors and refectories of a vast hotel. Strong character is a separate thing; and it requires a separate, individual nurture. Promiscuous intermixtures never produce it. It might very well be defined as *the power of standing alone;* single-hearted principle; independent abiding by the righteousness of God. And how we see the want of it everywhere, wherever men or women meet together; wherever majorities browbeat an unpopular faith; wherever the sound of many feet tempts you to join a crowd in doing evil; wherever you are likely to be a loser in money, or to be laughed at, or voted down, for not doing as those about you do,—staying away in your little Athens of hostility and desertion;—wherever Christ is on one side saying, "Come after Me, live with Me, suffer for Me," and the world is on the other side saying, "Here are mirth and ease, and here are wine and meat, and favors and good offers and fine establishments, and flattering notices of the public press." Righteousness never counts her companions. This is the heroic loneliness of all God's great ones from the beginning,—of Jacob left alone through the long night of his agony, wrestling with the angel, till he had power with God and prevailed; of Moses receiving his commission to emancipate and organize a nation, alone in the mountains; of Elijah, when he cried, "Lord, they have killed Thy prophets, and digged down Thine altars, and I am left alone, and they seek my life"; of Daniel in his exile, watched by an idolatrous monarch, kneeling three times a day with his face towards Jerusalem; of St. Peter when he answered the rulers, "Whether it be right in the sight of God to hearken unto you more than unto God, judge ye"; and higher yet, of Him who trod the winepress of His redemption so divinely and awfully alone as to exclaim to the most faithful of His followers, "All ye shall be scattered, every man to his own, and shall leave me alone; and yet I am not,"— never am, and never can be, utterly "alone, because the Father is with Me."

So St. Paul's striking expression opens its meaning. In three particulars, in order, we shall have the breadth and the point of the instruction.

First, the God of our lives puts into all of them some solitude, for a purpose of His own. Nothing else would do as well. He arranges it for us that we cannot be always in anybody's company. He keeps curtains about us, and drops them very often. Friend after friend departs. Something happens that tells you there is a space of mutual misunderstanding or want of understanding between you and the nearest and dearest heart on earth. There is a night between every two days. He ordains sickness, and shuts us in chambers, and sends us on journeys, and beckons away from us all our companions. Is it not plain that this is because the deepest and holiest exercises of the Spirit are where no human presence is by? Look back along your years past. If repentance ever took hold of you with its solemn hands, and held you still, and bade you look up for mercy; if the great choice between God and self was ever made, was it not when you were alone with your Saviour? The spot where the old selfish nature is cast down, and the soul passes from spiritual death to spiritual life,—the prodigal rising out of his hunger and husks,—is a solitary spot. Before the Spirit has done His deepest and best work in you He will have you all to Himself. The question of everlasting love is a private question: Wilt thou be Mine forever? The Bridegroom must stand at your heart's door when no human form, or face, or voice, can come in between you and Him. Each succeeding struggle, when we get the better of a besetting sin, when we wrestle with a fierce tempter and finally cast him behind us, when we make the terrible sacrifice which carries us clear of some entangling alliance or corrupting but fascinating acquaintance and sets our feet on a rock, or when God himself puts out His hand and cleanses us by some unsought suffering,—is solitary work. Conversions are solitary. Great griefs are solitary. The heart breaks "alone." When each one of us will hear a voice saying, "Come, walk with Me in the valley of the shadow of death," or a voice saying, "Come, walk with Me on the high places of purity and sacrifice,—arise and depart, for this is not your rest. Turn ye, for why will ye die eternally?"—it will be as if all mortal shapes had vanished from our sight. Salvation is an individual matter, and the starting towards it is in a desert place,—penitence, humiliation, self-surrender. Perhaps it is because in such separation from society there is an unwonted openness and honesty of mind which any human listener or looker-on would disturb. In this regard our communion with Christ only obeys the law of all lofty and delicate friendships. Intervention is interruption; and even the best society on earth is not good enough to divide your intercourse with your Master.

Secondly, loneliness sometimes becomes lonesomeness;—the excessively secluded life is embittered by a craving for sympathy. That would have been St. Paul's feeling at Athens, and he would have thought it not "good" but bad to be left there, but for the one Divine Friend who stayed with him. It is in *His* felt presence and affection, and nowhere besides, that those hearts are to find their consolation which are imprisoned in an unwilling separation from their kind. However thronged the streets, or however brilliant the season, these uncheered souls are all around us. Say what we will, and bear it nobly as they may, it is a daily crucifixion; and if we are not touched by it we are not Christlike. It is small comfort that you are not "interrupted" in your monotonous isolation, if all the while you have an aching imagination of a *possible* interruption which would call out every energy and aspiration within you into generous action. By far the greater number of us have hours when we long for nothing so much as to hear some fellow-soul say,—"I know how you suffer; I see your struggle; bear up; struggle on; one heart at least answers to yours." There are constitutions finely tempered which need continual protection, but have it only under coarse, sordid hands,—lacerating wherever they touch. There are self-distrustful, timid creatures, tortured with a despairing sense of failure and fatigue, who get never an encouraging look or reassuring accent. Oh, this is a loneliness that makes every other meaning of the word weak,—colder than Polar winds, and bleaker than Siberian deserts. What is the comfort? Only one. For all these the Man of Sorrows is the only companion, and His hidden love the only consolation. What would Athens have been to Paul but for his Saviour? Draw nigh, O every solitary soul, to Mary's Son! Let Him draw nigh to you; He understands the most reserved. He knows your unutterable secret without the telling, infinite in tenderness. He has watched your silent war, and waited with your waiting, and carried griefs just like yours. "If any heart will open the door to Me, I will come in, and My Father will come."

Take it finally for your encouragement in your more secluded and least noticed services for Christ, that His blessing rests upon you as graciously in your obscurity as upon the most conspicuous of His workmen. Paul the despised missionary at Athens is as sure of his Saviour's presence and benediction as when the priests and populace of Lystra are crowning him with garlands and ready to worship Him with their sacrifices. We are slow to learn that the spirit of the Gospel is no more in the assembly of ten thousand than where one tired laborer watches by the sick orphan child in his neighborhood all night, or one daughter of fortune and culture cheerfully crucifies every taste, every Sunday, to teach a group of unclean vagabonds how to pray to their Father, and how to live purely for Christ. We hurry into publicity, as if that were heaven, and are impatient to count converts and see results, as if that were salvation. Not among the thunders and blare of popular acclaim, but away from crowds, in nooks and corners of the earth, close down to the roots and fountains of the world's welfare, are offered day by day the worthiest sacrifices of Christian love. The most glorious chronicles and monuments of Athens,—called "the garden of great intellects,"—are not in her letters, her temples, or her arms, but are in that little record of the bent and friendless traveller who thought it good to be left there alone, to lift the cross, to herald a kingdom not of this world, and to preach,—"to the Greeks foolishness,"—Christ the wisdom and the power of God.

We reach then the one great principle which is the same for both parts of our Christian life,—the hours of retirement and the hours of action,—the soul in secret and in society. There is such a thing, attainable to us all, as a living heart of loving faith and faithful love which beats steadily for God and man, whether in the unsympathizing streets of a foreign city, or in the warm circle and communion of kindred souls at home,—out in the world, or around the altar. When Christ said to the weary disciples, "Come ye apart and rest," did He say, "*Stay* apart? Scorn society? Escape, like a sentimental hermit, from mankind, because mankind are bad"? Never that. "Rest *awhile*." But when the noisy comers and goers, fainting, sinning, dying, needed His gracious ministries again, he broke up His rest and went back to feed their hunger, to heal their sick, to wash their feet. When the people pressed upon Him out of their cities, and cried to Him, He had compassion on them, and came down from the mount, because they were as sheep having no shepherd; and then Master and disciples went on their way of work together. Our religion is one half the loving adoration of God; the other half is the loving service of the brother whom we have seen; our fellow-man. Get down on your knees, alone, or you will begin no work aright; and then up, and be doing!

Our Lord gave it for the *Creed* of His Church that faith justifies. He gave it for the *life* of His followers that faith without works is dead.

# THE HUMAN SOCIETY IN THE CITY OF GOD.

*Fifth Sunday after Easter.*

"THUS saith the Lord of hosts: There shall yet old men and old women dwell in the streets of Jerusalem, and every man with his staff in his hand for very age. And the streets of the city shall be full of boys and girls playing in the streets thereof."—*Zech.* viii. 4, 5.

I FIND this remarkable prediction in one of to-day's lessons, in the midst of a passage where a great Hebrew prophet is encouraging his countrymen in one of their dark days with promises of a bright time to come, when the desolations of war and famine shall be repaired, and a prosperous population will flow back into the empty highways. The dear old capital, the centre of their reverential affections and seat of their worship, beautiful for situation and holy for its history, will put on its thriving look again, and be the same blessed home to them that it was before. The words used are so vivid that the writer seems to become an inspired artist;—with a few clear strokes and strong colors he paints a fascinating picture of that coming glory of his nation, so that we, standing here so many hundred years afterwards, find it as fresh as if the artist's hand were just moved aside from the canvas. How thoroughly human the figures and impressions of that Bible-picture are; and how lifelike they represent our religion to be! For observe, first of all, this was the city of God,—a city that He has fashioned and filled after His own design, just as He wished it to be. This future Jerusalem was no mere mortal metropolis, built by human ambition, or populated by some sordid colony that had said, "Go to, now; let us go to such a city, and buy and sell, and get gain." It was to be modelled after a heavenly pattern. It was to embody the Divine ideal of a perfect, pure, and happy state. In the verse before, the prophet had told us this in the plainest language: "Thus saith the Lord: I am returned unto Zion, and will dwell in the midst of Jerusalem; and Jerusalem shall be called a city of truth; and the mountain of the Lord of hosts the holy mountain." There is no mistake, then, in the city's composition, and no accident in its arrangements. If the Lord does not mean to have old men and old women in it, they will not be seen there; if boys and girls are found playing in the streets of it, we may be sure they did not stray in as vagrants, or get dropped there as foundlings; they are there by the express appointment of the Father of all the families of the earth.

We may take these sentences, therefore, as a graphic outline of what God would have a Christian state of society to be, not in heaven, but in this world. In the scriptural imagery, or symbolism, Jerusalem is a type of the Christian Church. Where the Gospel of Christ has done its perfect work, where Christianity has realized itself in social institutions, and has penetrated all our private and public life with its practical regulation, there the whole of our being will come under its control; all its periods, from childhood to old age, will take the stamp and bear the fruit of this holy and gracious power in the heart; every capacity in us will be invigorated to its best exercise by Christian faith; our common work,—the handiwork of the husbandman and mechanic, the intellectual work of the scholar, the housework of woman, the shopwork of the trader,—will be better and safer and happier work for being done in the name of Christ, for the sake of Christ, out of that living union of the heart with Him which makes Him the real life and power of all our daily service,—done by a Christian will, with a Christian purpose, in a Christian spirit, with Christian hands and brain and feet.

And thus you have the subject before you. It seems to me to be greatly needed. There is, here in the midst of us, and everywhere about us, a painful and almost unaccountable separation between the vague notions about religion that float loosely through men's minds and those great interests and employments which occupy them from morning to night, six days of every week. It is as if a farmer should dig a deep trench, or build a high wall, between his granary and his table—spending the bulk of his time in gathering in his harvests, but then locking them up in barn and cellar, forgetting that they grew for the daily nourishment of the body. Our faith is really the bread of our life. This Word of God, what is said of it? "Men shall not live by bread alone, but by every word that proceedeth out of the mouth of God." Moses wrote that on the threshold of one great religious dispensation in the world's history, and Jesus Christ repeated it, at His temptation, at the opening of another, and He added, "I am the Word and I am the Bread." The substance of the creed you confess is not like a pew in church, or a Sunday suit that is put on and off, to be seen or occupied only when the labor and struggle and trial of life are interrupted; it is just as much meant for our soul's food as the corn which God's sunshine, soil, and air have ripened all Summer is meant to sustain the bodily forces that till and gather it. This Church is meant to open straight into your homes. The ideas you receive from the pulpit are not merely for the attention of the moment, for criticism, or entertainment, or a topic of conversation as you walk home from the sanctuary when the service is over. They are the seed-grain that is scattered on the ground, not to die there, or be caught away by birds, but to sink in, to act on the heart and be acted on by it, in the spiritual chemistry of assimilation and reproduction, to take root and get fastened there, to bear the blade and the ear. These prayers and sermons that he has heard ought to be found *in* every worshipper, a part of himself, absorbed into the constitution of His character. If not, how are they much better than the Chinaman's praying-mill, or the counted beads on the Romanist's rosary? I know of nothing in the whole religious condition of the people more wanted than some sharp sword of the Spirit to cut this curtain asunder that hangs between our abstract and speculative religious belief and our ordinary intercourse with men, hiding the one from the other,—some storm of holy light that shall smite through this artificial, half-atheistic wall of partition between a passive faith and an active operation of that faith, in secret dispositions and out-of-door doings. The men and the children in the street, as the text says, should be the constant signs and witnesses of the kingdom of God within them,—men about their business, children at their play, so toiling and trafficking, or so playing, if you please, as to make it plain that the stamp of the regeneration is upon them, the image of Christ within them, all citizens together of the great unseen city and commonwealth of new-born souls, baptized into Christ, and bound to His resurrection, having their conversation *in heaven and here* at the same time. There is nothing in our domestic habits, that I know of, too small to bear this stamp and seal of the law of Christ, nothing too commonplace to be a test of sanctification. If every disciple's love and loyalty to Christ went into the least of his transactions, making his speech gentle and pure, his bargains immaculate, his temper as even as that of Him who when He was reviled reviled not again but suffered patiently, his whole treatment of the world a testimony to the cross, why then you could judge a man's faith as you judge the growth in your orchard. Give the comparative anatomist the smallest bone of a bird, a fish, or a quadruped, that has been buried a thousand years, and out of that fragment between his fingers he is able to describe the entire creature, to name and classify it, and draw a likeness of the living body. If we Christians were as much alive with Christ as the apostles were,—as we certainly ought to be alive with Him who died for us, and who if He becomes our indwelling Saviour changes us from glory to glory,—we should hardly need our written covenants and formal professions; for every hour's life would be an embodied article of our creed. Then there would not be, as now, three classes of men, —unrenewed men on the one hand, true Christians on the other, and between these, a set of professing Christians whose whole Christianity stands in their profession; there would be only two armies, each under its own leader and banner—for Christ or against Him. In fact, every hour of our life *is* an embodied article of our creed; though it may not be the same creed that the tongue repeats. The tongue may say: "I believe in God the Father Almighty." But what if your life only says to your neighbors, I believe in myself and this world, in good bargains and paying investments, in getting the most I can and making it more, or in entertainments and dress and admiration? Is it likely that either your neigbors or God will be deceived?

They are not deceived. And this reminds us that the case is really worse than we have yet put it. We have spoken of inconstant and inconsistent religionists. There is another class which is largely created by them. In all these villages and cities there are a great many men who treat the whole system of positive Christianity, both doctrine and ordinance, with indifference. They live by the side of Christian institutions very much as they would live by neighbors speaking another language and following different pursuits. They pass the church door, but never go in. A Bible lies on their table or shelf somewhere, but it is let alone as if it had no message in it for them. They hear the ringing of the Sunday bell, but it stirs no Christian gratitude and signifies no Christian hope; the notes ring out and die away, freighted with no hallowed associations, kindling no premonition of "the rest that remaineth for the people of God,"—as unmeaning to these souls for which the Eternal Shepherd came as they are to the ears of the dumb cattle that eat and sleep on the Summer sod, and are buried under it. They never acknowledge any acquaintance with Revelation, in the street, nor invite it to their houses, till that one guest pushes in which they hold at bay as long as medicine and fear can do it; and then, inconsistently enough, they ask in, to meet that dark stranger on the way to the graveyard, the minister of the risen Christ, whom they had disowned all their lives. Now, no believer in the reality of his Faith, whether he be minister or layman, can look this strange problem in the face without painfully asking the question, again and again, What does it mean?

How does it come about? What can break up this strange and heathenish unconcern? The faith in Christ, the trust in God, the expectation of immortality, the love of the Church, for which we care more than for all the rest of life together, is nothing to those brothers and sisters, who, nevertheless, are made just as we are made. Solve us this mystery, O science or philosophy, and we will crown you as the prophets and interpreters of the secret things of the mind of man!

I do not pretend to suggest here the whole explanation. If we believe the Scripture, which knows a great deal more of us than we know of ourselves, the sad reason for much of it is the natural disrelish, in a selfish and self-indulgent character, for an unselfish, disinterested service; the natural man discerneth not the things of the Spirit of God; a life of appetite and accumulation, *i. e.*, has nothing in common with the glorious inspiration of the spirit of the Cross. Grant this, yet it does not cover, by any means, all the cases. Now and then one of that sort of men breaks the silence, and gives you, frankly, a different account. You find there has grown into his mind,—perhaps from mistaken and one-sided instruction, a settled impression that this whole matter of religion lies aside from his life, and apart from its vital interests. With those that have it, he tells you,— and he sincerely thinks so sometimes,—religion is a class-concern, or a periodical and occasional concern, at any rate a partial and narrow concern. It lays hold only on a peculiar and exceptional faculty in the mind. It takes a man, if at all, by unusual ways, ways over which his will has no control. It comes to some, and not to others, and those others must be excused. It is like the arbitrary gifts that make a man a mechanician or a poet,—that fix the complexion of his face or the color of his eyes. It lies off from the great body of his manhood or his business,—and is therefore not to be gone about, bred in, and made a part of every man's substance and best life, by any intelligible, practicable means. There is much of this sentiment abroad, and it kills, in not a few, all effort to be Christians.

Let us meet it as directly as we can. Nothing will be more convincing, in exploding the error, than a daily demonstration, in our own persons and conduct, of the opposite truth. We turn and look into the face of Christ as He walks the world in the majesty and beauty of His holiness. Is there anything there that looks like a class-piety, an occasional or intermitted sanctity, a faith for some exceptional souls, a limited salvation? No. All our humanity, every faculty, power, capacity, affection of it, is taken up into Him. His blessed incarnation, His coming in our flesh, includes everything that is in you and me. Until every element and fibre, every faculty and power, in us, is reached by His redemption, touched with the beauty of His righteousness, and made new by His transforming grace, we are not entirely His, —not complete Christians. He speaks, on the mount and along the hill-sides and highways and lake-shores of Judaea. Do you gather from anything He says that His followers are to have two divided lives, serving mammon a part of the time and God a part, the world with their business energies, and God only with some sentimental states brought out at special seasons? Does He say, Come unto Me, a part of you who labor and are heavy laden,—or, Let here and there one come? Does He say that He died for a portion of His Father's family? Which one of our faculties, of intellect, heart, or will, does He set apart, and say, My coming and My Gospel and My righteousness have nothing to do with that?

Analyze the very essence and marrow of the Christian life. What are the parts of it? Faith, Hope, Charity. Is any one of them a class-possession? Christianity is too divine and bountiful a blessing to be so hedged in and misapprehended. It intends that every man and woman and boy and girl shall be the better for it, and every corner and instant in the character and life of each shall be the better. It comes to make better workmen as well as better believers, better men for the life that now is and for that which is to come,—better citizens and neighbors, better husbands and fathers, better parents and children, better boys and girls. It would make strong men more manly, pure women more pure, light-hearted children lighter-hearted, because the love of Christ casts all fear out. The unseen city it is silently building is a city of truth, the mountain of the Lord of hosts, the holy mountain. Old men and old women shall dwell in it, and it shall be full of boys and girls playing in the streets thereof. It *comes down*, to be sure, like a bride, out of heaven, from God. But although it descends from above, it is human in its adaptations; it is a dwelling-place for just such people as we all are; human feet walk in it; human voices are heard along its avenues; human comfort lights its windows. The Gospel is sent into the world just as the world is. It is not some other race, but ours, in its own flesh and blood, in its habitations and occupations, that the Saviour comes to teach, to purify, to redeem, and to train up for His future service,—that heavenly labor which is perfect rest.

Accordingly, we must expand our ideas and give them life, by corresponding convictions of the *way of coming* to Christ and being made one with Him in this world. The pathways that run up to that Jerusalem are not all of one pattern, or graded after one scheme. It is enough that each one starts just where each one of us who is to travel it is found, and that they all end at the same Master's feet. It is a very simple road. Theology becomes only a blind guide when it complicates and mystifies it, and puzzles the unsophisticated mind with metaphysical cross-examinations. Do you *want* to be a Christian? Then you have already begun to be one,—but you have only begun. Do you wish that Christ were even now dwelling in you, with His glorious, animating, and satisfying presence, giving peace and power to your heart? Then have no misgivings or doubts that the motions of His Spirit are already stirring your soul, and that all you have to do is to renounce the sin that prevents His perfect entering and abiding, and believe that He is waiting to bless you with life everlasting;—repentance and faith. Do you say, in your timidity, that you wish you hated sin more? Be encouraged; what is that wish but the hatred and the repentance, in their first, feeble, incipient stage? What these feelings need is religious nurture, to grow, to strengthen, to have food and air and light and exercise. That religious life is yet but a little child, like one of the children in the streets of the new Jerusalem,—and it needs to be treated as little children, with their little life, are treated. Where shall this be done? Outside the Saviour's fold, or within His fold? Put the question in another form: are the flock and the lambs fed out in the wilderness among the briars and the rocks, where,—as I remember seeing it once in a very striking picture,—the poor creature lies caught and tangled, torn and bleeding, in the thorns, with the vulture wheeling slowly in circles up in the air, waiting for him to die, and the strong sea beating the rocky precipice below, and the shepherd is seen slowly climbing up, and looking everywhere, his own hands bleeding with the briars, his own feet torn with the edges of the rocks,— is that the place for the saved wanderer to be fed, to be healed, and grow strong? No. The Shepherd layeth it on His shoulders rejoicing, and carries it *home*. That is the place. Where is the Christian's home, but the Church? But you say you are afraid you have not faith enough to enter there. Listen to an old singing saint who knew the human heart through and through:

> "He that lacks faith, and apprehends a grief
> Because he lacks it, has a true belief;
> And he that grieves because his grief's so small,
> Has a true grief and the best faith of all."

The greatest part of salvation on our part is in the being willing to be saved. The great road to heaven is the taking up of the work, just as we take up any practical and earnest work, into which our whole heart goes. I fear we cover the matter up, and spoil the simplicity of Christ, with over-much will-work and system-building, and over-many requirements that Christ never laid down. I fear it more and more, the longer I live. The great ideas that the modern mind of Christendom needs to grasp and realize are the simplicity of the conditions of Christ's salvation, the practical character of faith, the fitness of Christianity to all the relations and positions of human life, the need and value of the Christian training of the young, and the using of the visible system of Christ's Church for that end. I join the Master at the beginning of His ministry. I see how natural and plain it all was. He showed Himself to men, and they loved Him. He spoke to them, and called them by their names,—Philip, Nathaniel, Andrew, Peter, James, and John. One by one they turned and hearkened. He said, Follow Me. They followed Him, attracted to

Him, and seeing something in Him that drew them on. He began to teach them, and as soon as He began, what He told them of was the kingdom,—the home, the family circle of Faith, where they were to learn to live and love and grow in Him, and become one in Him; the city of old and young. Oh if those unbelieving and indifferent men and women could only see how plain the way is, and how full of human joy and blessedness that divine city is, and how suited its ordinances of prayer and scripture and sacrament are to call out all that is best in them, and build them up into free and strong and noble souls, they could not stay away, or wait outside. They would say this day, "As for me and my house, we will serve the Lord."

Yes, as for me and my house! The children were seen by the prophet in the streets of the new Jerusalem. Christ has work for all of them to do,—gladness for all of them to feel. The city is wide and wide open. The old men and old women are there,—every man with his staff in his hand for very age. It is a healthy place then, a place to live long in. Between these two extremes,—the old man leaning on his staff and the boys and girls playing in the streets,—all the periods of human life are compassed, and so our blessed Faith is suited to them all. It is a comprehensive Faith. It comforts, guides, enriches, sanctifies them all. The city is a place by itself; a holy place; yet it gathers into it all souls that will come in by the door. You know who it was that said, "I am the Door of the sheep; by Me if any man enter in, he shall go in and out and find pasture."

Blessed are they that do His commandments that they may have right to the tree of life, and may enter in through the gate into the city. The Spirit and the Bride say, Come, and whosoever will, let him come!

# THE HEAVENS OPENED.

## *Ascension Day.*

"AND behold a ladder set up on the earth, and the top of it reached to heaven; and behold the angels of God ascending and descending on it."—*Genesis* xxviii. 12.

"Verily, verily, I say unto you, hereafter ye shall see heaven open, and the angels of God ascending and descending upon the Son of Man."—*St. John* i. 51.

"No man hath ascended up to heaven, but He that came down from heaven, even the Son of Man which is in heaven."—*St. John* iii. 13.

You are struck, first of all, in these transactions, with the fact that they all lie entirely apart from everything known to us in common history, or ever experienced on the level of this world. The heavens, generally shut up in close reserve and inexorable silence, are set open to the eyes of men; beings called angels are visibly passing and repassing; supernatural creatures are coming on errands to Christ and going from Him, He being at home in the midst of them, at once their object and Master; and finally this Lord himself is shown coming from heaven, and going up into it. Highways such as run between two of our earthly cities we see travelled both ways between this planet and the new Jerusalem. Outside of Revelation, we shall all say at once, there is nothing like this.

Materialism is our first danger. Church building and

the Lords's Day, prayer itself, ministry, creed, ordinances and sacraments rest on a belief in a supernatural world full of supernatural life, or else they are a slowly perishing pretence. If that faith in unseen beings and an unseen country dies, however silently or gradually, the whole fabric of what we call religion becomes a solemn unreality.

Before joining the several passages just repeated together, and drawing from them the comforting instruction of their joint doctrine, we will look at them a moment separately. Each of them pertains to a human person and place, and while what is written in them all alike is surpassingly sublime, the record of each one has a beauty peculiar to itself.

In the first, one of the principal characters in the earliest period of the world, a patriarch, being on a journey undertaken in obedience to God's special command, sleeps, after the Oriental fashion, in the open air, either under a light awning, or with no other tent than the sky, the stars in sight. The contact of this man with the sights and sounds of material nature is as direct and free, therefore, as that intercourse of his spirit with God which this out-of-door condition of things about him symbolizes. On one of these nights of Jacob's rest, the time comes when a promise is prepared for him. In an age of the future so far away that his thought can grasp no clear conception of it,—when the sinful and sorrowing race of men shall have learnt, by long trying and by many tears, how little it can do of itself, when the bad choice of the first pair has borne bad fruit enough, and when the time appointed of the Father is fully come,—then a descendant of this Jacob shall be born, of such a new and universal power of life to save men, that in Him all the nations of the earth shall be everlastingly blessed. This was the magnificent truth sent down through that Eastern midnight sky into the shepherd's mind. No doubt his idea of that wonderful salvation would be narrow with the narrow range of his shepherd-life and the scanty populations then scattered between the Caspian, Mediterranean, and Arabian Seas. Still it must have been to him even there a prospect inexpressibly glorious and inspiring. See, then, with what brilliant and yet simple heralding,—such as befitted the religious economy of that early time, this communication was made. There are no books, no sanctuaries, no pulpits, no anointed prophets yet; but there is that eternal and all-illuminating mind of the Jehovah-angel, out of which all true prophets are afterwards to be inspired, all true sanctuaries to be built, and all sacred Scriptures to be written,—the "Word that was in the beginning with God, and was God." *He* brings the message, in his own way; and it is a way answering to those childlike times on the earth when God's great men led their flocks over the plains. Jacob "went out from Beersheba, toward Haran. And he lighted upon a certain place, and tarried there all night, because the sun was set; and he took of the stones of that place, and put them for his pillow, and lay down to sleep. And behold a ladder set up on the earth, and the top of it reached to heaven; and behold the angels of God ascending and descending on it. And the Lord stood above it, and said, The land whereon thou liest, to thee will I give it and to thy seed. And in thee and in thy seed shall all the families of the earth be blessed." Now see. It is just as if, out of that thick darkness of the night, when mortal voices are still and the public daylight is veiled, the Creator carved out a temple for Himself, and opened a hidden window of Jacob's soul, and conveyed to him His assurance of His love. The "angels" that run to and fro on the ladder-steps are only the carriers of the message. He does so always to believing and obedient hearts, only without sight or sound. In the very earliest of all writings, the Life of Job, supposed to date back before the age of Moses and his books, and quite independent of them, it is written, "In thoughts from the visions of the night, when deep sleep falleth on men, then a spirit passed before my face; it stood still, but I could not discern the form thereof; an image was before mine eyes, and I heard a voice." Gradually these open visions became infrequent; they hovered awhile on the border-land of life, and so disappeared. Whether because man grew artificial, and his senses more gross and confused, or because it was necessary that other perceptions should be brought into play, at any rate the ladder was drawn up, and the angels were concealed. It is very certain that in the glare of intellectual light their forms generally become less shining. But the faith in their reality never lost its place in the old Church. Every devout Hebrew sang with David, "Praise the Lord, ye angels of His, ye that excel in strength." Chosen and ordained prophets, like Ezekiel, could say, "By the river of Chebar the heavens were opened, and I saw visions of God." The unseen pathway between heaven and earth was still trodden by angels. They kept their heavenly watch and their human charge,—ascending and descending, till the Son of Man came, who commands their legions, and makes them His ministers.

So we reach the second passage. This Son of Man has come. At the very beginning of His course, standing on the threshold of His kingdom, when He as yet discovers His real divinity to only a few open-minded and clean-hearted men like Nathaniel,—an Israelite in whom there is no guile,—He is careful to say, "Hereafter ye shall *see* heaven open, and the angels of God ascending and descending upon the Son of Man." That deeper sense, which the deeper readers like Origen and Augustine, and Luther and Tholuck, have never failed to recognize, is this. Our Lord's coming into the world flings forever apart the folded gates of the invisible. It throws the two worlds open into each other. It is the very *reality* which the ladder Jacob saw long before in Syria, with the condescending and climbing angels on it, typifies and prefigures. From the moment of Christ's baptism, the outset of His sacrificial and saving ministry, all the bars and partition-walls, and to the eye of faith even the veils of the holy place, are taken out of the way. A train of spiritual glories is from that hour set in motion, which will go on breaking and brightening over the earth, in gifts of the Spirit, in the awaking of love and trust in human hearts, in righteous conduct, and in the gathering of nations about His cross, which will have their consummation and crown only when He comes again with His saints. This, then, is your Christian privilege, you who believe and follow the Lord. And as there was a promise then, so there comes another promise: "Hereafter ye *shall see.*" It is a constantly increasing clearness, and culminating splendor, as the great plan of revelation proceeds. While the kingdom goes from strength to strength, its children move on from glory into more complete glory,—which is only their better knowledge of Christ and nearer likeness to Him. As they grow in that, Christian people will see that the whole heavenly world is actually in Christ's service, even when He is on earth. You notice that in the text "ascending" is put before "descending," as if these holy ones *started* from here, and *went up* first,—which only signifies that the person of Christ, wherever that is, is the real centre and starting-point of all spiritual life and spiritual fellowship. The stream of life flows outward and upward and onward from Him. He is the bond between things terrestrial and things celestial. Time and space are lost in that love and life. The going up and going down are but images of the eternal unity, where the true tabernacle of God is with men, and the separating and disordering power of sin is forever broken down and cast out. *Hereafter ye shall see it*, if not now,—ye who believe and live righteously. The flow and reflow of that blessed love and beatific light shall be unceasing,—without hindrance or cloud,—because *He* fills the universe who is all in all, the very fulness of God. And, as far as we are inwardly with Him, we are with His angels,—whether we see them or not,—moving with their motion, climbing when they climb, hearkening with them to the voice of His Word, ministering to Him with them in the satisfying communion.

Pass on and observe the progress of the doctrine. Jesus has entered on His public teaching, and is persuading a politician to accept the mysteries of the new kingdom, in the only way they *can* be received; viz., on the simple faith of Divine authority, coming in by the new birth of water and the Holy Ghost. They are talking of regeneration. Our translation, by the way, conceals the special signification. "Except a man be born again," we read. But Christ says, "Except a man be *born from above* (ανωθεν), by a power coming down into him from the world of life above him." Nicodemus represents the educated and fashionable class:—he is one of the prudent sceptics of a half-secularized and comfortable Church; and like the Nicodemuses of the trade and politics and learning of our days, he is so well satisfied and so much occupied with the life that now is, that he understands neither why anybody should want any other, or be born into any better. Christ says to him: O poor rich man, your intellectual acuteness and logical practice have never let you in at the open door, where the spiritual perceptions play at their pleasure, and God's truth is known. "Art Thou a Master in Israel, and knowest not these things? We speak that we do know, and testify that we have seen. No man hath ascended up to heaven, but He that came down from heaven, even the Son of Man which *is* in heaven." The heaven Christ gives to His followers, or into which He immediately receives those that join themselves to Him by faith, is a present heaven, always present where He is present. See how the walls of time and space spring back and vanish away before this One Lord of our souls. How the curtains of our little tent where we tarry for a night are lifted up, and these outward heavens roll together as a scroll! It would be something to stand at Jacob's side in the pasture, and see the ladder and the angels. But here we have a grander privilege. Heaven comes down *amongst us*, and we are its citizens already. Are we living so? Everywhere the Living Head carries the living members with Him. He comes down to us, that we may rise by Him. The ascension is immediately followed in the actual New Testament order, as in the Church's year, by a sending down from the place whither Christ has gone before of heavenly gifts upon His people; and most of all the one great Whit-Sunday gift of the Comforter. These gifts are impartial and universal, making Christians strong, safe, and joyful. They are the angels' footsteps on the ladder, coming down among men. "Unto every one of us is given grace according to the measure of the gift of Christ." Every one. There is but *one* Family, and *one* Communion. Our common dwellings and daily work are encompassed with the infinite glory of that heavenly presence, which once condescended to the smallest duties, and washed poor men's feet. This is what the Son of Man has done. This is the transfiguration of the Christian's life, wrought by the coming of Christ in our humanity. To believe it is life eternal.

There are three great conclusions that leave their blessed burden of religious consolation on our hearts.

First, to the believer heaven is *actually opened;* not opened merely in the sense of having a passage set into its wall through which, by and by, our souls may creep in to get their first acquaintance with its life, but open for *immediate* intercourse and a personal communication, if we will,—spiritual gifts coming down to us out of its silent streets, as actual as if we saw on shining stairs those radiant bearers of them that brightened Jacob's dream. The full truth shines out. We are not shut in from the influences of our Lord's Spirit, *here*, where we need them so much,—fighting temptation, or bearing hardship and pain and sorrow. The heavens over us are not brass, even if the earth under us seems sometimes to be iron. The fainting and weary soul of the disciple has her refreshment. All her fresh springs are near at hand. Working on, as we may often think, to little purpose, suffering with no clew to the mystery of our pain, finding the ordinary path parched as Baca, and our own spirits almost as dry, nevertheless heaven lies around us. Now and then its dew moistens our thirst. We are able to hold on our way by its invigoration. Life is not the horrible mockery it would be if this world were all. The land we are travelling through is not comfortless or forgotten of its Father; it is a part of Emmanuel's country. "I will not leave you comfortless, I will come to you." And so, with all its sicknesses and graveyards and the crimes that are worse than either,—this world where we are, to a Christian resident in it, is an outer room at least, and one of the many mansions, of God's house.

Secondly, this opening of heaven to us, both here in these *beginnings* of the better life and hereafter, is made for us only by one Lord, who is at the same moment and forever the Lord of angels and the Friend and Master of men,—who fills the universe with His holy life because He has in Himself the fulness of God. Blessed and glorious as the *fact* is that in these days of the Son of Man, and to the members of His body, the heavens stand open, He is certainly most blessed and more glorious who has opened them. And hence how plain it is that whether we are moved by thankfulness for what He has done for us, or by a hope of peace hereafter, our first business is to *come to Him*, in the only way that we can come, the way He has Himself marked out. If we are in any doubt—He being out of sight—whether the service is genuine, He has shown us marks that we can test it by. He has left His representatives among us, and said distinctly, "These My poor people,—ignorant and forlorn, sinning and sorrowful, lost, and most lost in not knowing that they are lost at all,—I leave with you; ye shall have them always with you; by this shall ye know that ye have been discipled by Me, if ye love them, and love each other. Inasmuch as ye serve and visit them, for My sake, because I have loved you, ye do it unto Me." Do that service, and then you are yourselves angels; for angels are but messengers and ministers. You, too, wait on the Son of Man, who has put from Him the kingdoms of the world, and the temptation of bread, and the flattery of ambition. Do that, and your own feet climb the ladder. You ascend with Christ in heart and mind, whither He goes before. Because He lives, ye live also. No matter if, like the patriarch, you have to take the stones of that place where you are,—hard and cold,—and lay them for your pillow, —behold, the pathway of light opens up none the less. The angels travel it both ways: they come down bringing God's help as well as go up with the burden of your prayers. You have been given by His Church to be His, and where He is there you shall be, and that *is* your heaven and your home.

And whatever helps you in Christian living, helps you also to realize spiritual things more clearly. Increased watchfulness helps, a larger and freer faith gained through the habitual exercise of the faith we have helps; so do a pure and upright practice, Church worship, and cordial communions by the Body and Blood. Prayer helps, and helps the more, the more unaffectedly and naturally and trustingly we use it; for nothing, more than these petitions and praises sent upward, with the certain answers sent down, can be like the ascending and descending messengers between us and our Lord. Make great ventures in that heavenly interchange; let your supplications and your alms come up together before God, and prove Him whether, in the old image of the prophet, the windows of heaven are not open, pouring you out blessings. *Live like Christ* your Brother, and Christ your risen King will give you service and honor in His kingdom. He is Master and Lord.

"Of the angels He saith, He maketh His angels spirits and His ministers a flame of fire. But unto the Son He saith, Thy throne, O God, is forever and ever."

# UNPROFITABLE GAZING.

*Sunday after Ascension.*

"AND while they looked steadfastly toward heaven as He went up, behold, two men stood by them in white apparel; which also said, Ye men of Galilee, why stand ye gazing up into heaven?"—*Acts* i. 10, 11.

THE question put is not a question of curiosity but of correction. It comes not from an inferior knowledge needing to be enlightened, but from a higher knowledge having light to give. The "two men in white apparel," according to the habit of Scripture language, are divine messengers. They make a part of the grand supernatural array which the common scenery of the earth put on as the Lord was leaving it. The supernatural is most natural; just as, when God makes His deepest revelations to us, the mystery of faith becomes the plainest reason, and there is nothing so irrational as not to believe. The best philosophy is the largest. The material world without the spiritual is but half a universe. When we get to the bottom of the matter,—as perhaps not all fine modern theologies do,—we shall see that there is a spiritual world without us because there is a spiritual world within us; that among the laws of the system we live in is the law of the spirit of life in Christ Jesus,—as natural and orderly in its divine operation as the law of the life of the wheat and the eagle, and that we want the Church as much as we want a house for the body, and a table for our food. From the entrance of the Saviour into the garden, the night before His crucifixion, on through the following forty-three days, the spiritual world and the material world seemed to have the doors between them swung open, and to become one. So at Gethsemane, so around and within the sepulchre on the morning of the third day, and so on the mount at the ascension. If we believe the history, or credit the great fact of the incarnation, at all, is not this just as we should expect? He in whom the realities of both heaven and earth were united and embodied; He who could say,—even while He was here amongst us, handling this world and handled by it, hungering and sleeping, aching and weeping, and working and loving, as we do,—"The Son of Man is now in heaven," *i. e.*, has His interior and secret life abiding there,—He is passing back personally into the unseen communion, where all His friends, down to us gathered here this morning, are to follow Him. You ask me why I believe in any New Testament miracles. Because I see the greater miracle before me,—Christ of Nazareth,—alive, grander than all this world's men, and yet lowlier, saying out that He comes forth from God, and goes to God, and is one with God, and that no man cometh unto the Father but by Him,—saying it as simply as my child shows me the flower found in the garden,—yet so saying it that all the scribes and proconsuls and philosophers and critics of eighteen hundred years have not been able to break the authority, or explain the secret:—this more than all else, tlfe best "evidence," is why I believe, and cannot help believing. Surely it will be nothing strange if the common order is disturbed to let a higher one in; if this striking together of the two spheres sets free the life that lives in the one as well as in the other. For the time, either the film by which human eyes are ordinarily holden is thinned, or else the veil that hangs before the mysteries of the holy place is lifted up;—and who knows but these are really only two different expressions of one and the same fact?—so that the home of the Christian family below and the home of the Christian family above appear,—as they actually are,—opening into one another.

We go to the mount of the ascension, my friends, thus to bring back help for our life, in the lower levels where we are living it, this week, and henceforth.

Remember that this question, "Why stand ye gazing up?" is the first thing in the order of events, and in the Bible narrative, after the closing of Christ's earthly ministry. Only a little breathing space was to be given them first to gather up their energies; and even that was not to be an interval of idleness. They were to go at once to Jerusalem, as the chosen head-quarters of the great warfare for the world's conversion, and their waiting there was to be like the waiting of the still midsummer elements, before the mountain winds sweep down and the tongues of fire leap out,—a busy waiting,—a preparation for this long campaign of many ages. They were to occupy the ten days from Ascension to Pentecost, with its mighty wind and flame, in making ready incessantly for the coming of the Holy Spirit to inaugurate their work. They were to be earnest and constant in prayer and praise. They were to read and settle in their minds the definite doctrines and precise directions their Master had committed to them during the forty days, pertaining to the constitution and discipline of the new kingdom they were to set up among men. They were to fasten and cement the bonds of a visible unity and worship between the members of the body, because, it is written, they continued "*with one accord*," in their "prayer and supplication." Especially they were to fill up the vacant place in the apostolate, made by the defection of the traitor, with the formality of a solemn election. Nothing could be done till the organization was complete, after the pattern shown in the mount.

Thus their business had been marked out clearly before them, as every Christian's business is clearly marked out before him from the time that his baptismal and confirmation vows are laid upon him and the Spirit is given him, onward. But how is it? The apostles are not turning to that business; they are still resting in a kind of sentimental trance between their commission and their ministry. The eleven had not yet comprehended the new duty of the hour, because they had not turned forward from the past to the future. They were living as some Christians do nowadays,—in their feelings more than in their convictions and their will, in fruitless memories not in daring hopes,—eyes turned towards the sky where a past glory had vanished, not with their hands turned faithfully towards the men for whom that Master had *become* a man and had died. Indulged any longer, this would become a mere life of religious sentiment, not a life of religious service,—and so not a healthy life at all. How long they had been gazing up into heaven we are not told; it may have been minutes, it may have been hours. At any rate, it required a voice from God to rouse them and send them to their work. That proved to be with them, as it always has since and always will with useful Christians, a life of intense, incessant, laborious activity:--the daily work that witnesses for Christ,—Christ that died; Christ that is risen; Christ that ascended and ever liveth to make intercession; Christ in His eternal humanity; Christ in the heart of His Church.

If those eleven men that had companied so long with Christ needed to be startled out of a false indulgence in the mere idle luxury of feeling, most of us certainly need it much more. It makes the whole matter real to our sympathies to watch the gradual unfolding and ripening of the full measure and stature of manhood,—which is likeness to Christ,—in men that had just our temperaments, our weaknesses, and the same inward and outward difficulties to contend with that we have. I have no doubt that if these disciples that we now rightly call saints,—James and John, Peter and Thomas, Philip and Matthew,—were to appear in our cotemporary society, as they were at any point in their biography previous to the Day of Pentecost, we should be surprised at their resemblance to the men we met in these streets yesterday; and after that time the visible difference would lie chiefly in their having a more single-hearted and enthusiastic devotion to Christ than the men that we are accustomed to see. It must have been meant to be so, or they would not have been chosen from the average social condition and ordinary associations as they were. Their very faults and doubts are encouraging,—when we see how steadily they struggled against them and rose over them; how, instead of fostering doubt, and growing ridiculously vain over their scepticism, as some frivolous deniers do,—as if to put self-will before God's authority were some mark of intellectual vigor, instead of a wrong to intellect and heart alike,—they rather longed for faith, crying, "Lord I believe, help Thou mine unbelief"; and when we see how patient their Lord was with them, so long as He saw sincerity and the germs of a genuine truth in them. So in this particular case: a mother is not more gentle with the lingering or straying steps of the child she attends along the street than the heavenly Master was with these apostles, who were letting their personal feelings detain them from their appointed task. Probably our personal religious preferences and pleasures, our tastes for some emotional stimulus or intellectual entertainment in religion, are, in kind, to us, very much what the absorption in Christ's merely *external* presence was to them. It is something that must be put aside as soon as it interferes with the more substantial business of carrying Christ's truth out in self-denying habits into the living world. I hear a man say it makes him "feel better" to say his prayers; so far so good; but how far does the good feeling go, and the power of the prayer keep him company, as a law of regulation to his lips and a purifier of his conduct and conversation, among the people that he meets who tempt him and try him? I was reading lately in the life of one of the most spotless and brilliant of modern religious devotees and orators,—from whose eminent honor in breaking up the tame monotony of the prevalent continental piety nothing ought to be detracted,—Lacordaire,—this remark, and it is mentioned by the biographer as a sign of high perfection: "I desire to be remembered only as one who believed, who loved, and who prayed." Well, it is true the Son of Man has not yet on the earth so much believing, loving, and praying that these graces can be overvalued; but why say only these? Taking the world around us as it is, ought there not to be an equal desire to honor the Lord in an active following of His steps and proclaiming Him in life? Taking Christianity as it is, must not a religious system which truly represents it be as conspicuous for its action as the mediaeval Church was for its contemplation, or the Wesleyan for its emotion, or the Puritan for its introspection? We need never be afraid that in that hearty and holy fidelity to Christ we shall lack His real presence. Invisible to sight He will, in the constant freshening of the disciple's living heart through the doing of His will, be only the more present to His faith.

And this is the other requirement contained in the angel's question. The eleven, we may say, are dropped suddenly from their high privilege to the same position with ourselves. They must walk, henceforth, as you and I here must, not by the light of an outward leader, but, what is a great deal better, by a secret and steadfast trust in Him who is forever with us by an inward possession, by His gifts and ordinances in His Church, by His intercession within the veil. There is for all of us also a "Jerusalem," a "Judaea," a "Samaria," if not an "uttermost part of the earth,"—some well-dressed city with its ragged fringe of want and wickedness, some country district with its neglected and untrained families, some sophisticated brain that has gone astray from the old standards and home of the Faith and set up its Gerizim rivalry,—some that you can minister to by your charity and win back by your witnessing, if that witnessing is only as zealous as Peter's, and as patient as Paul's, and as loving as John's. They, no more than you, "by their own power" or holiness, made any lame creature leap and walk; it was by a Name that is as ready to be taken on your tongue as theirs, as mighty for you as for them, and through a faith in that Name which you can have without measure, though now you see Him not.

If, then, the question of the heavenly men be put into some paraphrase for ourselves here, this would be its import. Reduce your privileges to Christian practice, and your faith to action. Life is not given us for speculation, or gazing, or mere delight, even though the relish be religious,—not for reverie and dreaming, even though it were the reverie of devotion, or a dream of Paradise. This world, our own little corner of it, wants sacrifice and labor, running feet and open hands, busy thoughts and gentle tongues,—all for Christ and the honor of His Church. The world's ways are not clean; there is too much oppression of the weak by the strong, of the fatherless and widow by cunning and power, of the nobler spirit in man by the meaner senses of him. There is too much cruelty in its habitations; too much darkness on its face; too much filth on its breast. Come and work for it. Its surface is rough, and wants much levelling down and casting up to make it smooth for the Messiah's feet. Believe in Him, and for this end. Confess Him before men, to follow Him in these pathways among the multitude; worship Him in sincerity, that you may gain inward power and love and light and grace for this faithful witnessing from on high. Wait for Him by watching at the gate, by working in the field. Why stand ye gazing up into heaven?

Without departing in the least from the direct force of the text we find in it, thirdly, a demand, on divine authority, that our Christian life, as to its inward supplies and the steady operation of its energies, should be independent of any particular external support, so that it may be only the more completely and religiously dependent on God himself. Not that we are to cast away any outward prop so long as God's providence holds it in its place and comforts us by letting us lean upon it; but that we should not be perplexed or disheartened when any such help that has been familiar to us is taken away by Him, or enfeeble ourselves by letting our integrity, or our purity, or our prayers depend on it instead of depending directly on Him. It would be greatly useful to us to take it up as a matter of careful and honest inquiry, how far our Christian character would be undiminished and unhindered by the striking away from it of all human safeguards. Try it to-day upon yourself. Take out all the considerations of social respectability and the good opinion of others, especially of those to whom you have a selfish motive for appearing well; take out all reference to the effect of a moral or a religious standing, or your business success, or the accomplishment of your professional ends; take out the check imposed on your worse propensities by the dread of domestic misery, of public disgrace, or of a loss of confidence; let go prudence, self-preservation, fear, interest; part with all those manifold and half-conscious restraints that are piled up about your religious performances,—the current proprieties that bolster up your invalid virtue; in short, let the simple allegiance of your soul to God stand out alone, unshielded, undraped, unbraced by any mortal device or accessory; how much of it would there be left? how staunch and steadfast would it stand? how long would it hold out? how constant would be your worship here? how spotless and unbending your warfare with "the unspiritual god of this world"? Oh for the rooted life, the grounded principle, the settled faith! So we are told of an old Christian hero,—and it is true of them all,—that the secret of his spiritual greatness was that he inwardly united himself to the cross, made it through life "his refuge, his remedy, his passion"; and that the cross which he upheld, *of it he was upholden*, until it became part of his very frame and structure, even as the old fighter of the northern mythology "felt his arm and sword grow together in the combat, welded into one by the blood that oozed from his wounds, and then knew that every blow he dealt told sure." No character is perfectly *sure* till it has this mystical interlocking and inrooting in the living sacrifice.

There is no danger, my friends, that our eyes or our hearts will be turned too much upwards, heavenwards,—provided we look there, in faith and prayer, for the light and the strength to do our Christian service here. At present this is our place; and the judgment before us is a judgment for deeds done in the body. Let us waste no time in vain regrets for what we have lost, or in equally vain longings for what we cannot have, or what would only dwarf and enfeeble us if we could. These eleven men, when they were bidden to stop gazing into heaven and go to their work were not turned away from heavenly things to earthly things,—very far from that. It was exactly the opposite. They were to stop looking into the air, that by a truer and God-appointed road they might travel, in God's time, higher up into the Christian heaven. They were to rouse themselves from a dream, that they might work out their salvation and the salvation of the world. They were to cease wasting their time on the empty cloud through which the Saviour's form had gone, that they rather might find and follow and possess forever the living Saviour himself, in doing by faith the substantial service of His love, for His sake.

To that end, the present line of living, however agreeable and prosperous, the present residence or occupation, however delightful, or the present apparent helps, however prized, as soon as they become tempters to sluggishness, must be given up,—a sacrifice to Him whose sacrifice for us is the only assurance of life. All true religious power and progress are attained by frequent breakings up of familiar and dangerous securities, by moving forth away from them into less agreeable surroundings, less easy roads, less sweet-tasting diet. "Why stand ye gazing up into heaven?" Hence God's personal providence with us is continually pushing us on, loosening our feet, changing the scene, displacing one or another scheme, or vision, or staff, or companion. He does it for what he would make of us,—better men,—and for the farsighted love wherewith He loves us. He does it because He will not let our feet cleave to the dust, our hearts grow thin and weak, our faith dwindle and die out;—the dropping of every such dear delusion liberates our real life, increases our durable riches, replenishes our strength, sets us forward, lifts us up. How many of you here are satisfied as you are? How many have not some secret suffering and sorrow, either for what you have had and lost, or else for something that you have not and are longing to reach? Answer that, and I shall not need to argue with you about this way of pain and parting being God's common way. That we do not see it oftener is only because we are blind to the deeper working of His hands, bent upon our little plans, and too eager for ourselves.

The summing up of the whole lesson, this morning, then, is this: Inquire whether the attitude of your soul is visionary or practical; your great aim in life self-indulgent or self-sacrificing; your daily desire and endeavor the mere enjoyment of the hours, however refined, or the ready going upon Christ's errand, the faithful witnessing to Him, everywhere, always, be it near or far, be it easy or hard, be it with human sympathies sustaining you or in the solitude of that obedience which treads the winepress all alone. On this it depends whether you waste your life's best faculty and vision upon a cloud, and then sink, a lost thing, into the dark, or whether you shall be endowed with immortal power from on high, and be taken up also yourself, into the Eternal Light, there continually to dwell.

# LEADINGS OF THE HOLY SPIRIT.

*Whitsun-Day.*

"I WILL lead them in paths that they have not known; I will make darkness light before them, and crooked things straight."—*Isaiah* xlii. 16.

"As many as are led by the Spirit of God, they are the sons of God."—*Romans* viii. 14.

BOTH Isaiah and St. Paul are speaking of good men,—men that believe, and pray, and work, from the only right motive. Both affirm the reality of a very intimate and tender connection between such men and God, existing constantly, even here in this world. There is a pervading, loving care on the one side, and a trusting dependence on the other side. There is a *leading* and a *being led*,—with a privilege mysteriously grand and gracious growing out of that relation on the part of those who are led. So far the two writers agree. But every thoughtful reader is still aware of a certain difference in the impression coming to him as he reads. The prophet says, speaking in Jehovah's name, "I will lead them in paths that they have not known; I will make darkness light before them, and crooked things straight." The Apostle says, "As many as are led by the Spirit of God, they are the sons of God." Each declares a divine promise. What is it, then, that distinguishes the second from the first?

Isaiah represents that more advanced and ripened stage of religious culture, in the elder Church, where the original meaning of the revelation at Mount Sinai had begun to come out into a clearness approaching that of the Gospel-day. The dawn was mounting into the sky, though the day-star had not yet quite risen. The conception of God's character had become, at least among the purest minds, more simple and satisfying. There was more of the graciousness of His fatherhood mingling with and balancing the fearfulness of His sovereignty. The idea of a free forgiveness to the believing and penitent heart, which is the central comfort of Christianity, was modifying the old regimen of inexorable statutes and animal sacrifices. Men were getting underneath the letter to the spirit of the commandments, and the nation that had bowed its head so long over the stone tables of the Law began to feel the freshening fore-tokens of the pentecostal wind which swept through the chamber at Jerusalem amid the tongues of fire. It heard something from the lips of those later prophets that sounded like the anthem of peace and good-will at Bethlehem. You have only to read the first chapter of Isaiah's Book to see this, with its contrast of the fat and blood of beasts with the inward washings, the new heart, the justice and liberty, the snow-white cleansing of the scarlet sins which were to come. Worship had become more spiritual. More confiding impressions of the unseen Father were certainly stealing into the worshipper's soul. Hence comes that promise of divine guidance, personal and gentle, which breathes itself into words so beautiful in the text. "I will lead them in paths that they have not known; I will make darkness light before them, and crooked things straight." There cannot be a human heart among us that is not moved by these assurances, because there is no one among us all that has not found out by rough experience that there are crooked things in his life which *need* to be made straight, and dark places which need to be made light; that there are spots where the ways part, with no guide-post, leaving the judgment and conscience perplexed, and where one is almost certain there must be paths better than that one he is walking in, safer if not smoother, and running to a better end. This common need of heavenly leading puts us into one company with those wandering Hebrews, and makes us prize the promise that was so comforting to them.

In fact, if we inquire of our own nature, we shall probably learn that this instinct which desires and follows leadership, even apart from religion, is nearly universal with men, and that religion takes advantage of it and employs it to train our best attachments and confidences up to heaven. With all his self-reliance and self-will man likes to trust and follow a leader,—identifying himself with his strength and skill, and making him, as it were, a part of his own foresight and individual energy. It appears among bands of youth, in those literary and athletic games which anticipate the serious competitions and conflicts of maturer years. It appears in tribes of travellers, in exploring parties and discovering voyages, in political combinations and social reforms, and especially in the military spirit which makes the general to be. half the army, gathers up the temper of a hundred thousand soldiers into the breast of one captain of captains, sways them all with the courage of his command, and in some manner spreads out the personality of his own will till it reaches to the remotest private in the ranks. This natural deference to a master-spirit, like the natural filial sentiment, or the natural feeling of hope and veneration and loyalty, is one of the prepared elements in us on which revealed religion lays hold, to elevate and sanctify it, and then to bind us by it more firmly and blessedly, in the bands of a spiritual piety, to God.

The next step in the doctrine, however, rises far up above all our natural and human ties; for it shows us this guiding love of the heavenly Father as entirely independent of anything that we think, or do, or feel. It leads us in paths that we had not known. The love is undeserved and condescending. It comes out to us before we go after it. It is like a hand of compassion reached down to us out of an inpenetrable cloud,—a seat of mercy where our sight cannot penetrate or any claim of ours be held. "I will lead them in paths that they have not known." It deals with us as a mother handles a child just beginning to know only her face or her voice. A little farther on the same prophet clothes the thought in other phrases of equal beauty. "There is no God besides Me; I have called thee by thy name, I have surnamed thee; I girded thee though thou hast not known Me." We were too infantile, in the childhood of our spiritual life, to know God when He took us up, put His arms around us, quieted the fierce cry of our passions, and carried us to Christian rest. There must have been a great deal in the national memories and the daily temple thanksgivings of those people to lend a vivid significancy to these words. They were always thinking of the time when they were all together but a weak bondman in Egypt, and the eternal kindness came down to unfasten their fetters, and bore them, as their great earthly leader says, "on eagles' wings" across the wilderness. Every man has been treated like that Israel. Who of us cannot recall some trying time when the utter dismay came over him of not knowing what way to take,—the sun gone down, human helpers away or feeble, human advisers indifferent or undecided? But God was there before us, and when we waited on Him we found He was waiting for us. It is when we are least capable that His love is most busy in our behalf, and when we are farthest from being sufficient to ourselves that His preventing goodness comes in; and then, very often, the one path which, of all those that opened, was the least inviting, was the one into which He led our unwilling feet.

I just used the words *His preventing goodness*. It is an Old Testament expression which has been preserved in the old English of the Prayer Book,—as we pray in the Easter collect for God's special grace "preventing" us. It is a curious example of the degradation of the meaning of words that whereas to our forefathers the term "preventing," *i. e.*, literally *going before*, bore with it the idea of God's going before His children only to do them good, to open their way and help them on, to guide them and attract them forward, in the modern usage an exactly opposite, a harsh and hindering sense, has been put upon the same term,—to "prevent" meaning now to keep back, to distract, to fail and baffle one in his purpose. We return now on Whitsun-day to the old and gracious acceptation: "Let thy tender mercies prevent us." God goes invisibly before His child, like the good shepherd of the Eastern pastures before the feeblest and timidest of his flock, to reassure the alarmed and doubting, to take the briars and stones and to scare the beasts out of the way, to straighten what is crooked, to hold a lamp over the dark passages among the rocks, to lead those that have faith enough to be willing to be led in paths that they have not known.

From this promise we pass over to that given us by St. Paul. "For as many as are led by the Spirit of God they are the sons of God." We see at once that there is an advance into another plane of religious thought. Instead of Jehovah we are told of "the Spirit," "the Holy Ghost," and that the leading is by Him. Then, instead of being taught of a mere outward change wrought by this leading, as in the material world around us,—paths opened, the dark made light, and the crooked straight, lo! there is a transformation of our whole interior nature and condition. They who were before merely creatures and servants, or children only as by creation, become children in a new and profounder way, as coming into a spiritual union and a certain filial, birthright likeness to God. Nothing is denied or taken away that Isaiah had said, only much is added,—as Christ said of the entire Gospel-system when compared with the old Law;—not a particle is destroyed, but all is fulfilled,—*i. e.*, filled full, rounded out, or made complete. To be led of the Spirit, as a Christian disciple is, is something far richer and higher than to be guided on, in hope, and in the day-dawn, as the best Israelite was.

If we ask what especially is signified by being "led by the Spirit," the first part of the answer depends on the use of words, as used by a man, St. Paul, who uses them with unsurpassed precision and power. In his exact Greek there are two terms for "leading," which correspond respectively, in a striking way, to these two views I have presented, as conveyed in the two parts of the text. The one signifies a violent and rather irregular act of propelling a body,—a driving or pushing on, as by winds, or waves. This St. Peter uses when he speaks of the moving of the minds of the Old Testament saints by the mind of God. The other, employed in the text, refers to an even, constant, unbroken force, acting not less powerfully on the mind because it acts gently and steadily:—the leading of a Spirit who abides always at His gracious work on the heart, in His chamber within it, and does not come and go. You can illustrate this for yourselves by any mother walking with a little child, or shepherd with sheep. The hireling, who only follows after, and, when the charge wanders or falls into danger, hurries up and catches hold irregularly, pushing the body here or there over a hollow or through a thicket, does not *lead*,—as that blessed Comforter leads whom the Saviour promised to send, choosing the tenderest possible images to describe the gift, and especially insisting, "He shall abide with you forever, even the Spirit of Truth." This is that Spirit whose coming into the Church and into the believer's heart we commemorate and celebrate to-day.

What then is the peculiar privilege of those who are so led, and are willing, in the yielding up and surrender of their hearts, to be so led, by this faithful Spirit of God? They are called by the noblest of all titles, and it declares the most exalted of all honors. "They are the sons of God." Is this possible? How can it be?

There is One only-begotten Son of God, brought once into the world, for the one mediation and redemption, becoming also the Son of Man, born of Mary, our humanity being forever taken up into His divinity and glorified by it. It is only our spiritual union with Him, in a personal ingrafting and adoption by repentance and faith, water and the Spirit, that we, in an accommodated and secondary sense, yet a most vital and precious one, are made also "sons of God." Our sonship to God comes only through Him who is THE Son, only-begotten and dearly-beloved; just as through Him, our great King and Priest, all true Christians are said in a sense to become "kings and priests unto God." Hence the expressions "Spirit of *God*" and "Spirit of *Christ*" and "Holy Spirit" are often used as equivalent. *Christ* gives the Comforter. When He is received into the heart, ingrafted there by faith, a new blood pours itself along the veins; a new nature is born; a new man is created,—a man of God, a son of God, in the *image* of Christ. Hence too, on the name "Spirit of God," wherever introduced, there is a kind of Gospel accent, —something that suggests, and is suggested by, the mediation of Jesus,—an evangelic power, a sweetness, a richness and unction, altogether peculiar to the religion of the Cross.

Thus, my friends, between the two members of the text, Isaiah's and St. Paul's, both inspired from the Word of God, there is just that difference, and just that advance, that there is between the two systems or dispensations,—between him who might be greatest born of woman under the Law, like John the Baptist, and him, as Jesus says, who is least in the true kingdom of heaven;—the same that there is between the old Jewish Pentecost, or Feast of Weeks, falling seven weeks after the Passover, and our glorious Whitsun-day, or Christian Pentecost, following at the same interval after our Lord's resurrection. The one is all that faithful men *could* have, in the leading of God's hand, in finding darkness made light, and crooked things straight, without the supreme glory of Christ's manifestation in the flesh, His sacrifice, and all the Gospel powers and splendors of His reconciliation. The other, dear brethren in Christ, is what we are permitted, in the wondrous mystery of God's grace, in His Gospel and His Church, to have by our membership, our incorporation and sonship in Him.

Here "the Spirit" is not a mere influence exerted on character, as by a foreign benefactor; it is an inwrought and essential principle of the believer's life. He is a new creature, a son (and the apostle in one place makes it still more personal by saying that the believing woman is a *daughter*) of the Lord Almighty. And as there are two New Testament terms, in the original, to signify two kinds of leading, so there are two terms to signify *children*. One has reference to mere natural descent or begetting, irrespective of any tender, filial feeling. The other, used when sons of God in Christ are intended, includes an affectionate and sacred dependence, or lovingness of the child's and the parent's hearts. So, you are more or less *influenced*, doubtless, by the life of any eminently great and unselfish man whose biography you read, or whose career you watch. The force of such an example enters in among the other forces that mould a character. But here, in sonship, there is something deeper and more interior than that. The tree may take an influence from the sun, and that foreign influence tends to make the tree tall, vigorous, green, and fruitful. But the tree is not the child of the sun. The tree gets the nature of its life, what makes up its whole characteristic quality, by secret channels from a seed. If it is altered at all, afterward, it must be by a graft, taking away the old and bringing in a new vital element. The law of the Spirit of life in Christ is not merely an external impulse giving us a movement in a particular direction; it is rather a silent, inward, secret element, transforming, regulating, and sanctifying everything; it is poured into the Church by the Holy Spirit, to quicken and revive it, and by secret visitation, by word and prayer and sacrament, it is granted to every heart that seeks it.

With this comes a special characteristic of our service to Christ. It is not a service of compulsion or restraint, rendered "grudgingly or of necessity." That would be no Whitsun-day religion. It is labor in a free and joyous spirit, such as befits the thankful receivers of an unspeakable gift in its true character. It is not done for wages, in view of a future settlement or emolument, still less to avert a future scourge. It is done in liberty, from a choice of the heart, and therefore, as all such service is done, with double energy and efficiency. Wise employers always select workmen that love their work. This distinction between sonship and servantship runs through all that pertains to a Christian's obedience. God gives Himself to those that are led by His Spirit. It is His highest gift: no other is perfect, and no other could satisfy this perfect love.

And so we are brought finally to understand why it is that the apostle, just after he has written these sublime words of the text,—"As many as are led by the Spirit of God, they are the sons of God,"—and before he goes on to write, "The Spirit itself beareth witness with our spirit, that we are the children of God, and if children, then heirs, heirs of God and joint heirs with Christ, that we may be also glorified together," puts in this sentence: "For ye have not received the spirit of bondage again to fear, but ye have received the spirit of adoption, whereby we cry, Abba, Father." Did the question ever arise, in reading this chapter, why that unusual Chaldaic word, "Abba," is left there untranslated? Probably because, like the familiar words in our English that are most easily pronounced by the very youngest lips, it expresses the childlike feeling in the childlike form, and is therefore untranslatable. St. Paul, the robust and intellectual man, would say to us, "When the Holy Spirit that Christ gave, as on this day,—the great promise of the Father,—has been really welcomed in its living and loving energy into your hearts, you will speak in your prayers to your Father as little children supplicate their parents from whom they took their life, and expect the warmest love"; and it is to answer that earnest human need that the Spirit was sent.

These sublime truths, of the higher offices of the Holy Spirit on Christian men, furnish a key to the interpretation of a very difficult passage in the second of St. Peter's General Epistles. His words are these: "Grace and peace be multiplied unto you through the knowledge of God, and of Jesus our Lord, according as His divine power hath given unto us all things that pertain unto life and godliness, through the knowledge of Him that hath called us to glory and virtue; whereby are given unto us exceeding great and precious promises, that by these *ye might be partakers of the divine nature.*" Human thought can be lifted no higher than that. It carries us up to the mysterious boundary between the finite and the infinite mind. True Christians do become "partakers of the divine nature," if not in its essence yet in its spiritual qualities, in such relation and measure as the difference of capacity admits, not in the infinity of the attributes of deity, but in the holy character and pure affection that pervade their action. This is the actual sonship in which the covenanted and genuine disciple stands toward God. It is not that literal and eternal sonship in which He is who is "Begotten of the Father before all worlds," and the "Only-begotten." But it is obtained *through* Him; we reach it by the faith which is a spiritual union with Him; it is real, conscious, practical, and transcends all other possible honors of our estate in its glory. It is a life going on now in every new-born and obedient heart. It brings us into the circle and the sympathy of the privileged Family. In other language, repeatedly employed in the New Testament, it is our "adoption,"—the "adoption of sons," by "the spirit of adoption"; and so great is the inward change wrought with the outward incorporation that it is called a second "being born,"—born not of corruptible seed, but of incorruptible. You were of the family of the flesh and its selfish impulses; you are now of the family of the Spirit and its holy constancy. "That which is born of the flesh is flesh, and that which is born of the Spirit is Spirit,"—and it is the Spirit that accomplishes the regeneration,—that Holy Spirit which we therefore praise and celebrate and magnify this day. He came and led us in paths that we had not known. He made darkness light before us, and crooked things straight. As many as are led by the Spirit of God, yield themselves to that attraction, and are willing to be so re-born and re-fashioned,—these find it out. To them the blessed, peaceable secret is opened. It opens more and more as they are led on, till they know as they are known.

THE END.

www.ingramcontent.com/pod-product-compliance
Lightning Source LLC
Chambersburg PA
CBHW051245300426
44114CB00011B/901